Forbidden Replicas
HONOURING THE UNKNOWN
by Ravinder S. Manocha

DEDICATION

This book is dedicated to the Manocha clan
for their support and affection.
*Gurbachan, Diljit, Malvinder,
Meenu, Ravinder, Grace,
Geeta, Nikhil, Tanisha,
Rikhael, Sharmin and Ishshal.*

CONTENTS

3 Preface

5 Poem by Ravinder Singh

6 Brief Historical Analysis of Chinese Replica Ceramics

12 Evaluating Antique, Replica and Fake Ceramics

19 Non traditional Sources of Chinese Ceramic

25 Gallery of Replica Ceramics

146 Bibliography

146 Chronology of Qing Emperors

147 About the writer and collectors

148 Acknowledgements

NOTICE OF DISCLAIMER

The writer, (which shall include but is not limited to all parties involved directly and indirectly in this publication) hereby makes known by this notice of disclaimer to any third party that the publication of any information, including but not limited to descriptions, articles and photographs of the ceramics in this publication, shall not directly or indirectly be construed as providing any express or implied warranty or representation on the accuracy or completeness of any information, description, content of articles or authenticity of any ceramics contained in this publication.

Third parties shall ensure that they undertake their independent investigations, authentication and due diligence on the content of this publication.

While reasonable care and due diligence has been taken by the writer in completing this publication, the writer will strictly not be liable for any express or implied liability under any law or equity for any damage or loss caused to any third party by any action whether innocent, negligent or otherwise including and not limited to any third party's reliance on the content of this publication.

Copyright 2013 Ravinder Singh Manocha. Publisher

All rights reserved. No part of this publication may be reproduced, stored in a retrieval system, or transmitted, in any form or by any means electronic, mechanical, photocopying, recording or otherwise, without the prior written permission of the publisher.

ISBN: 978-981-07-8433-1

PREFACE

The first time my wife Grace and I saw a Qing replica vase, we were mesmerised by its beauty and even more shocked by the price. A collector wanted to sell it for the original price he had paid decades ago and saw no commercial reason to continue to hold on to it. We were novice collectors and were only vaguely aware of ceramics and antiques, but the fine and detailed hand painted designs and the colourful, elegant paintings impregnated with thousands of dots fascinated us. As an artist-in-training, I could imagine the hundreds of hours and the sheer talent required to paint the vase. Later, as we studied ceramic history, we learnt that the paintings, reliefs and decorations on these ceramics were just the final part of a long and complicated process to create this unique canvas for this art. From our first piece to our last, we continued to collect strictly immaculate and artistic replica ceramics of the highest quality based on our personal discernment of artistic and aesthetic value. Long term commercial appreciation remains purely an incidental motivation when compared to the joy and excitement of finding these ceramics over the years.

Whether the ceramics were produced during the last century or earlier, no credit has been given to the seventy-two anonymous skilled artisans and the many other skilled workers described in Jingdezhen literature. However, the dynasties, the emperors and even the kiln administrators are acknowledged in history. These unknown craftsmen led terrible lives on a bare subsistence level, either serving the dynasties or governments in the 20th century. It is often said that ceramics of the past are mixed with the sweat, blood, bones and tears of these unknown souls. Most modern collectors only critique these ceramics on their potential commercial value and rarely acknowledge the many craftsmen behind their creation. This period of anonymous creation has disappeared forever from Chinese history and these ceramics are all that remain. To downgrade or dismiss them on pure commercial grounds is to dishonor these talented unknown craftsmen.

This publication is our attempt to create a permanent record of honouring these unknown heroes of the past and to remind us that beauty can be created even in extreme times and conditions.

We urge readers to discard any preconceptions and bias and appreciate these ceramics at face value for their craftsmanship and the spirit of creation embodied in these works.

Finally, I would like to acknowledge my partner-in-crime, my wife Grace. She is always been my passionate supporter, critic and joint collector. She helps me to communicate and diplomatically negotiate with the many Mandarin speaking collectors who sold us their best replica collections. I thank her for tolerating the many years of dust and clutter of our many ceramic displays and boxes of ceramics around our house. Without her support, this book would have remained another uncompleted project.

Ravinder Singh and Grace Manocha, 2013

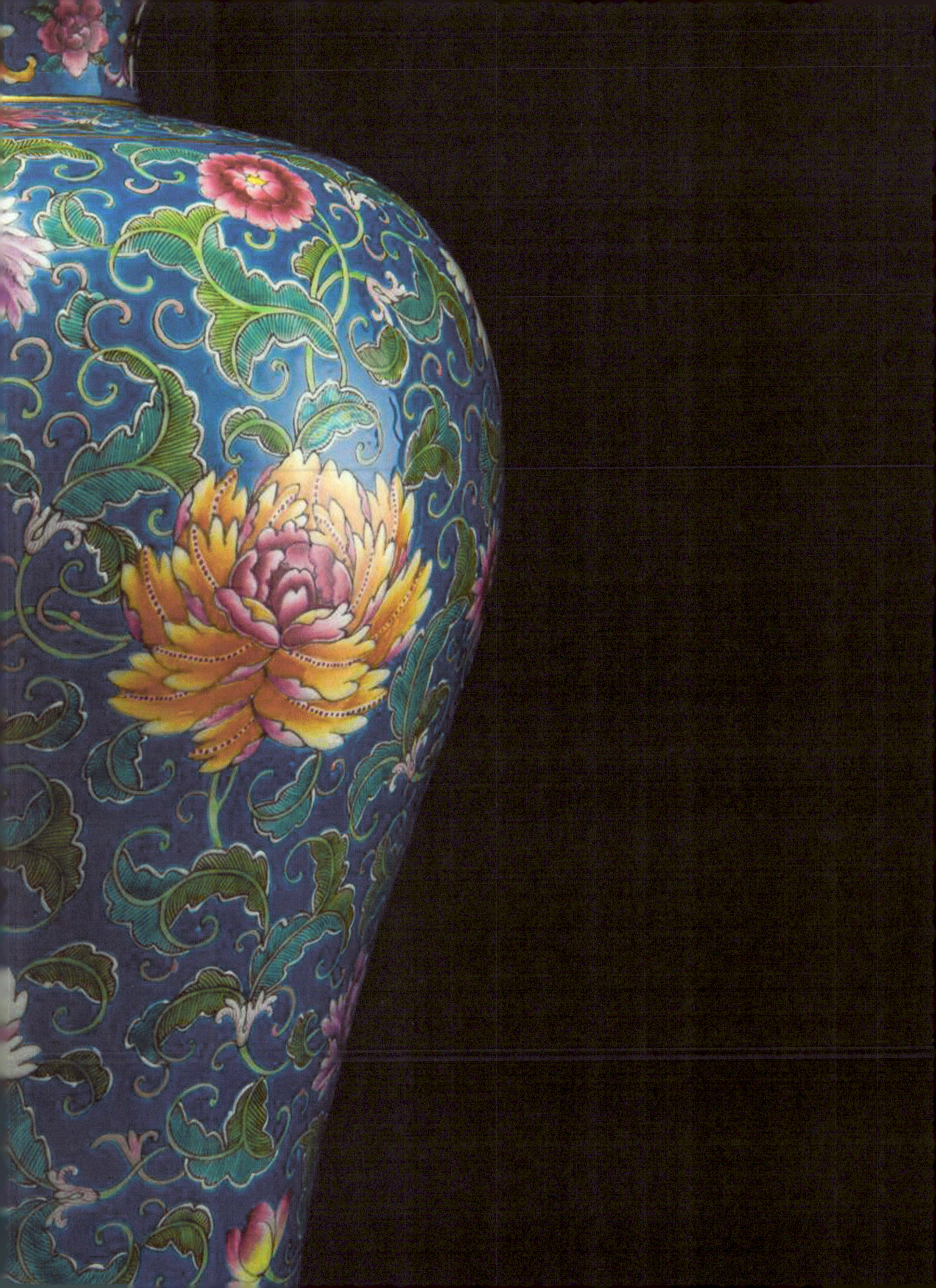

HONOURING THE UNKNOWN

The son of heaven rises
To claim his birth right

Dress he must of the best
Eat he must of the best
Lust he must of the best
Tire he must of the best

Emptiness as vanity fades
Knowledge he thirsts for peace
Beauty he seeks in mind and craft
Suffering he must inflict for this new lust

The lives he destroys to hold beauty in his hand
Credit he denies
Reward he claims
The people cry out in pain

The son of heaven will not rise
Only beauty remains.

Ravinder Singh Manocha, 2013

BRIEF HISTORICAL ANALYSIS OF CHINESE REPLICA CERAMICS

Reigns of Kangxi, Yongzheng and Qianlong, Qing Dynasty (1644 to 1911)

Ceramic is one of the great inventions of China. The creation of ceramics began about 2000 years ago during the Han Dynasty and since then, Chinese ceramics and their heritage kilns have gained worldwide recognition. An interesting development related to replicas occurred between the end of the Yuan dynasty and the early Ming dynasty. In response to demand, Chinese kilns started to produce historical replicas of the past. The popularity of replicas may have arisen out of veneration for antiquity or from an admiration and preservation of the craftsmanship of the past. The private kilns owners recognised an opportunity for a potentially profitable venture for the domestic and export markets. Huge quantities of replicas were produced during the Ming dynasty, reigns of the Qing emperors Kangxi, Yongzheng and Qianlong, in the late Qing and Republican era until the 1980s.

Replicas ceramics of every type and grade were produced, some of which are of such excellent quality that they were indistinguishable from original ceramics. This has resulted in considerable difficulty in authentication by modern researchers and experts.

During the reigns of the Qing Emperors Kangxi, Yongzheng and Qianlong, ceramics production reached a peak of technological development. Much of the quality and diversity of the ceramics produced at this time is attributed to Tang Ying, the Qing official in charge of the imperial kilns under emperors Yongzheng and Qianlong. Tang Ying had a deep understanding of the technical processes involved in ceramic production. He was also a competent administrator who implemented quality control and increased the efficiency and production capacity of the kilns. Under his supervision, he implemented many innovations in ceramic production. New and improved glazes and designs were introduced and many original and high-quality ceramics were created under his administration.

In the early 17th century, Chinese ceramics from a heritage and domestic trading commodity gradually morphed into an export revenue generator for the Chinese royalty and nobility. Demand for Chinese tea, silk and ceramics by Western traders led to opening of a trading outpost in Canton in 1699 and subsequently to a growing trade in Chinese ceramics.

This export trade in Chinese ceramics peaked around the 1750s but continued to be significantly active towards the end of 18th century. The Dutch, French and English were the biggest buyers of ceramics. During the late 18th and early 19th century, American traders became the largest importer of Chinese ceramics.

The 19th century was a period of gradual decline of export of Chinese ceramics because of competition from the new Japanese and European ceramic factories and introduction of Staffordshire pottery. The low cost, mass-produced ceramics from these countries displaced the dominance of Chinese ceramics after the 1820s. Another contributory reason for the decline in export was the deteriorating quality of ceramics produced after the 18th century.

The extravagance of Emperor Qianlong exacted a severe strain on the finances of the empire. The power of the Qing Empire declined from the Jiajing period. The destruction of Jingdezhen by the Taiping rebels in 1853 during the Xianfeng reign had a devastating effect on the ceramic industry. Although the imperial kilns were revived during the Tongzhi period, the quality of ceramics produced could not recover its previous glory. A positive sign was the revival of blue and white porcelain during the Guangxu period when high quality replicas of Kangxi blue and white were produced. The Qianjiang porcelain was an important innovative decorative technique which influenced the production of high quality and artistic new fencai paintings during the Republican period.

Replicas from the late Qing Dynasty to the Republican Period

In the declining years of the Qing dynasty trading in antiques and replicas developed. The demise of the Qing dynasty resulted in the closure of the imperial kilns. To satisfy the demand and increase revenue, foreign and local traders who were working cooperatively with private kilns, began producing replicas for export. Many former craftsmen from the imperial kilns were employed to produce replicas. They replicated the ceramics made by the imperial kilns during the reigns of emperors Kangxi and Qianlong They included replicas of blue and white, five-coloured, tricoloured-glazed, kidney-bean red and porcelain decorated in peacock green and eggplant purple developed in the reign of Emperor Kangxi. They also made replicas decorated in blue and white, pastels, doucai and sacrificial red that were produced in the reign of Emperor Qianlong. There were replicas of the Junyao kiln of the Yuan dynasty, blue and white bowls from the reign of Ming Emperor Hongwu and blue and white cups from the reign of Ming Emperor Yongle. Among these, the most distinctive replicas were of the larger wares. These replicas were sought after by rich and high ranking government officials and foreign collectors who were willing to pay high prices for them.

Especially popular were the overglaze polychrome ceramics that carried the Qianlong reign mark. Many were decorated in the falangcai style and they carried the Guyuexuan mark. There were also many painted with European themes and decorations. The Republican president Yuan Shikai commissioned the production of replica ceramics for his personal use. They were modelled after Qing imperial ceramics. Famous artists such as Wang Xiaotang and Wang Dacang were believed to have anonymously painted some of the pieces. The Republican period produced some of the highest quality Qing imperial replicas as the former Qing dynasty craftsmen and imperial kilns were also sponsored and supported by the Republican government.

An important development during the Republican period was the re-emergence of the market for decorative art porcelain. They were produced by private workshops in Jingdezhen. The artists personally composed and executed these works. Their creations were essentially a continuation of the literati style of paintings on ceramics first popularised by the Qianjiang artists during the late Qing period. The drawings were in glossy and brilliant fencai enamels. The artists' mastery of the fencai enamels was well developed and they were able to use delicate and fine shading in their compositions. The most famous pioneers of this new fencai porcelain were Pan Taoyu and Wang Xiaotang. Pan was very versatile and produced images of human figures, landscape, birds and flowers. Wang was famous for his work on the human form. Unfortunately, both these pioneer artists died before the age of forty and only limited pieces of their art survived them.

Among Pan Taoyu's students were Wang Yeting, Liu Yucen and Cheng Yiting, all members of the famous Eight Friends of Zhushan. The Eight Friends of Zhushan is recognized as the elite group of the best fencai master artists of the Republican period. They were members of the Yue Yuanhui, a society where members met monthly at Zhushan to interact and exchange ideas on art. Each of the artists specialised in particular themes and had their own distinctive styles. It is now generally accepted that there were 10 premier artists of that period who were members of the Society. The names and individual painting styles are described below.

- Wang Qi - specialised in drawing human figures. His earlier works were done more in the gong bi style, which is characterised by fine outlines of the human figures. However, his style subsequently evolved into a more free and calligraphic style.
- Wang Dafan - also known for human figures. He adopted the gong bi style for his human figures.
- Deng Bishan - specialised in fishes and reeds in a style influenced by Japanese paintings.
- Wang Yeting - specialised in landscapes.
- Tian Hexian - specialised in plants.
- Xu Zhongnan - specialised in bamboo, rock and pine trees.
- Chen Yiting - specialized in birds and flowers.

- Liu Yucen - specialised in birds and flowers.
- He Xuren - known for his paintings of winter landscapes.
- Bi Botao - painting of birds and flowers.

Some of the contemporaries of the Eight Friends of Zhushan also produced comparable quality of art. Among them were Wang Bu who is known for his blue and white paintings; Wang Dacang known for his landscapes, Fang Yunfeng for his human figures and cats and Zhang Zhitang for landscapes.

These early pioneers germinated the growth of the contemporary ceramic industry in the 1980s and 1990s. This trend significantly impacted the future prominence and survival of replica production as it shifted the artistic and skilled talent to this new area in the late 20th and early 21st centuries.

Contemporary Artist Replica

There is evidence of a new type of hybrid replica related to the above contemporary artists produced in the early 20th century until prior or after the 1960s. They were produced by students or descendents of such well known artists or by individual talented obscure artists. This group of artists was producing high quality replica works of the mentioned famous artists. The replica artwork in most cases is comparable to the original art of such famous artists in terms of style, quality and theme. However, there were obvious original modifications and emphasis in colours and strokes incorporated in these replicas that clearly differentiated them from the original works. The calligraphy and seal of the original artists were loosely copied, probably to indicate the source of the work but evidently, there was no concerted or intentional attempt to make these works exact forgeries of the original work. The high quality of these works indicates that they were likely produced within the cultural context of replicas and were not intended to be forgeries. The replica artists, in the spirit of replica production, unfortunately failed to indicate their own names or seals on these art pieces. They were probably sold as replicas during the Republican period and priced accordingly.

The writer believes that many high quality ceramics of the early communist era were similarly produced within the same spirit of contemporary artist replicas. They have been similarly and casually downgraded by experts as "non-genuine" ceramics despite their historical context, high-quality craftsmanship, original drawings and themes. The government probably tacitly sanctioned and allowed these grades of ceramics to be produced for the domestic population and for export. They would not have been classified as fakes and were probably accepted and traded as replicas during this period.

The risk of classification as forgeries by international buyers deterred many talented artists to significantly reduce or stop producing contemporary artist replicas despite the strong demand. This resulted in the deteriorating quality of such replicas produced by inexperienced struggling young artist until the 1970s and 1980s when these works were classified into the low quality fake ceramic category. These early contemporary artist replicas were, unfortunately, broadly labelled as fake ceramics in the later part of the 20th century.

The writer believes many of that the early contemporary artist replicas were produced by the artist's most talented students and descendents. The problem of classification as true replicas is further compounded by a limited number of these famous artists including their personal calligraphy and seals on these replicas produced by their descendents or favourite students.

The writer's opinion is that early high quality contemporary artist replicas should be clearly differentiated under the Chinese cultural and historical context and should be distinguished from modern definitions of fake ceramics.

Chinese Communist Party Replicas 1950-1980s

The Communist Party of China assumed full control of the government with Mao Zedong heading the People's Republic of China in 1948. If art was presented in a manner that supported and promoted the government, the artists were acknowledged and rewarded. Any clash with the communist party manifesto would reduce the artists to farmers for "re-education" under the regime's rules. The most severe governmental control on artistic freedom was during the Cultural Revolution. The most notable event was the Destruction of the Four Olds, which had major ramification on ceramics, paintings, literary art, architecture and countless other areas of Chinese art history.

Artists were encouraged to portray socialist realism in their work and painters were assigned subjects and expected to mass-produce paintings on these themes. This was considerably relaxed in 1953 after the Hundred Flowers Campaign from 1956 to 1957, when traditional Chinese painting experienced a significant revival. During this period there was a proliferation of peasant art depicting everyday life in the rural areas on murals and at outdoor painting exhibitions

During the Cultural Revolution, there was an overhaul of many of the arts, with the intention of producing new and innovative art that reflected the benefits of a socialist society. As a result of this, many artists whose work was deemed to be anti-socialist were persecuted and prevented from working.

China's historical sites, artefacts and archives suffered devastating damage as they were thought to be at the root of the "old ways of thinking". Many artefacts including ceramics were seized from private homes and museums and were often destroyed on the spot. There are no records of exactly how much of Chinese art was destroyed, stolen or seized. Western observers suggest that much of China's thousands of years of history was in effect destroyed or later, smuggled abroad for sale to Western collectors and auction houses during the ten years of the Cultural Revolution.

Although this uncontrolled destruction was undertaken by some of the Revolution's over enthusiastic followers, the destruction of historical and cultural relics was never formally sanctioned by the Communist Party, whose official policy was instead to protect such items. On May 14th 1967, the Chinese Communist Party central committee issued a document incorporating recommendations for the protection of cultural relics and books during the Cultural Revolution. Archaeological excavation and preservation continued successfully during this period. Several major archaeological excavations during the Revolution led to the discovery of the Terracotta Army and the Mawangdui tombs and were protected from any further potential damage by the new legislation.

Though never officially acknowledged by the Chinese government, the writer's opinion is that replica ceramic production was supported and continued during this period. Several reasons suggest this to be the correct assumption. The replica trade offered potential export revenue from overseas markets to a newly cash-strapped government. Secondly, it offered a unique opportunity to replace high-quality replica ceramics with valuable original ceramic antiques moved to Taiwan from the 1930s to 1948 by the Republican government. Thirdly, it enabled the replacement of the uncontrolled destruction of much of the heritage ceramics during the Cultural Revolution from 1966 to 1976. Finally, in order to restore national pride, there was a need to replace many stolen and destroyed ceramic artefacts. This was caused by the many instances of illegal plunder by foreign powers in the past and subsequent foreign occupation and looting of Chinese treasure from 1911 onwards.

The Forbidden City Palace Museum and museums in Shanghai, Beijing and other parts of China needed to be replenished with the lost historical symbols of Chinese ceramics and the only way was to create perfect replicas (probably secretly) as replacements. The writer has in his possession several high quality replica pieces acquired through older collectors who had acquired them in the 1960s and 1970s. These have Chinese museum markings and serial numbers at the base of the ceramics. All these pieces have excellent craftsmanship and design. However, on closer examination one can detect minor imperfections and flaws in colouring, glaze or drawings on some of these ceramics. These could have been rejected or surplus pieces that were manufactured by private kilns as museum replacements. It is likely that these rejected or surplus pieces were supposed to be destroyed but were instead secretly exported by private kilns and sold to foreign collectors to defray cost of manufacturing such museum quality ceramics for the government.

Many foreign collectors around the world are in possession of high-quality ceramics replicas acquired during this period. Whether these replicas were produced, by the private kilns independently for export or jointly with the support of the Communist government or were authentic dynastic ceramic smuggled out of China to avoid persecution, remains a moot question based on today's questionable authentication tests.

A dormant period of inactivity of replica production would have left all skilled replica artists unemployed and redundant. These artists would not have been able to maintain, upgrade, refine or transfer their knowledge and skills to the new generation of replica artists in the 1980s. The 1980s era of ceramic replicas would not have been achievable if this talent was left to disintegrate and vanish if the government had not directly or indirectly supported the ceramic replica industry and ensured that its expertise and knowledge remained intact.

If the converse view is correct and no replicas were made during this period, then the replicas made during the 1980s were of a much lower quality and design due to the lack of talented artists transferring their skill and knowledge to the new generation of craftsmen.

Replica Porcelain After 1980

Economic reforms by the Chinese government introduced free market principles to the ceramic industry in 1995. Increased general affluence in the region promoted a revival of interest in antiques and collecting Chinese ceramics. Antique ceramic auction prices continued to appreciate and this ignited a strong demand for high-quality replica ceramics. The sheer variety of replica ceramics available reached a historical record, with every design replicated from the colourful pottery of the Neolithic age to ceramics produced in the Republican period.

It is the writer's view that the replicas produced in the 1980s yielded a variety of different and varying grades and quality of ceramics. The volume was astronomical and probably higher than any other replica-producing period in Chinese history but the overall quality was probably the lowest.

In a free market economy, the private kilns and traders will have to tailor products to meet the demand and capacity of the consumer at the top by offering high-end replicas with imperial and museum quality material and workmanship. These commanded high prices and were bought by affluent local and foreign collectors who paid for the quality and craftsmanship of such replicas. The writer has in his possession a 1980s ceramic catalogue titled, *China's Best Arts and Crafts, Volume 2 Number I 1981*, which advertised pictures of immaculate replicas for high retail prices. It was clear that the market for such high end products existed. Though it was small and exclusive, it was flourishing and many forward-looking collectors had invested and purchased such excellent replicas during this period. The skills were very personal and only mature artists with skills acquired during the Republican period or someone trained under a dedicated master artist working with professional private kilns could have produced such museum or imperial quality replicas. The price of a high-end replica during this period based on the catalogue and writer's research was estimated to be between US$2,000 to US$5,000 and above. The main replica retailers were in Hong Kong and Singapore. This demand probably germinated into several famous and specialized kilns such as the Jiang and Huang kilns that still continue to produce quality-high replica as contemporary works of art.

The second category was the mid-range replica produced in large numbers by small private kilns using cheap material and talented young artists. This satisfied the novice collector and the general retail market. Workmanship probably varied and there were always gems of craftsmanship and talent in the vast numbers produced, but they became rare as the industry developed its commercial emphasis in the late 1980s. Such mid-range replica pieces would have been sold at an average price of US$500 to US$800 and higher.

The last category was the low-end replica which would have been the forerunner of the fake porcelain industry. The main objective was to produce these ceramics quickly and in large volumes. The quality of material and talent was the cheapest available and these were sold as curio pieces or decorative ceramics. The average price was about US$100 to $300 because of the low operational and labour cost in China during this period.

This was an era of commercialization and the whole process was geared towards quick profit. Most of the replica ceramics produced was limited to ceramics that would not have required 72 assembly line stages with an experienced artist at each phase of the production process. This age-old tradition of producing imperial quality products is documented in Jingdezhen literature. Due to the astronomical cost, time and failure rate of replica production, the majority of 1980s replicas were produced in the more simple and profitable contemporary style. Mid and low-range replicas tended to be produced from cheap outsourced ceramics vases from small kilns. Painting involved simple common or pasted patterns and themes, minimal use of expensive industrial gold, cheap imported chemical pigments and individual large repetitive or contemporary drawings. The works were done by young and inexperienced artists to keep production cost low. Though the salaries and other costs were low, the replica profit margins were equally low because traders wanted low prices. The growth and prominence of contemporary ceramics in the 1990s as a viable alternative for the talented artists and craftsmen depleted talent from the replica industry and left a low-skilled workforce to continue with replica production.

The quality of work, craftsmanship, material or design from 1980s never reached the standard of the Republican and dynastic replicas except in rare instances when individual artists or where private kilns and organisations sponsored and invested in the quality of the ceramics. The 1980s represented the apex of the early incubation period until the early 20th century of the proliferation of fake ceramic artefacts. This was a period of unscrupulous free market enterprise where traders and kilns only wanted to maximize profits by any means. In fairness, it must be mentioned that the economic plight of the workers in the ceramic industry, the decline in export of quality Chinese ceramics and unethical foreign trading practices exacerbated this unfortunate trend.

In the past, replicas were revered as collectibles. Low and high-quality replicas were produced but there were no concerted attempts to pass them off as fake antique ceramics. By the 20th century, opportunistic foreign traders financed small independent private kilns in different parts of China to specialise in producing fake ceramics. Many of the forgery and fake ceramic techniques such as artificially aging ceramics were developed and refined during this period. Without the hold of dynastic control and the fear of persecution from the government, the era of fake ceramics emerged in high volume and destroyed the reputation of the high-quality replicas.

Ravinder Singh Manocha, 2013

EVALUATING ANTIQUE, REPLICA AND FAKE CERAMICS

Scope

In evaluating the categories of ceramics, the writer's emphasis will be strictly limited to its commercial valuation derived from criteria evolved by free market forces. The cultural, historical and social values of these ceramics are only relevant as far as they relate to the commercial valuation of ceramics under discussion.

Antiques- Commercial Criteria

Period of manufacture
This is determined by expert opinion, provenance and scientific tests. Non scientific tests are generally inconclusive. However, these tests are still heavily relied on to estimate the commercial values of ceramics.

Purpose or usage of the ceramic
Ceramics produced specifically for the use of imperial dynasties, the nobility or the common man can determine its lineage. Dating of a ceramic can be substantiated by its connection to religious, artistic or other purposes. Generally, an imperial ceramic has a higher commercial value due to its rarity and general commercial fascination with imperial dynasties.

Quality of the craftsmanship
The fine details of workmanship, the degree of quality control, complexity of designs, themes and drawings are indicative of respective periods. The materials used, production methods, glazes and pigments are also used as evidence by experts to support dating of ceramics. Reign marks, seals and calligraphy are similarly used as markers to determine the period of manufacture. The aesthetic, artistic refinement and objective beauty of a ceramic will generally assume a higher demand and commercial value.

Condition of the antique
It should be relatively flawless with no damage or imperfections except age-related wear and tear. Any damage or flaws will reduce its commercial value. A poor quality antique can be merited if there is evidence of its age and can be collected for that purpose. However, it will not have the high valuation of flawless and high-quality antiques.

Historical versus commercial value
Many ceramic antiques are valued as historical and museum grade pieces. However, based on current market trends, these pieces are less likely to have a high commercial valuation. Only an increase in demand from commercial buyers can potentially raise the valuation of ceramics in this category.

Rarity
Antique collection is driven by the desire to own rare and potentially unique artefacts. The commercial value of an antique can appreciate rapidly if there is information and evidence that supports that it is in fact, rare and limited.

The criteria above are parameters determined and promoted by auction companies and their experts. Right or wrong, these are the main commercial basis of valuation of antiques in recent times. It allows auction companies to potentially control inclusion or exclusion of ceramics on criteria of suitability. This ensures that their preferred clients have priority in auctioning selected products that will ultimately bring the greatest financial return to all parties.

In recent auctions of ceramics, it has become evident that the buyer can by his auction bid materially change the valuation or authenticity of a particular ceramic. This is despite the contradictory original expert valuation on the said ceramic. A New York auction in 2011 of a pear shaped famille rose porcelain vase, illustrates this principle most aptly. This particular vase was estimated by Sotheby's experts as "probably a Republican period" ceramic. They valued it at US$800 to US$1,200. It was aggressively bidded for by seven parties and was finally sold to an anonymous buyer for US$18 million.

"It's outstanding if it's genuine," remarked Giuseppe Eskenazi, one of the leading dealers in Chinese art in a post-auction statement. This illustrates the commercial reality of antiques valuation. Experts can call a piece an antique or replica all in the same breadth, depending on the commercial valuation by buyers.

Similarly a "potential replica" of a Qianlong vase was sold for £43 million at a Bainbridges' auction in November 2010. The winning bid was more than 50 times higher than the pre-sale estimates by their experts. The price, including auction house fees, was a record for any Asian work of art offered at an auction. Due to a dispute between the buyer and auctioneer over the additional £8.6 million auctioneer fee, the vase was re-brokered by London-based auction house Bonhams. It was subsequently, sold by private treaty at an estimated sum of £25 million to another buyer in January 2013.

Multiple expert opinions, which were mostly unsubstantiated and based on hypothesis from oral information without any scientific tests, concluded that the porcelain vase was probably made for the Chinese emperor Qianlong, who ruled between 1736 to 1795.It was supposedly looted from the Old Summer Palace during the infamous raids by the British and the French forces in 1860 and subsequently sold to the buyer. How these conclusions were reached and accepted despite sketchy records of ownership remains a mystery.

Mr. Ivan Macquisten, editor of the *Antiques Trade Gazette* expressed the view that the auctioned vase was one of the finest pieces ever made in China. He was further quoted as saying, "Last year there was an exhibition in Beijing of great historical Chinese objects and a similar vase was listed as being in the top dozen items in Chinese art history and that wasn't as good as this one".

Experts can differentiate ceramics by tests of unsubstantiated ownership, provenance and purely by craftsmanship and give one imperial lineage and other less refined pieces can be denigrated to replica or non-imperial status.

In mid 2011, a similar but less elegant vase with crudely drawn images compared to the Bainbridges' vase was sold. It was documented in the *2012 Chinese Art Auction Records* as having been sold by a Macau-based auction company at slightly more than RMB 191 million (approximately £12.5 million).

In each of the first two instances, experts and the auction houses involved in the original valuations and authentication of the ceramics for auction have not publicly contradicted the results of the buyers' bids. In essence, we can assume that they have by their silence, invalidated their own original valuation of authenticity and value. Concurrently, they have discredited the methodology and principles they applied in reaching their conclusions. For all intent and purpose, both these vases stand in auction book records as authentic antiques and precedents for future sales. The third mentioned auction sale in 2011 seems to have taken its value and likely an assumed authenticity on the auction precedent determined by the Bainbridges' sale. From available published information, none of these vases were subject to any scientific tests to establish their authenticity.

Ceramic provenance of the Chinese dynasties should be distinguished from other art forms such as paintings and 20th century contemporary ceramics. These are mostly accredited with specific artist names, craftsmanship styles, seals and calligraphy as indicative markers of authenticity. The modern provenance test applied by experts to Chinese dynasty ceramics is of scant documentation or oral evidence of alleged ownership tracked from the earliest period the ceramic was assumed to be in the owner's possession.

This authentication test is often applied to ceramics which were in the possession of dynasties, governments, museums, prominent families and individuals. Whether these pieces were substituted with fakes or replicas is rarely ever questioned by experts in their evaluation and investigation of provenance of these sources. The reliance on this method of authentication makes an unrealistic assumption, that there is no reason for ceramics in this category to be anything but genuine antiques because the source is assumed to be unimpeachable. Until more advanced scientific tests are developed to verify the age of these ceramics, we will never really know whether these expert assumptions of ownership track provenance can be justified.

Chinese dynasties imposed the accreditation on ceramics to the specific reign or dynasty for ceramics produced during the respective dynastic period. The seventy-two different highly skilled and anonymous artists, potters and craftsmen involved in ceramic manufacture are irrelevant as long as they created high-quality artistic ceramics that were consistent with the historical period. The assumption by modern experts is that the quality control was relatively superior in all dynastic periods. This assumption can potentially be supported with respect to imperial pieces produced by the royal kilns and the handful of private kilns subcontracted to produce imperial ceramics. It is unrealistic, however, to assume this premise for all other non-imperial ceramics. The further assumption is that the many artists involved in the production of ceramics were all equally skilled and painted in a particular and highly consistent manner in the production of millions of ceramic artefacts. This is one of many unrealistic assumptions made by ceramic experts as they judge the authenticity of period ceramics. No man can sign his name consistently over 365 days in a year. Nevertheless experts assume this is possible and that every signature is identical and every artistic stroke has the identical consistency, even if made by different artists.

In fairness, the examination and valuation methodology used by experts for dynastic ceramics involves more than the anonymous artists' craftsmanship and ownership provenance. They also evaluate the materials used, glazes, pigments, patterns and themes consistent with the relevant period based on archaeological and occasional scientific evidence. However, in the many recent authentications of dynasty ceramics in the absence of proven scientific dating tests, the best qualified expert's conclusions based on visual examination and aesthetics to determine its consequent commercial value is in the writer's opinion at best, a fairly good subjective guess.

What is a Replica?

What then is a replica and why are replicas nominally priced against antiques? Are there genuine differences between these two categories of ceramics or is it an artificial difference created by third parties to justify the business and value of antiques?

It is important to mention the cultural and historical context of a Chinese replica ceramic for completeness. The Chinese do not consider the manufacture and sale of replicas as an affront or illegal act. Replica production was sanctioned by the dynasties as a cultural activity and replicas were produced with the same fervour and dedication as other ceramics. There may be marked differences in the seals, colours and patterns used for imperial ceramics, but the quality, finishing and craftsmanship of high-quality replicas were in the writer's opinion, of comparative standard. Replica production allowed for the retention and enhancement of old skills as well as development of new methods and design of new ceramics. It cannot be denied that the production replicas contributed significantly to the current stage of development of Chinese ceramics. The natural acceptance and bias for replicas has prevented modern Chinese authorities from legislating against the proliferation of fake ceramics, as the latter is a blatant attempt to deceive consumers and encourages the production of ceramics outside the spirit and purpose of replicas. The broad classification of replicas by ceramic experts as an inferior product has contributed greatly on the misunderstanding and lack of appreciation for replica ceramics.

Below are the categories of replicas that have evolved since the Ming dynasty first started to produce replicas in the 15th century. The list is by no way exhaustive but, it is important to examine the different categories of replicas to appreciate the lack of consistency and confusion caused by this unique product of Chinese history.

Period Replica
These refer to ceramic made during a particular dynastic period but imitating the design or style of an earlier dynasty. The standard of finish would be more or less equal in terms of craftsmanship and material as original non-replica ceramics made during the relevant period. To differentiate between replicas and imperial dynasty ceramics, there would likely be marked differences in the seal, use of royal colours, calligraphy, designs and artwork such as the five clawed dragon reserved exclusively on ceramics produced for the emperor. These were originally produced, sold domestically or exported as replicas within the Chinese cultural context.

Imperial Quality Replica
These refer to ceramic made during the relevant dynastic periods. The quality and design is equivalent to ceramics for imperial use. However, these replicas were never used or intended for use by the imperial dynasties. They were most likely, secretly produced by the private kilns and sold exclusively to Chinese nobility or exported to foreign markets through foreign traders.

Non Imperial Replica
These refer to ceramic made during the relevant dynastic periods. The quality and design of these replicas for non-imperial use and were probably produced for the Chinese nobility or the general population. The craftsmanship and quality control would not have been as stringent as that of imperial ceramics and any defects and imperfection would be tolerated as part of the cost and expectations of the buyers. They would most likely have been produced by private kilns and openly sold domestically and exported through foreign traders.

Imperfect Period Replica by Imperial Kilns
There is archaeological evidence that imperfect imperial ceramics made by imperial kilns during the Ming dynasty were destroyed and buried deep within the compounds of the kilns. However, during the Qing dynasty, kiln administrators were authorized to sell imperfect pieces to defray the cost of the imperial kilns. Many slightly imperfect imperial ceramics would have been sold domestically or exported. The writer's view is that these imperfect pieces would be exported rather than sold domestically as the royalty would not have accepted or allowed the local Chinese population to use anything reserved for royalty, imperfect or otherwise. The exported ceramics did not remain within the Chinese territory and there was tacit acceptance of this profitable channel to dispose of the imperfect imperial ceramics. It is highly likely that some perfect imperial quality ceramics may have been branded as imperfect by unscrupulous kiln administrators and secretly sold to the Chinese nobility or exported through foreign traders.

Modified Period Replica
During the Qing dynasty, artistic freedom and innovation were encouraged and improved designs and modified replicas were produced. The problem is that these improved or modified ceramics are loosely classified as replicas because they were based on historical designs and craftsmanship. What degree of innovation in design and what

percentage of originality or modification can take these ceramics out of the classification of replica and into the area of original period ceramics? There is general apathy to address this issue by historian and experts. The failure and inability to accurately date such ceramics only compounds the confusion in the area.

New and Original Designed Replica

Using the artistic theme, influences and colours of antique ceramics, the craftsmen during the dynastic periods were able to individualise ceramic wares in terms of drawings and designs to create a completely original work of art. These products were probably made as single unique pieces or as a small collection of original pieces. The question that arises is whether these original creations would fall under a category of antique ceramics. This class of replicas were probably sold domestically to Chinese nobility or exported to Western buyers under the label of replicas or non-imperial ceramic.

Modern Replica post 1911

The end of the dynasty did not spell the end of the craftsmanship and talent of the many ceramic craftsmen during the dynasty period. The strong demand from the Republic government and export markets kept these artists producing and transferring their skills to new artists of the 20th century. Many dynastic equivalent quality ceramics were produced post 1911. These pieces matched the technical and artistic brilliance of early dynasty ceramic, yet have been poorly valued by ceramic experts purely because they were not made during the dynastic period and were produced openly as replicas. It is probable that many artists working in the imperial kilns were employed and sponsored by the Republican government and private kilns to produce these high-grade replicas. However, as commercial considerations became a prime consideration in replica manufacture, many mass-produced low-grade and cheap replicas appeared on the market. Commercialisation led to the growth of the fake ceramic industry that blurred the line with high-quality replicas produced in the early and later part of the 20th century

Contemporary Replica

The 1980s saw the rise of two pioneers of the modern contemporary replica industry: Jiang Xunqing and Huang Yunpeng. In the book, *Traditional Jingdezhen Wares from Contemporary Kilns* published by the University Museum and Art Gallery and University of Hong Kong, we are introduced to the Huang and Jiang kilns founded by the aforementioned pioneers. These kilns have been devoting their efforts to re-establish the art of replica manufacture to its original dynastic intent. Young artists and craftsmen are trained in the use of old production and artistic processes and skills, which are concurrently documented in theory and in practice. These kilns produce high quality replicas with the original intent to honour the past and to make them accessible to the general public to appreciate Chinese culture and art without paying the exorbitant price of antiques. The replicas are credited to the kilns that manufactured them without naming the artists and craftsmen involved in its manufacture. It is similar to the approach adopted by the dynasties.

However, in recent times there has been a radical shift away from the practice of artist anonymity. Individual artists have begun to credit their names and seals on such replicas and are moving these ceramics into the area of collectible contemporary art. Huang Yunpeng the founder of Huang Kiln, has won numerous national awards for replica ceramics. He was awarded the prestigious title of Chinese Ancient Ceramic Master in 2007. His work has been described as integrating innovative modern designs with the aesthetic emotions and integrity of the past. Prices of such contemporary replica ceramics continue to rise slowly and are becoming comparable to works of the best contemporary ceramic masters of the 20th Century.

To complete the analysis of antique and replica ceramics, it is necessary to evaluate both the modern fake ceramic and ceramic craft industries in China.

Fake Ceramics

What caused this industry to arise and grow exponentially in the 20th century? Several factors triggered this phenomenon. The advent of cheap, mass-produced ceramics from foreign factories greatly impacted the export market for Chinese ceramics. In 1995, the Chinese government moved from a planned to a free market economy and the subsequent establishment of the Jingdezhen ceramic industry to free market forces resulted in a large pool of talented albeit unemployed ceramic artists. Fake ceramic production provided a potential avenue for earning a living for the many workers and artists in a deteriorating ceramics industry. The absence of a regulatory framework in China on fake ceramics strongly contributed to the growth and legitimacy of this industry. This was further fuelled by the growing market for antique Chinese ceramics and demand from novice collectors. Producing replica ceramics was not an acceptable commercial alternative as the cost of producing high quality replicas was prohibitively expensive without dynastic or government-sponsored support.

Fake ceramics are now the beyond original scope of antiques and cover all areas of ceramics including crafts and modern contemporary works.

Fake ceramics are manufactured using modern technology and utilise cheap labour of artists of varying talent. Materials used are often of poor quality. However, sophisticated techniques are used to age the ceramic to avoid detection by modern authentication methods. Fake ceramics are usually manufactured by small independent kilns that employ struggling young ghost artists who copy genuine works and sell them to the many unsuspecting collectors.

Fake ceramics are produced in large volumes and sold at low prices. Unfortunately, the retailers raise prices significantly to guarantee good profit margins. Profits earned perpetuate this unethical industry.

Poor quality fake ceramics can easily be detected by an informed buyer or amateur expert. However, as manufacturing technology improves, the fake ceramic can achieve a very high quality visual finish as comparable to genuine products. It is difficult for seasoned buyers to tell the subtle differences purely on visual examination. Forgers lured by easy profits have become good at hiding the identifying features of fake ceramics and furthermore, expert valuation is expensive and not always reliable.

The future of the fake ceramics is alive and strong. As long as regulations remain weak or nonexistent with poor enforcement, the industry will thrive. The greedy and reckless collector will never disappear and a new one is born every minute. Many experienced collectors have switched to collecting contemporary art to ensure that there is a clear provenance from the artist. Even then, there are risks of innocently acquiring fake ceramics. In the end, it is the responsibility of the buyer to exercise caution and diligence and obtain proper certification, photographic evidence and when necessary, expert valuation before investing in suspect ceramics.

Ceramic Crafts

It is pertinent to briefly distinguish between crafts and replica ceramics. Both were produced during the same periods. Craft replicas were marked with the reign of dynasties or the historical period in early history and later the commercial organisations and kilns that produced them in the 20th century.

Craft replica ceramics were produced earlier by small private kilns. They were mostly for utilitarian and decorative purposes and were sold cheaply and abundantly to the general population. The most common and recognised ceramic crafts are sculptures that have gained prominence as artistic artefacts. The highest quality of this category of crafts was probably produced in large quantities during the Republic and Communist era.

Soon after, with advancements and innovations in ceramic production, private kilns began producing large numbers of craft replica ceramics in varying designs and grades of quality to meet the expectations and demands of the domestic and export markets. Many varieties of ceramics crafts were produced with high artistic standards with a growing number accredited to named artists. These pieces are generally categorised as modern collectible art. The line between traditional art and craft has become blurred in the last few decades with these recent developments.

Period and old replica ceramic crafts have evolved into antiques and are valued against the same criteria as traditional antiques. The modern fake ceramic craft industry is similarly gaining prominence as craft appreciation and valuations rise.

The Future

What is the future commercial valuation of replica ceramics?

The authentic ceramic replicas of the past, whether of high or low quality, will in time evolve into antiques and their future value will be judged in exactly the same criteria as traditional antiques.

Fake ceramics however, will never evolve into anything of artistic significance, but will continue to remain a representation of human deceit, gullibility and greed.

Ravinder Singh Manocha, 2013

NON-TRADITIONAL SOURCES OF CHINESE CERAMICS

Despite recent history and clear documented evidence of loss of many valuable ceramic pieces, the core of Chinese ceramic collections held in its museums remains relatively intact in its breadth and diversity. This is because of the large number of high quality ceramics produced from the earliest dynasties under imperial patronage starting from the Yuan to Ming and becoming most fervent during the Qing.

The loss of national treasures from China was both legal and illegal and the causes were both internal and external. This loss impacted Chinese art, culture and history. For our purposes, the discussion on lost national treasures will be focused on both dynastic and replica ceramics produced between the 15th to the 20th century.

The legal export of Chinese porcelain, silk and tea to the Far East and Europe started a trend that led to a bustling trade. This gradually incited wars and use of military force by foreign powers to gain commercial and trade concessions from China. These conflicts led to massive illegal plunder and looting of Chinese heritage ceramics particularly, from the 17th century and its illegal export and smuggling by Chinese and foreigners.

It is important to study the impact of historical trends and to assess the quality and quantity of such loss of Chinese national treasures and the countries they were removed to and held until their disposition publicly and privately in the 20th century till the present.

Qing dynasty 1644 to 1911

Export trade
During this period, both private and imperial kilns had the capability to produce imperial quality ceramics. The replica industry was similarly flourishing and these grades of ceramics were being sold overseas through foreign traders. It is likely that imperial quality ceramics were ordered and sold to Western traders openly or secretly. The export revenue earned by the Qing administration probably made them less inclined to control the grade and quality of porcelain being manufactured for export. The private kilns often acted as subcontractors of the imperial kilns to produce imperial ceramics when the demand from the royalty exceeded the capacity of the imperial kilns. It is not inconceivable to conclude that foreign traders wanted to buy imperial quality ceramics whether labelled as replica or otherwise. The private kilns recognised this opportunity and would have supplied a mix of imperial and non-imperial quality ceramics, including varying quality of replicas to foreign traders. Fear of persecution and discovery would have stopped any private kilns from supplying any ceramics strictly related to the imperial family.

Damaged and rejected ceramics from imperial kilns
It was only during Qing dynasty that the administrators of the imperial kilns found a legitimate avenue to sell or smuggle out imperial quality ceramics to foreigners. Until the Qing dynasty, all damaged or imperfect imperial ceramics were destroyed and buried within the compound of the kiln. The damaged or rejected pieces from the imperial kilns during the Qing dynasty were sold to private kilns to resell to foreign traders These rejected imperial pieces were unlikely to be sold domestically as they were associated with royalty. If they were sold, it was done secretly. The majority of these ceramics were probably exported through foreign traders.

The Qing dynasty allowed such imperfect ceramics to be sold to foreign traders to defray operating cost of the imperial kilns. Quite likely, this spurred many corrupt kiln administrators to falsely label and smuggle out perfect imperial quality ceramics to foreign traders who were willing to pay high prices for such quality pieces. Domestic sale must have been limited to the imperfect pieces. The risk of selling a perfect imperial grade ceramic imposed a high risk of detection and severe punishment. It can be assumed that a limited number of imperial quality ceramics must have reached foreign shores and an even larger number of near perfect pieces may have landed in the hands of western traders, Chinese nobility and high level Qing officials. Those ceramics sold in China were probably kept as family heirlooms until they were sold domestically or smuggled out of China as part of the export trade.

Theft by Qing officials and Chinese nobility
The Chinese society had a distinct class of quasi-official nobility under the patronage of the emperor. They were amassing great wealth and power through trade and other benefits of monopolies bestowed on them. The Chinese society was broadly categorised into the royalty, high officials, nobility, low officials and commoners. Ceramics were produced for each segment of society but we are concerned with the top three strata of society. These groups had the capacity to acquire national treasures secretly or otherwise and the ability to dispose of them when the risk of detection became high.

Historical evidence illustrates that high ranking Qing officials like Heshen (1744-1799) could accumulate vast personal wealth in their official roles. Heshen's historical prominence is highlighted by his love of snuff bottles and the large number he amassed at the time of his death for corruption. Other Qing officials must have similarly acquired imperial quality art and ceramics as corruption was rife during this period. Many were taking bribes from foreign traders for granting trade concessions and benefits. The removal and execution of Heshen was meant to serve as a warning to Qing officials to stop using their position and power to enrich themselves. It did not deter the many detractors but probably had the reverse effect of making them more cautious and ignited secret hoarding of such treasures and outflow of many illegally obtained Chinese treasures to foreign traders.

Internal and external looting

Taiping Rebellion (1850-1864) Yangminguan (1860) and Boxer Rebellion (1900)
There were many periods of looting, smuggling and destruction of Chinese imperial treasures from the mid 19th century by foreign powers. These continued unabated until 1948 when the communist government assumed power and started another more destructive ten year phase in 1966 during the Cultural Revolution. These stolen national treasures ultimately followed the lucrative trail to western auction houses and foreign collectors. Many famous London-based collections such as the one by Sir Percival David were probably collected from purchases of imperial ceramics during this period of Chinese history.

Western intrusions on Chinese soil were designed to assert control and secure trade concessions. They led to humiliating defeats for the weak Chinese military and plunder and looting of Chinese national treasures on an extreme scale. The French and British forces openly held makeshift public auctions and sold illegally seized valuable and rare imperial treasures at low prices to the many foreign traders and officials. This buying faction probably included a small group of wealthy Chinese traders and officials. The collected bounties from these "sales" were often, officially distributed among the military staff of the invading forces.

The Taiping Rebellion was one of the most devastating civil wars in Chinese history. It was a period when Western mercenaries were employed by the Chinese royalty to subdue the Chinese rebels. This introduced, yet another foreign force that looted Chinese treasures during this period.

The burning and looting of Yangminguan summer palace in 1860 was another period of illegal theft and abuse exacted by western powers in the thirst for favourable trade concessions.

The most reliable accounts of these incidents are documented by several Western missionaries in their written letters and journals. They minced few words in describing the greed and avarice of their countrymen in destroying and plundering Chinese cultural and historical treasures.

Because of the embarrassment of Western scholars of their countrymen's behaviour, there is little evaluation of the quantity of imperial ceramics lost through this channel. However, one can assume that the extent and number was much higher and than any official historical estimate.

Looting from within
The Chinese nobility and traders were no less guilty because they were not the invaders. They enjoyed the spoils of lootings by buying up national treasures at throwaway prices. These were subsequently sold to wealthy overseas Chinese and foreigners or smuggled and hidden away in obscure regions in China to avoid detection.

Theft by kiln administrators, artist and potters
Though this must have been on a small scale, we can conclude that the lure of Western dollars and the lack of control must have allowed these activities to continue for many decades until the fall of the dynasty.

Theft by eunuchs
Eunuchs persisted during the dynasties until their fall in 1911. Many of them held privileged positions and were given the rare opportunity to travel outside the walls of the Forbidden City to interact with foreigners and the Chinese nobility. Eunuchs were highly resourceful and often acted as official translators and as a conduit of communication for foreign dignitaries and traders. The last Qing emperor Puyi recorded in his memoirs that there was massive plunder by eunuchs and palace officials during the last days of the dynasty. The palace ceramic collection was massive, diverse and unrecorded until the establishment of the Forbidden City Museum in 1925. Theft could have been by replacement of imperial ceramics with replica ceramics, so it may have gone on indefinitely. Complicity among officials to enrich themselves and the lack of accounting particularly in the late Qing period could have contributed significantly to the loss. The presence of foreign traders and local Chinese merchants with ready cash and access through the eunuchs provided an outlet to this plunder to overseas markets with a low risk of detection.

Puyi

Puyi, the last Qing emperor and his officials were not blameless in protecting national treasures. The exacting costs of maintaining the imperial household without revenue from the country forced the royal household to secretly mortgage such assets for loans with local banks that were rarely redeemed. Palace officials were secretly assigned to sell imperial treasures to traders and nobility to fund the costs of the royalty. Bribes to Western dignitaries, officials and traders for opium or other western luxuries were given in exchange for imperial collections. Puyi himself secretly moved many imperial treasures to Manchuria after the fall of the dynasty and continued to fund his imperial household by selling these treasures in China and Hong Kong through traders and antiques dealers.

1911 to 1948

The end of the Qing dynasty and the emergence of Yuan Shi Kai as the Republican president did not stop the outflow of national treasures. Yuan Shi Kai's fascination with imperial ceramics started a revival of high quality replica ceramic production and probably encouraged an export of many high quality ceramics to fund the extravagance of the new government. The writer has in his possession several immaculate ceramics with the approved export seal of the

Republic period affixed to the base of these pieces which were packed in convincing period boxes. Whether these were legitimate replicas made during the Qing period or later or antiques exported to avoid detection is just another mystery to add to the expanding list in this area of Chinese ceramics.

During the early 20th century, government supporters of the Republic and early Communist era such as Sun Yat Sen, famous Chinese artist Xu Bei Hong, and many others visited South East Asia particularly Singapore, Malaysia, and Hong Kong. Prominent Chinese from the mainland did so with the intention to solicit financial donations for their causes from wealthy overseas Chinese in the region. It is probable that replica ceramics, antiques and other art pieces, tacitly approved by the Republican and the Communist governments, may have also been given as gifts to many prominent overseas Chinese in the region for their financial support during this time.

There is little documented evidence of Japanese seizure of Chinese treasures during the Japanese occupation of China. There is a historical account of Chinese treasures being packed into a convoy of trains before the Japanese invasion and transported all over China to prevent Japanese seizure of these assets. Though many accidents and fires were recorded during the chase, the Chinese government maintained that the national treasures remained intact and fully accountable after the Japanese surrender in 1945 and restoration of the treasures to Nanjing in 1947. It is not improbable based on related historical evidence to assume that a significant percentage of national treasures were either being secretly hidden in China or stolen at that time or subsequently exported through foreign traders.

The famous 3,000 year old Zhou dynasty bronze artefact known as the Great Yu Cauldron is an example of a national treasure that was ingeniously buried under the Pan family home by their descendent Pan Da Yu during the Japanese occupation in 1937. It escaped detection despite the Japanese conducting seven extensive searches and interrogations to locate this treasure on the Pan ancestral home. It was subsequently unearthed and donated by Pan Da Yu to the People's Republic of China in 1949 and displayed in the Shanghai Museum in 1952. The government paid RMB 20 million Yuan to Pan Da Yu for her donation which she graciously donated to the Korean War fund. This gesture by the government was probably to encourage the rich Chinese nobility to return national treasures that had been secretly acquired by their families in the preceding centuries. (Source: CCTV documentary *National Treasures Lost and Found, Part I and II*)

Another illustrative incident relates to The Five Dynasties scrolls, Night Revels of Han Xizai by Gu Hongzhong. These scrolls were purchased for 500 taels of gold by Zhang Daqian in Beijing's famous Luilichang antique market in the late 1940s. Zhang graciously and out of patriotic concern resold this historic painting back to the Chinese government in 1952. How these historic artworks were acquired by Beijing antique dealers is never been openly addressed by Chinese authorities. This is just one of many known examples of lost treasures of China acquired by wealthy Chinese and foreigners through these illegitimate channels during this period.

The Taiwan National Palace Museum boast more than 655,000 artefacts removed from a Beijing museum in the 1930s to prevent them falling into the hands of Japanese troops. (Source: *Standard Newspaper*, Taiwan). The Communist coming into power in 1948 forced Chiang Kai Shek together with 3,800 crates of national treasures to move to Taiwan. (Source: Holdsworth, May, and Caroline Courtauld. *Forbidden City:* Frances Lincoln, 2008). The actual number of these treasures transferred to Taiwan during this period remains another unanswered question.

1948 to 1980

Fearing the threat of communist persecution, many legal and illegally acquired family heirloom ceramics were smuggled out to Asia and the West. They were most likely marked as replicas or poor quality antiques. The owners of these ceramics could not get high prices domestically because it was the post-war era and fear of getting caught with a potential national treasure was always a huge risk. There were probably many sellers and very few buyers during this time. Many wealthy Chinese wanted to leave the Communist regime in the 1940s and selling heirloom antiques was a means to fund their passage out of China. Others might have moved these treasures to tombs or secret hiding places believing that they could sell them after the communist regime was overthrown. As the communist regime became entrenched, many owners of these treasures feared that the opportunity to dispose of these valuable ceramics may not arise in their lifetime. The real or imagined fear of persecution for ownership probably prompted them to sell these ceramics through local domestic trading companies at any reasonable price.

It is not inconceivable to assume that a large number of heritage or illegally obtained ceramics were similarly exported before and during the Cultural Revolution. This was to protect them from destruction and to avoid potential persecution against the owners. There is no evidence that these grades of ceramics were being produced during this period by the communist regime and they could have potentially come from these and other sources.

My discussions with seasoned ceramic traders from China and Singapore on this issue revealed that there was a fear and unwillingness to sell these particular grades of ceramics openly in China after the 1950s. The domestic antique markets were well established in Beijing and Shanghai in the 1900s but were tightly controlled when the communist party came into power in 1948.

According to these sources, from the early 1950s government agents were interrogating and harassing antique dealers in Beijing and Shanghai who displayed or openly sold these types of ceramics in the domestic markets. This was probably a reaction to the Five Dynasties scrolls incident, among others. The supposed government agents were particularly adamant in knowing the source of the ceramics and the details of the owners. This, coupled with colourful stories of illegal arrest and harassment of domestic antique dealers probably, led to many of these ceramics being secretly exported out of China. Whether this was a sale strategy concocted by Chinese and foreign traders to sell these ceramic at higher prices to foreigners or to mask the ceramics with a degree of mystery or simply the plain truth is another issue to add to the long list of unknowns surrounding ceramics from this era.

By the 1980s, there was supposedly considerable relaxation or nonexistence of these alleged official checks. Despite this, traders preferred to avoid any confrontation with government officials and continued to sell these high grade ceramics overseas. These ceramics were supposedly acquired from many old family collections. The opposing view is that the traders were probably motivated by the higher prices in foreign currency rather than any real or rumoured government checks in exporting these pieces. There is no means of verifying the existence of independent Chinese kilns manufacturing these grades of ceramics at that time so we can only wonder where these antique traders were getting these sources of ceramics.

The 1980s policy to revitalize the ceramic industry crystallised a new avenue for all illegally obtained heritage ceramics to be legitimately and easily exported out of China. Demand for high quality ceramics created an opportunity for astute foreign collectors to pick up imperial quality ceramics mixed with modern commercial ceramics from Chinese and foreign traders.

Where, where and where

The writer estimates that the bulk of these high quality ceramics, whether replicas or otherwise, is in the hands of farsighted individual collectors and wealthy families in Asia Pacific, America and Europe. These collectors bought or acquired these ceramics for their craftsmanship and as works of art rather than as antiques. American and

European traders imported containers after containers of Chinese art and ceramics through Hong Kong from 1911 till the late 1980s. The Eight Allied forces that invade China provide a general distribution pattern of these export regions. They were the United States, France, Germany, Japan, Russia, Italy and Austria.

The British and French colonies and their overseas Chinese populations from Singapore, Malaysia, Taiwan, Indonesia and Philippines continued the oriental tradition to acquire Chinese art during the 20th century. Most prominent locations were Hong Kong, Singapore and Malaysia where the wealthy Chinese population was the largest in the 20th century and antique and art collection trade had developed and started to mature.

It is common commercial activity in the last two decades, for all the prominent auction houses from China and Europe to regularly advertise in large press releases soliciting Chinese art and antiques from countries in Asia. They regularly send their authentication experts to all these countries to meet with local collectors to value and propose auction terms for their ceramic collections among others. This is a strong affirmation that a substantial number of historical Chinese ceramics are in these mentioned regions.

Prices of ceramics for most of the 20th century, for one reason or another, were undervalued and the high quality and craftsmanship in most instances is in the writer's view not replicable for the similar value in the future.

My final words

It is a sad reflection on many "experts" and ceramic traders to label any grade of replica ceramic that they wish to dismiss as "unsuitable" as a product of the 1980s period. I have experienced many such interactions but on persistence and forced closer examination, the same expert discovers to his surprise that a particular piece is equivalent to an "imperial" quality ceramic. The expert is dumbfounded, except to say, "If you can find someone to accept this you will be laughing all the way to the bank". When asked to source a similar high quality ceramic from China, they are unable to find a similar piece even after months of searching. These experts spout generalities and cannot conclusively identify the location or name of 1980s private kilns that supposedly manufactured such high-quality ceramic pieces. The 1980s commercial manufacturing period for Chinese ceramics continues to add more confusion on the age of older high quality replica ceramics. Until a scientific test is available to accurately date these ceramics within years or decades, the jury is still out and experts can continue to put high reliance on sketchy provenance and biased expert knowledge to authenticate period ceramics. The serious collector should not be swayed by such opinions and rely on his own research, valuation and instinct in collecting quality replica ceramics.

Besides luck and opportunity, the first three guidelines applied in this collection are, beauty, beauty and beauty. Anything that has beautiful craftsmanship will appreciate in value in time and evolve into an antique. Anything that is beautiful and takes human effort, creative energy and spirit to create will not be easy or cheap to replicate commercially. Lastly, beauty must have an objective dimension and be appreciated by a majority of people to have a potential commercial appreciation. Subjective beauty is purely for individual aesthetic appreciation and commercial appreciation, if any, is incidental.

Collecting replica ceramics is an art investment with a long gestation period. It can take several years and probably decades to realise its real commercial appreciation. It is not an investment for the speculative art trader or collector who cannot appreciate the value of beauty while he patiently enjoys its ownership. As such, the last three guidelines applied in this collection are patience, patience and patience.

Ravinder Singh Manocha, 2013

GALLERY

OF

REPLICA

CERAMICS

THE COLLECTION

We have decided to display the collection without any captions or explanations on dynasty reign, sizes and other historical information. First, because we view the collection strictly as artistic pieces and should be viewed unadulterated. Secondly, several pieces are original designs and are rarely seen or published and we do not want the pieces to be copied or replicated in poor quality by the modern fake ceramic industry. We have generally limited photographs to each piece for these reasons. The visual experience cannot equate the feeling of holding and touching a beautiful piece of porcelain but it's the next best thing. Enjoy.

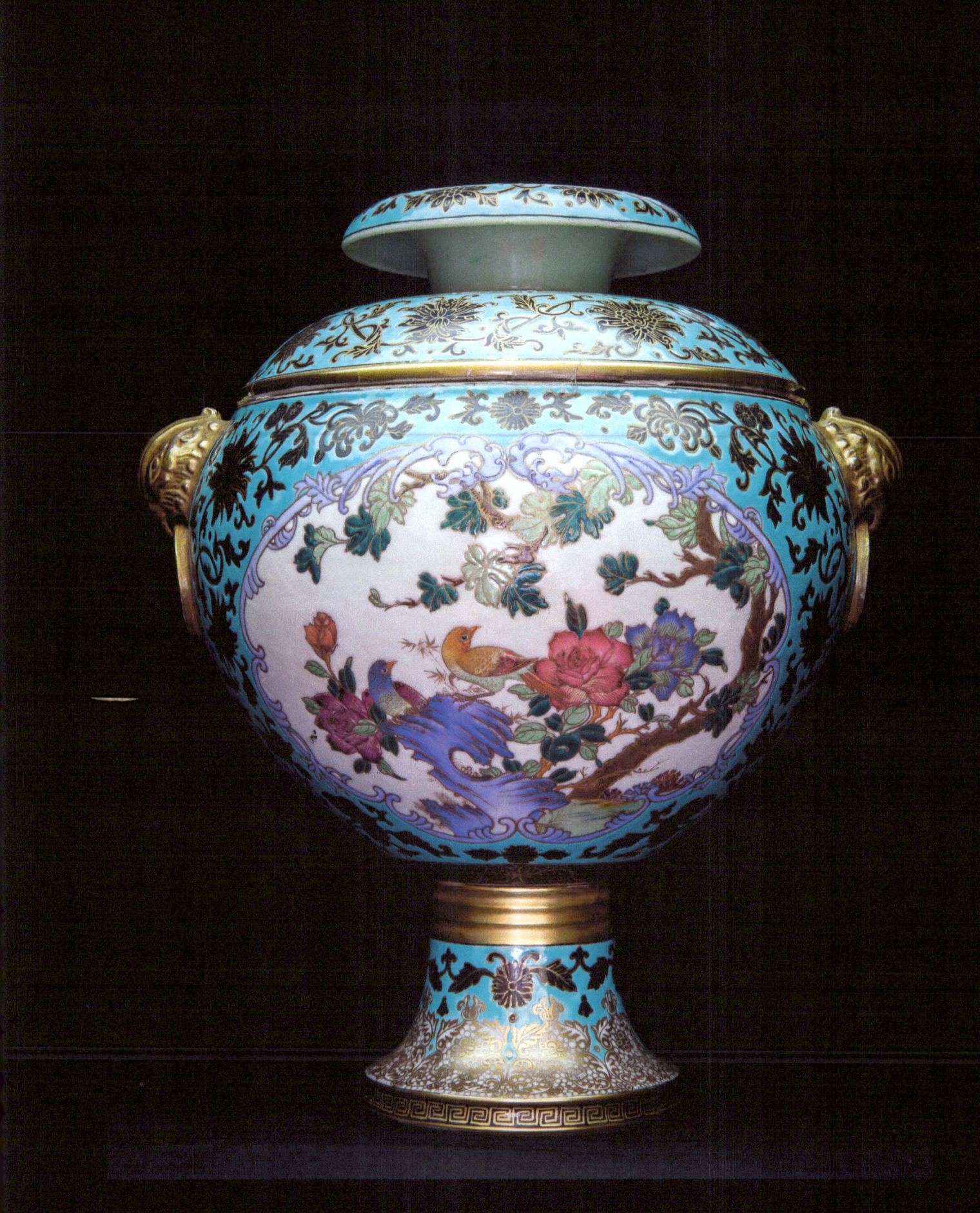

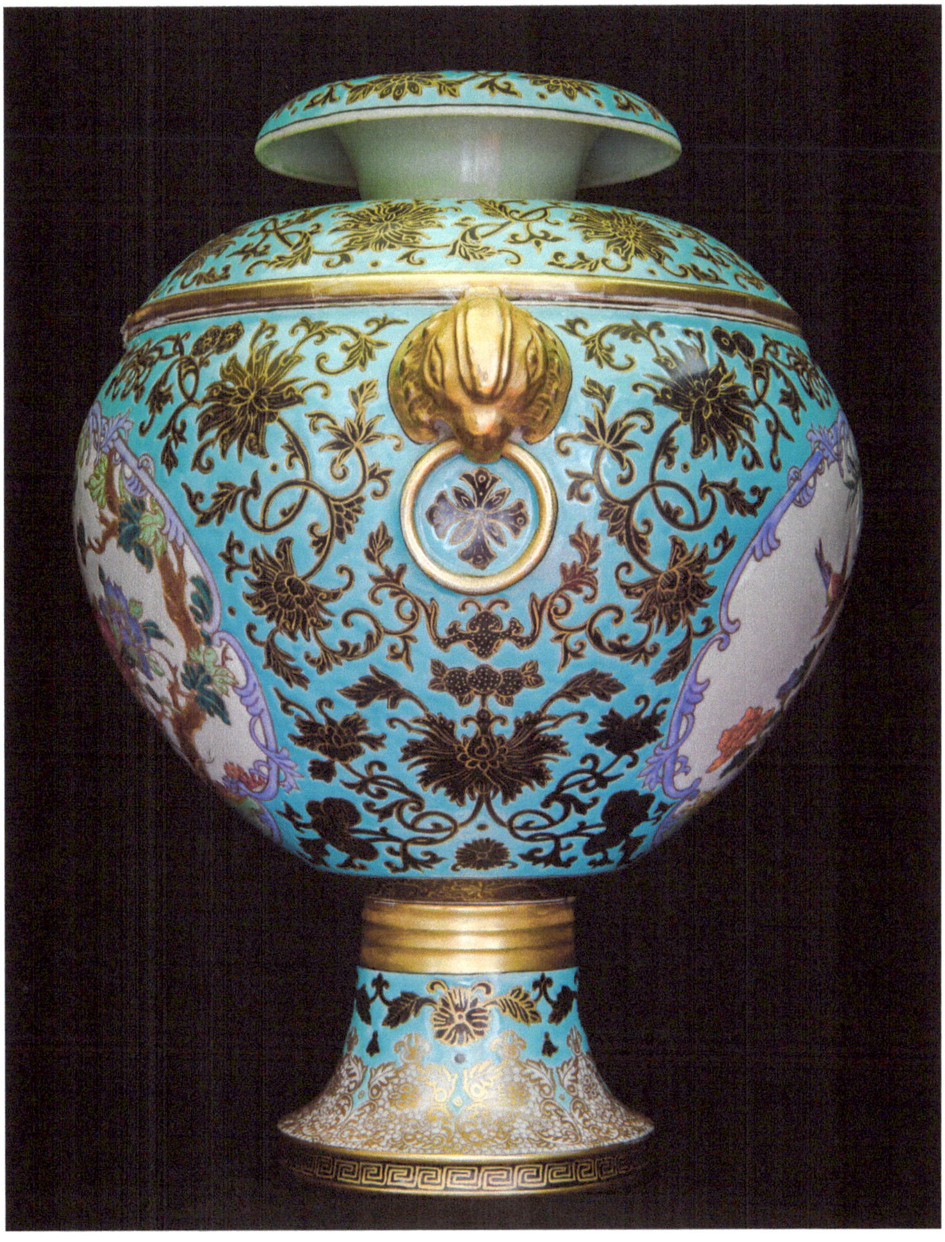

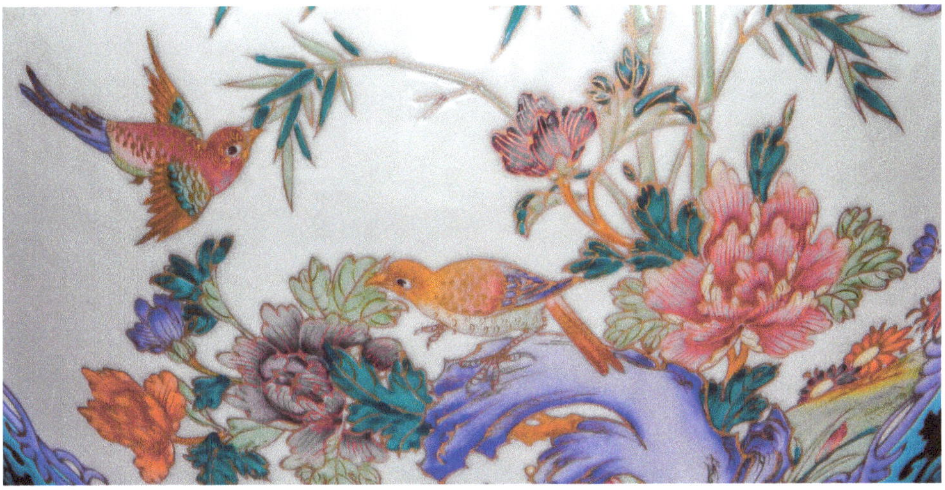

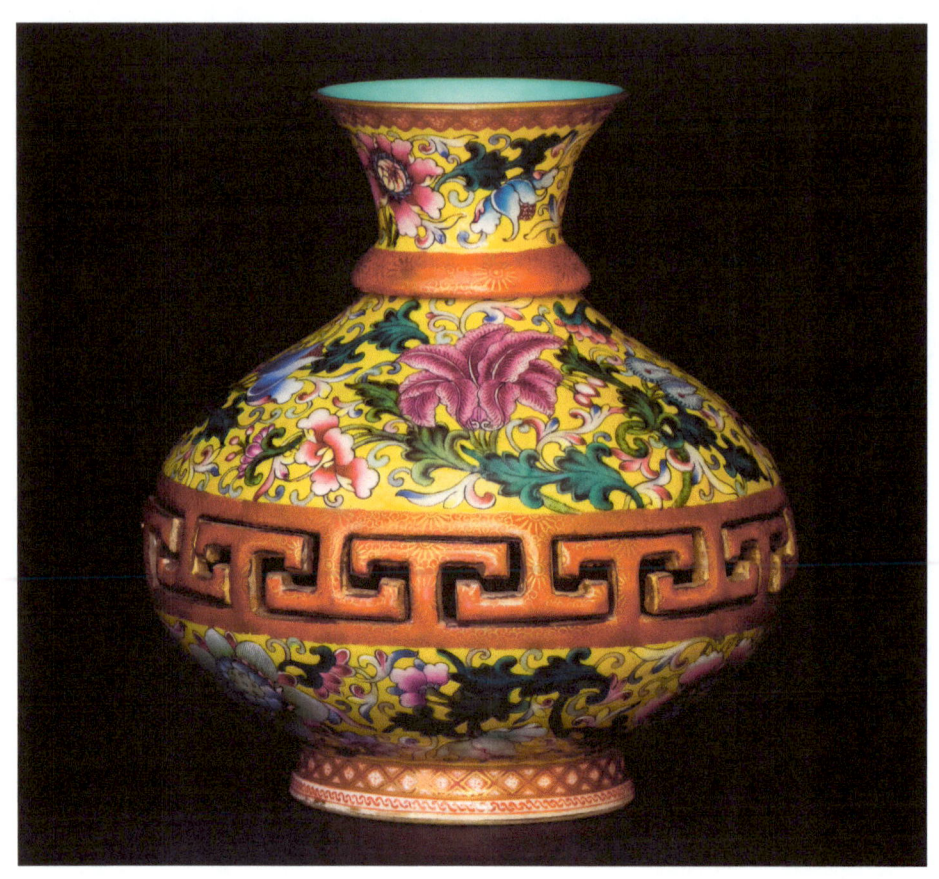
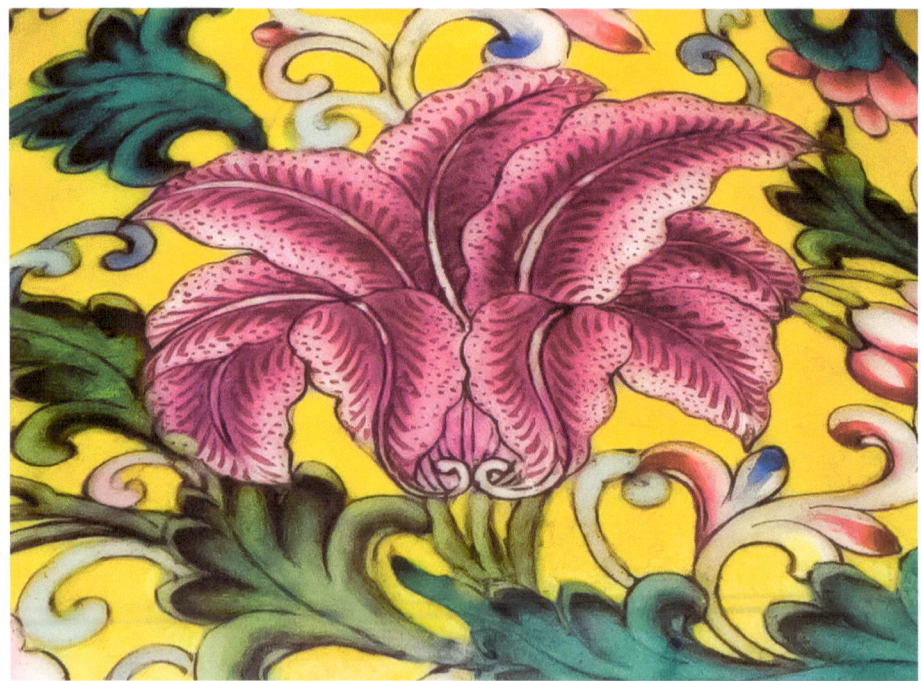

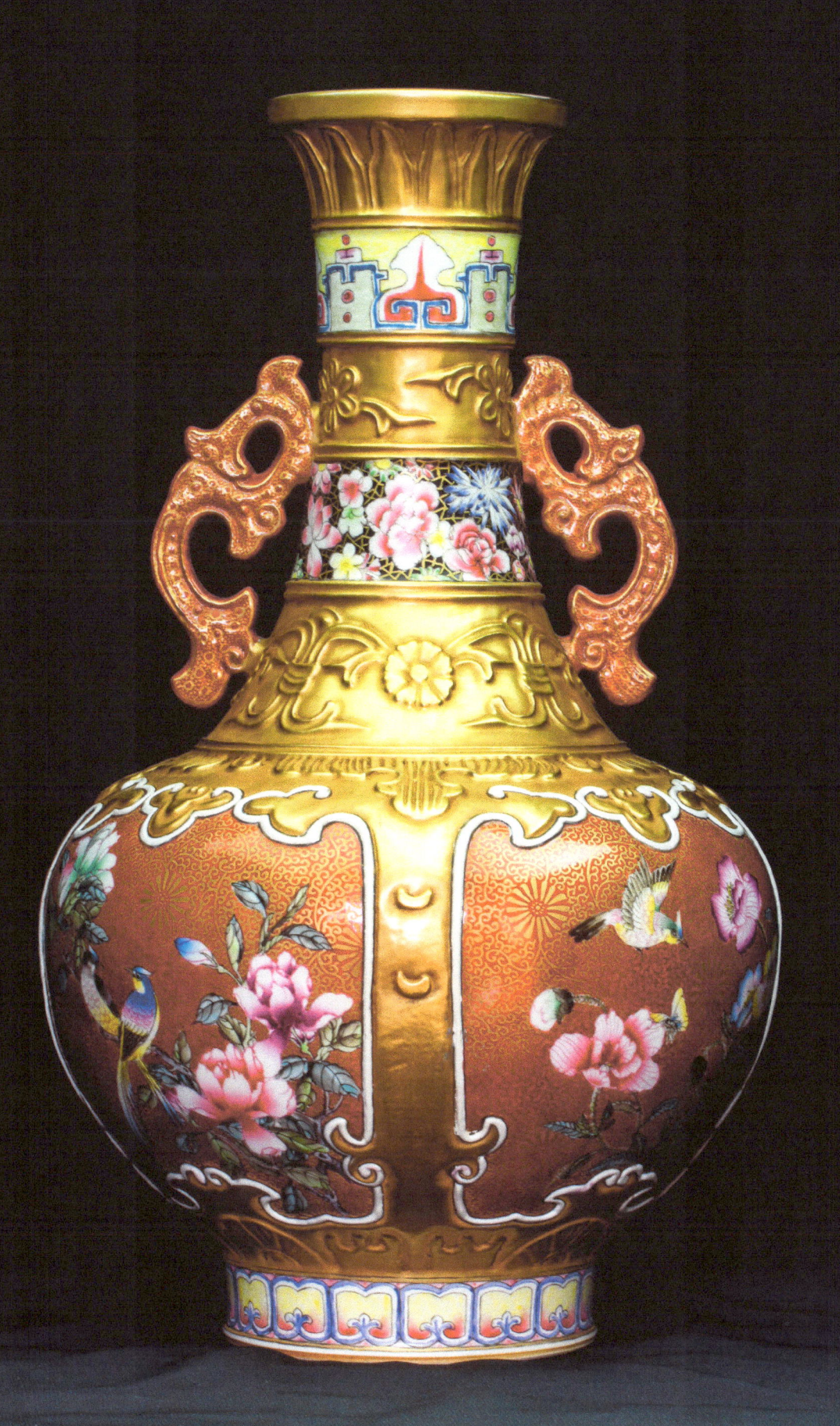

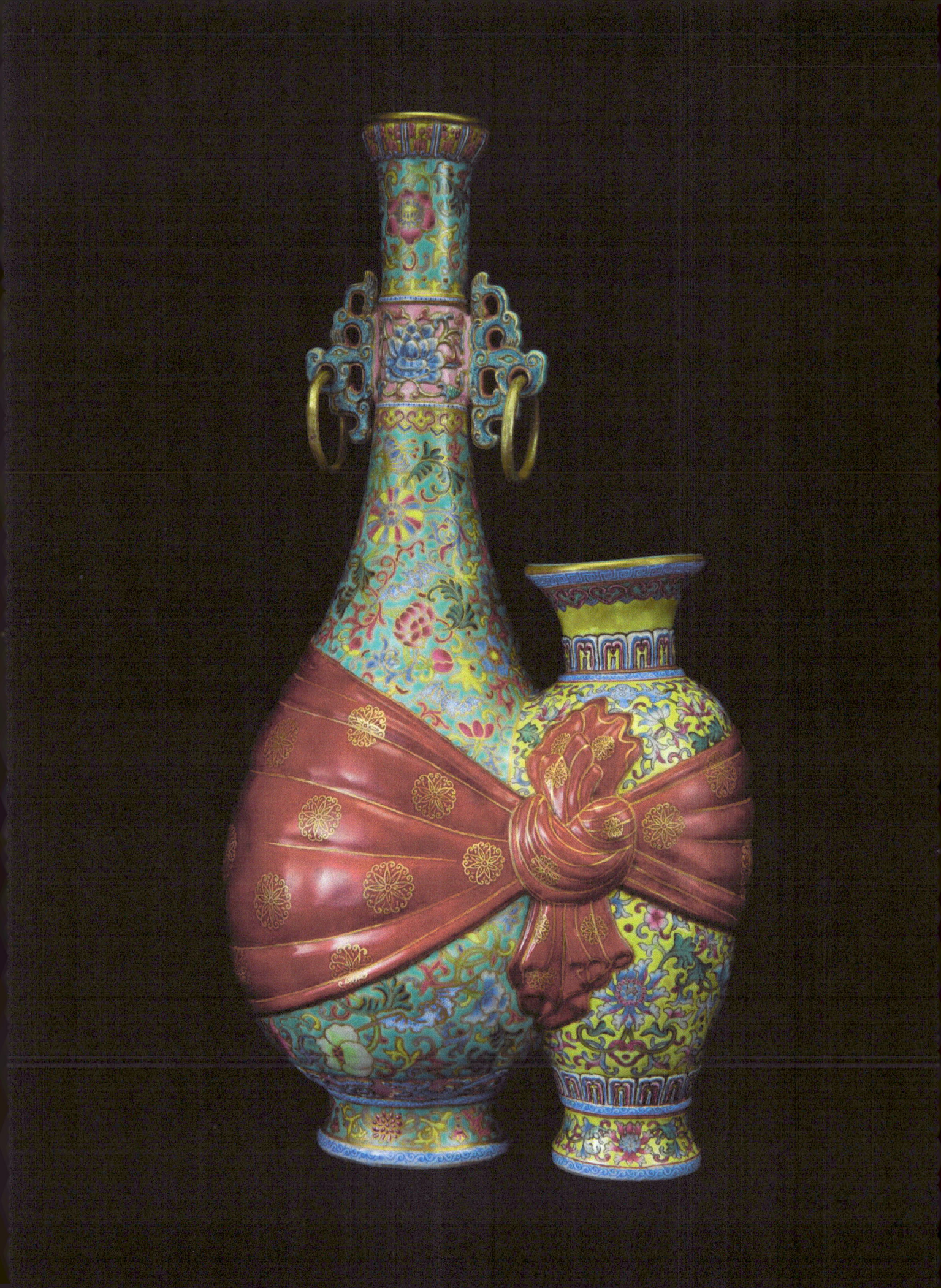

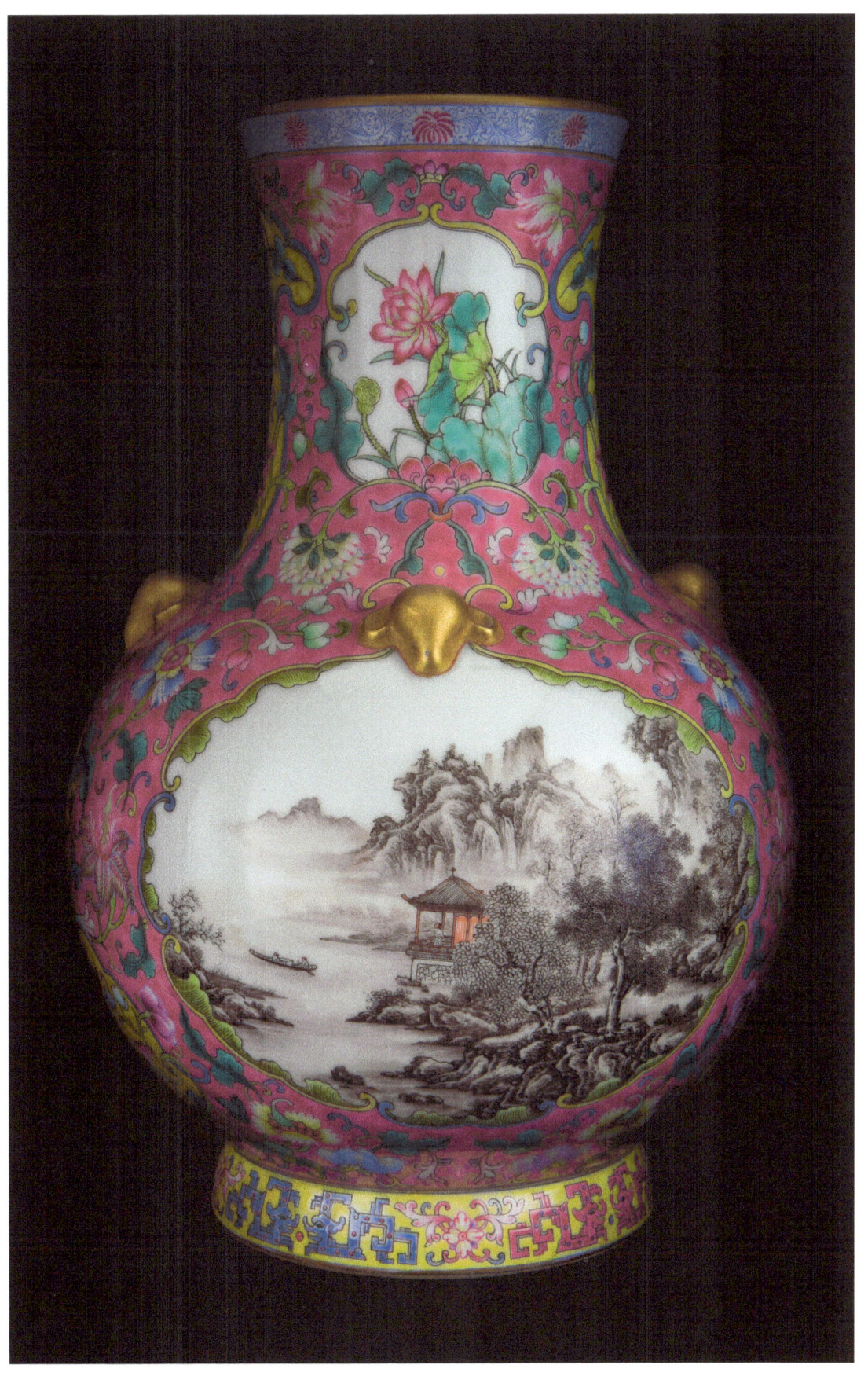

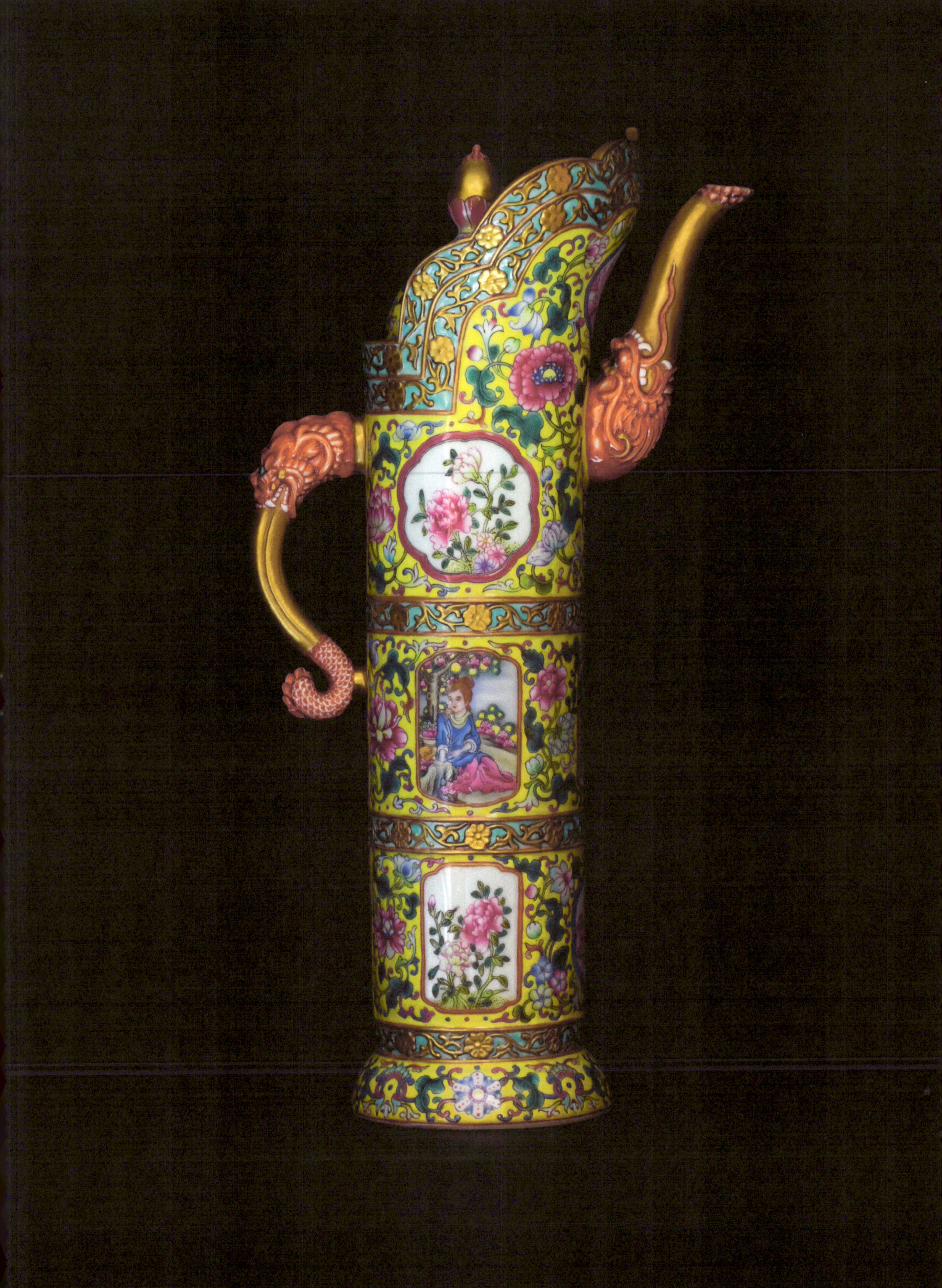

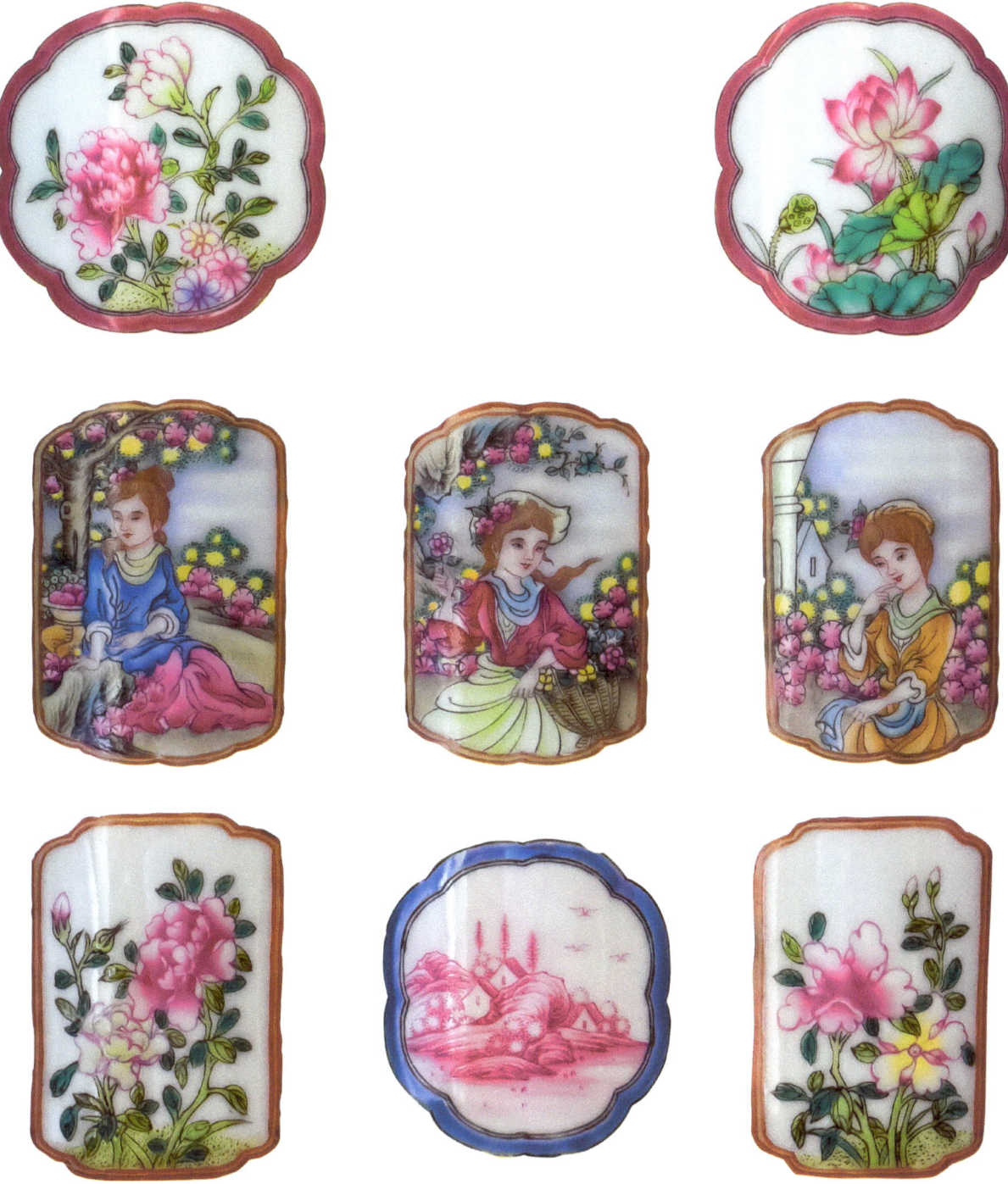

HONOURING THE UNKNOWN 33

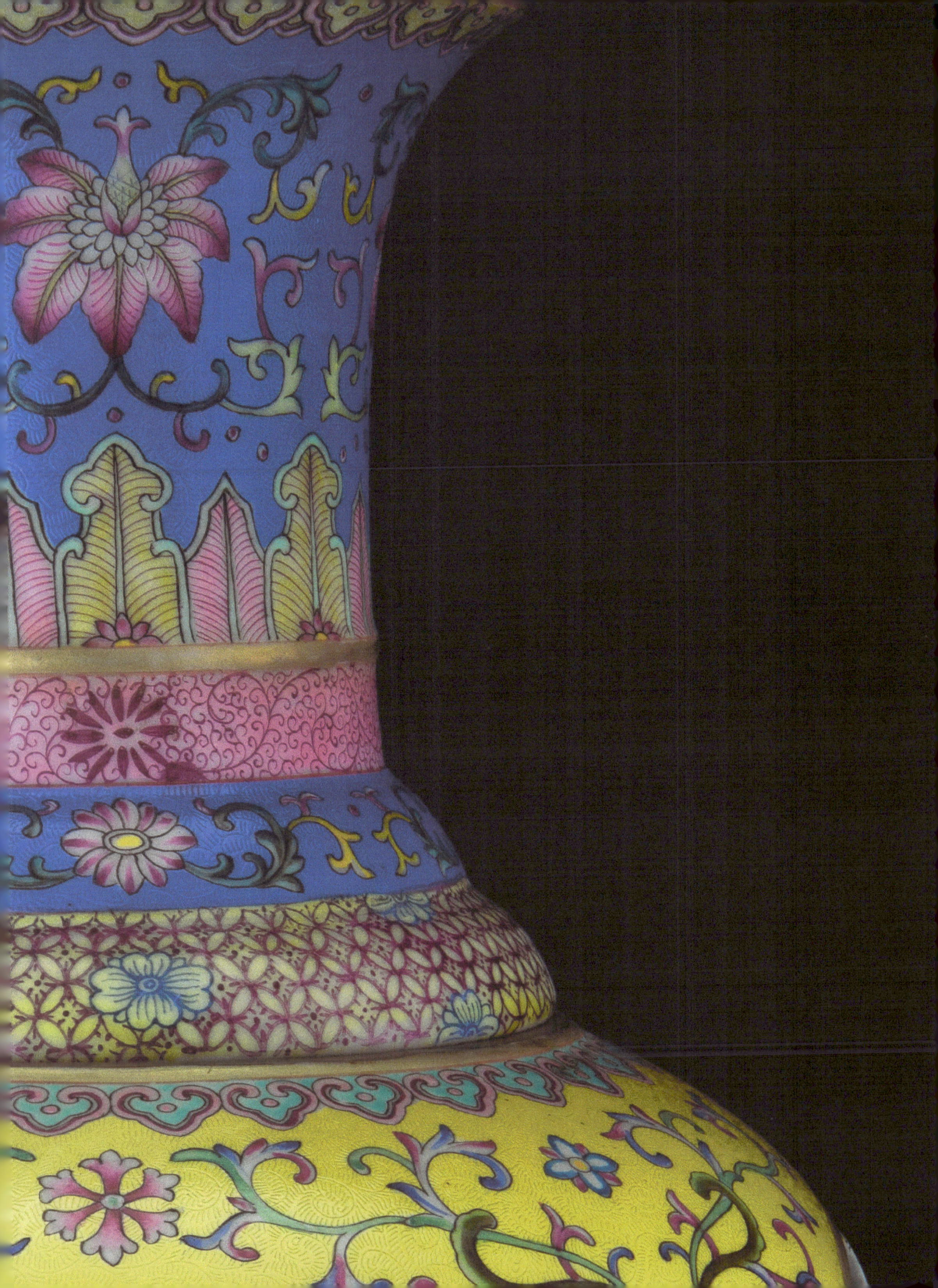

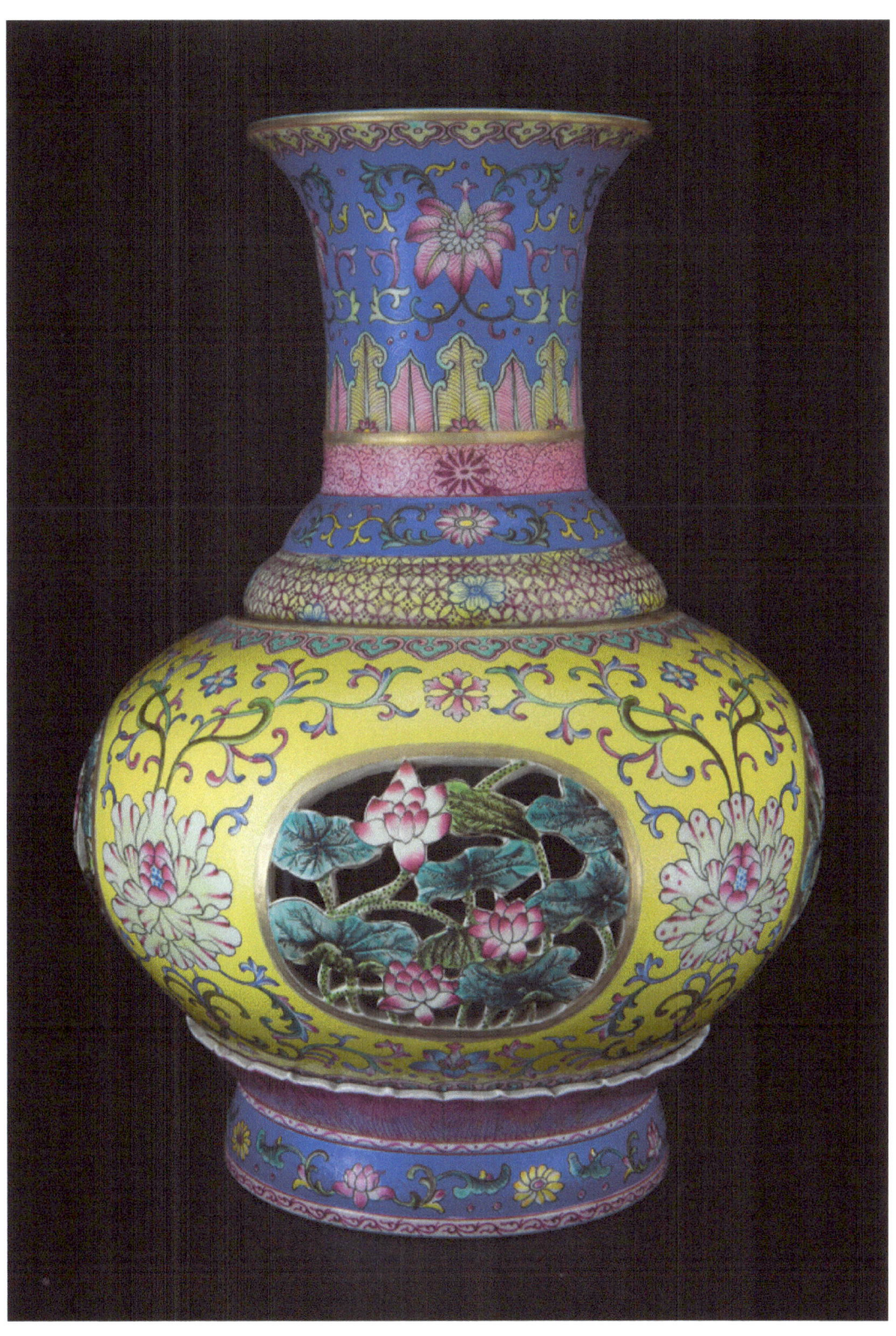

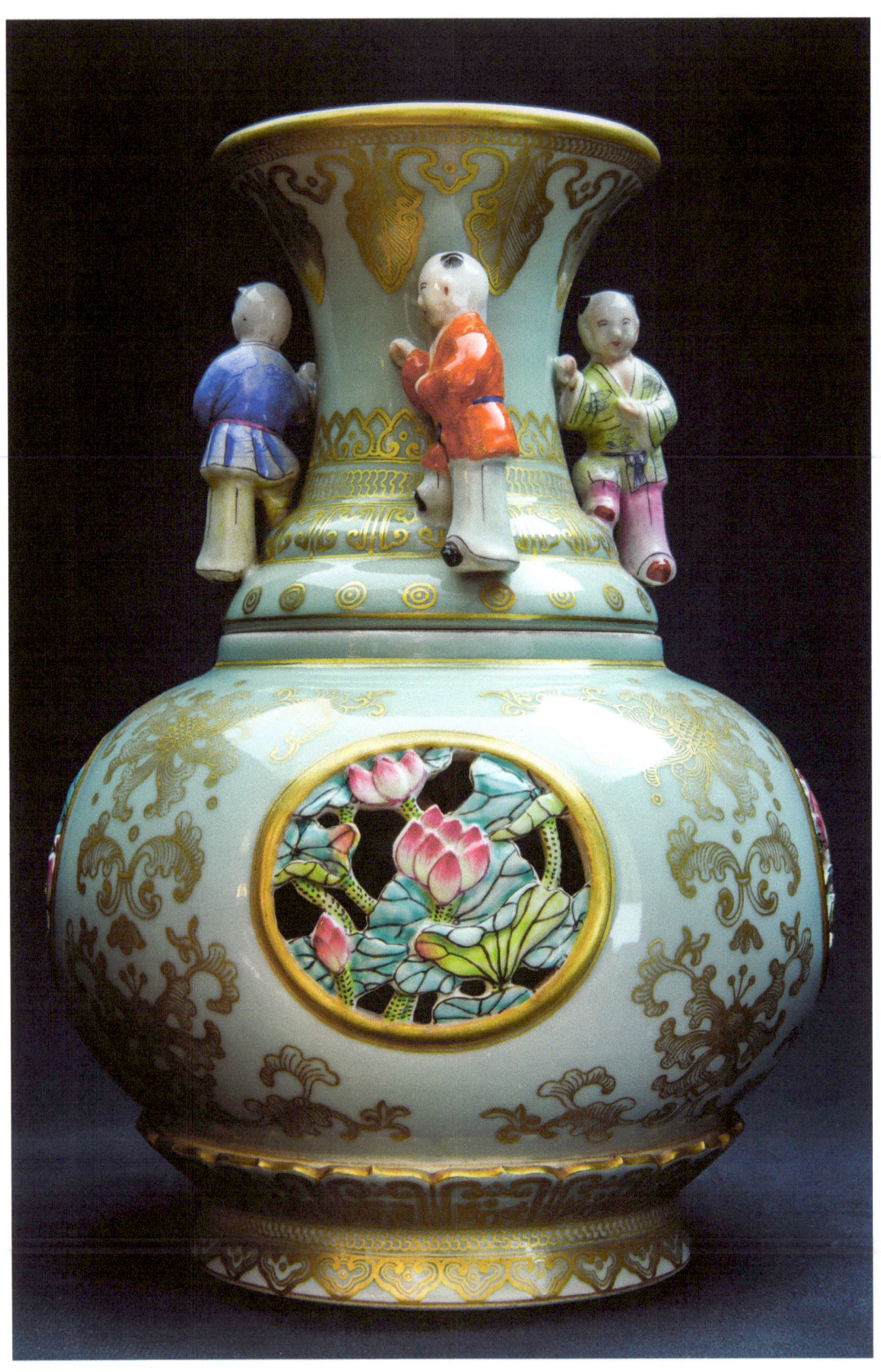

36 FORBIDDEN REPLICAS

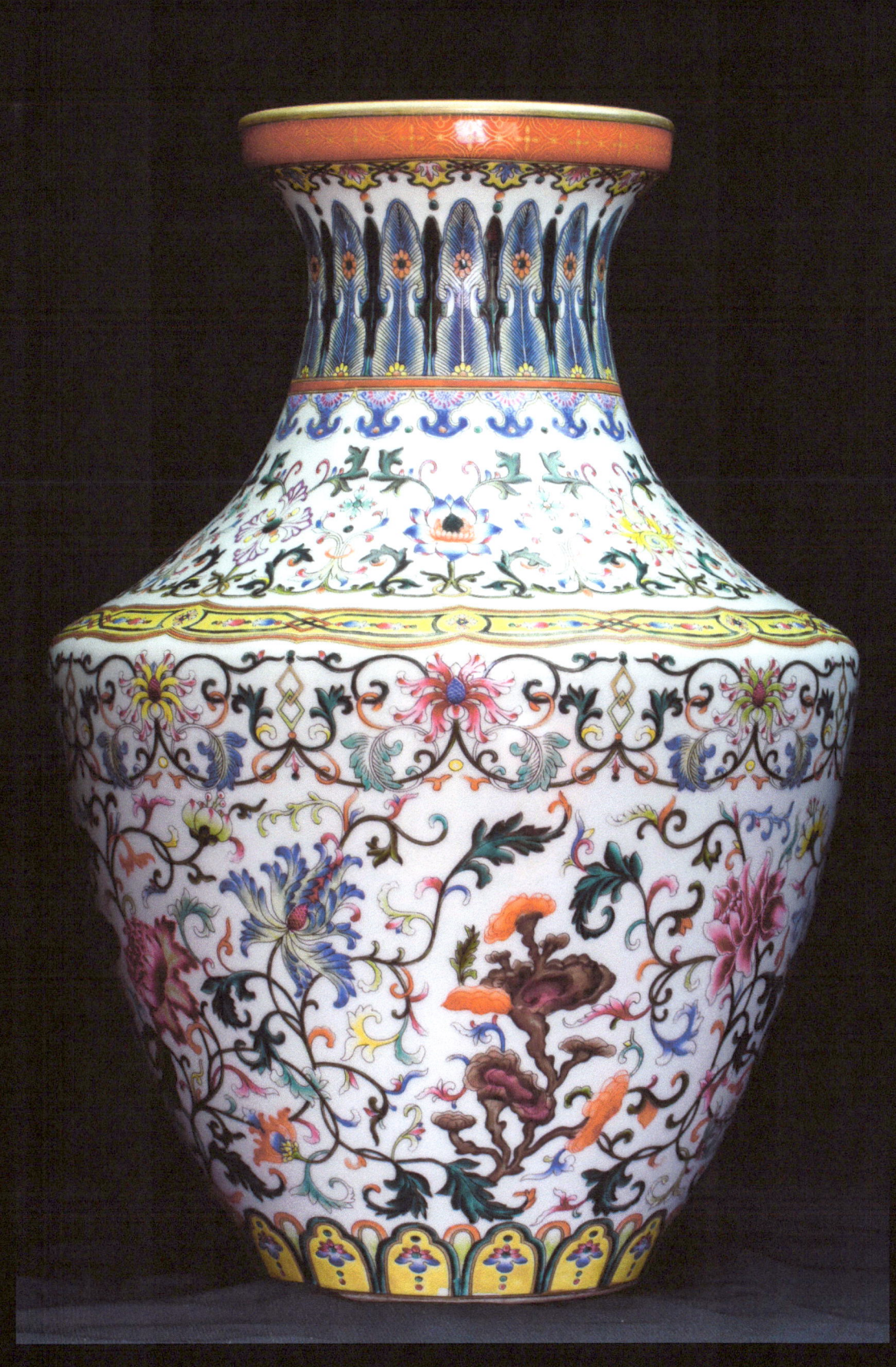

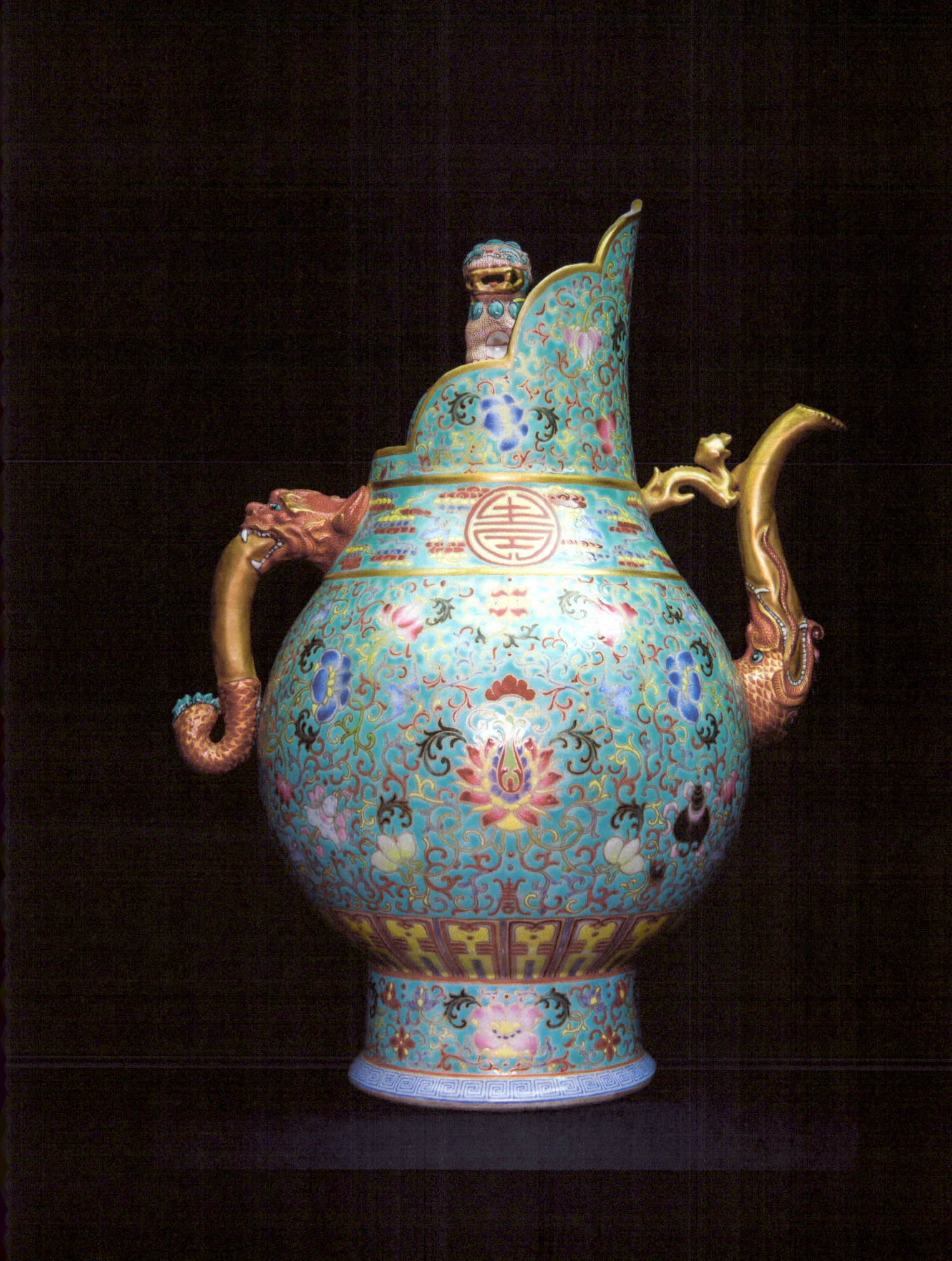

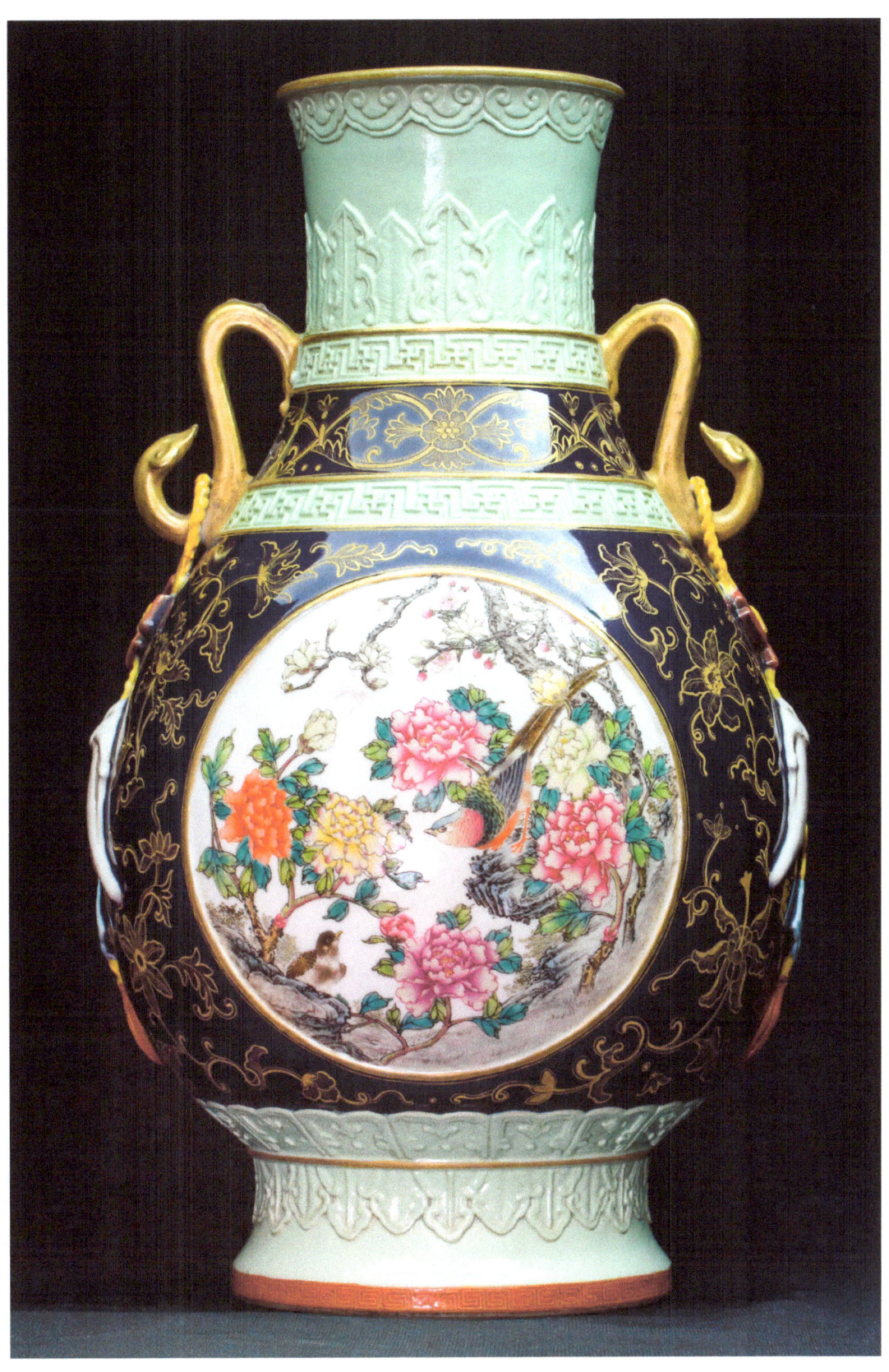

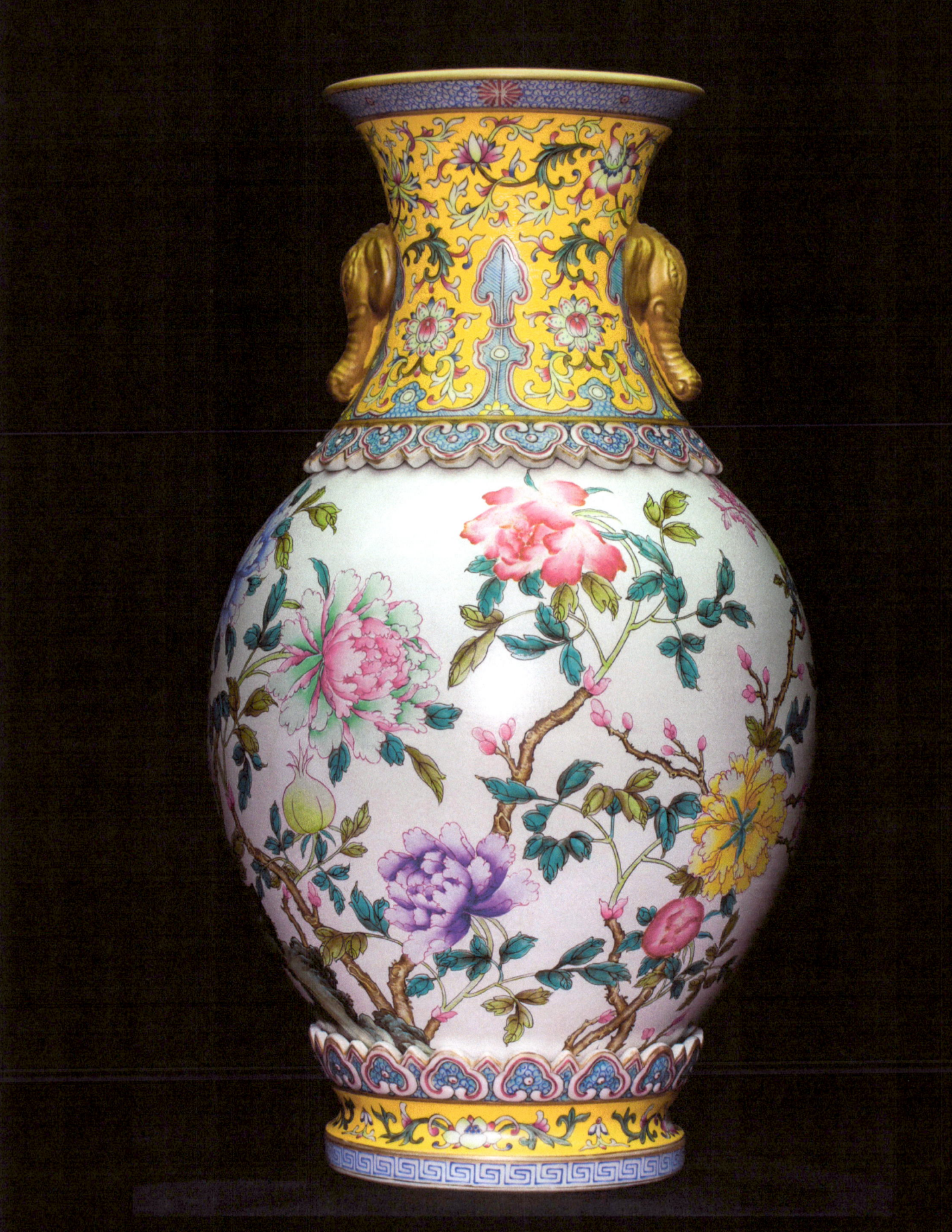

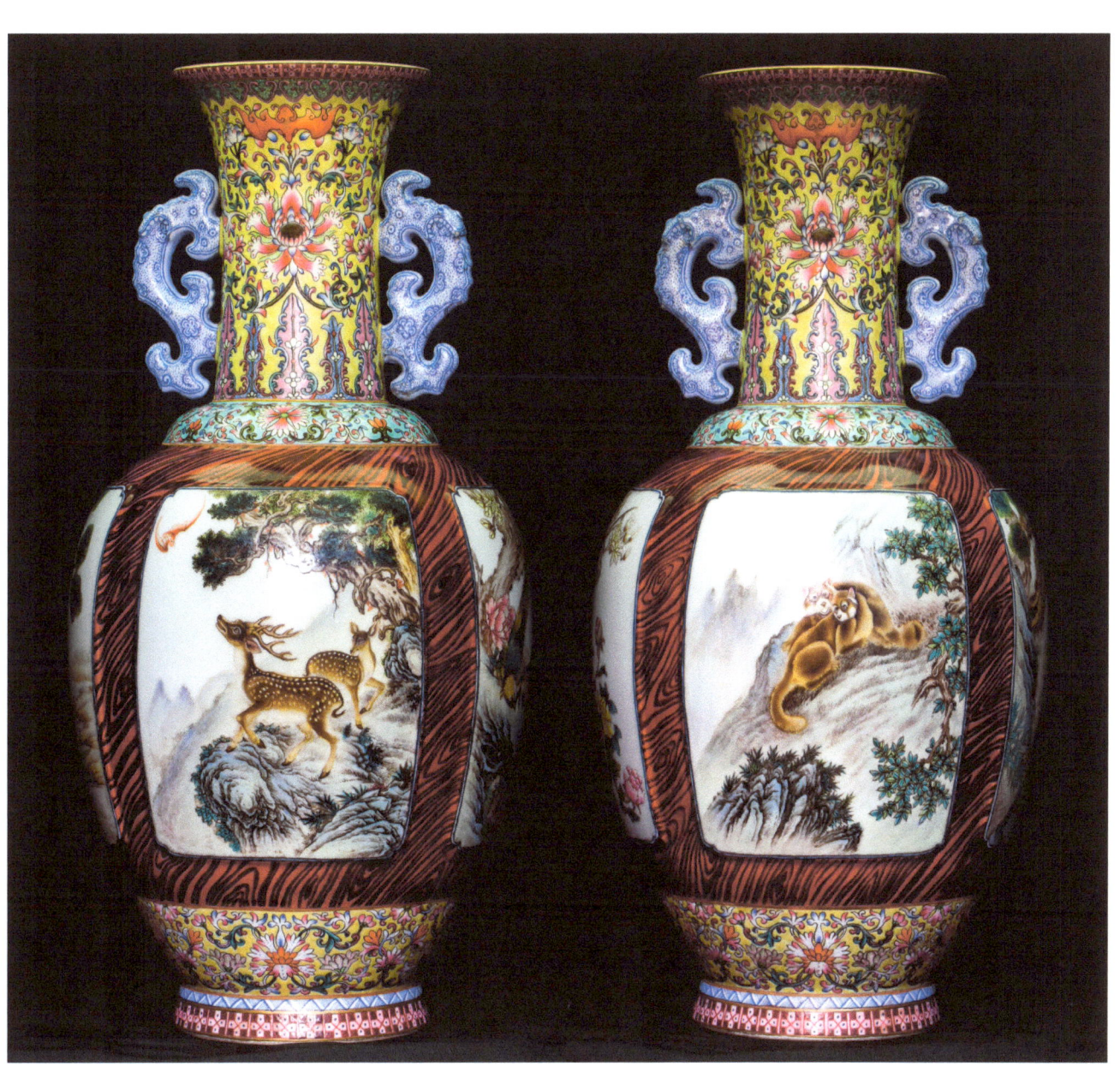

HONOURING THE UNKNOWN

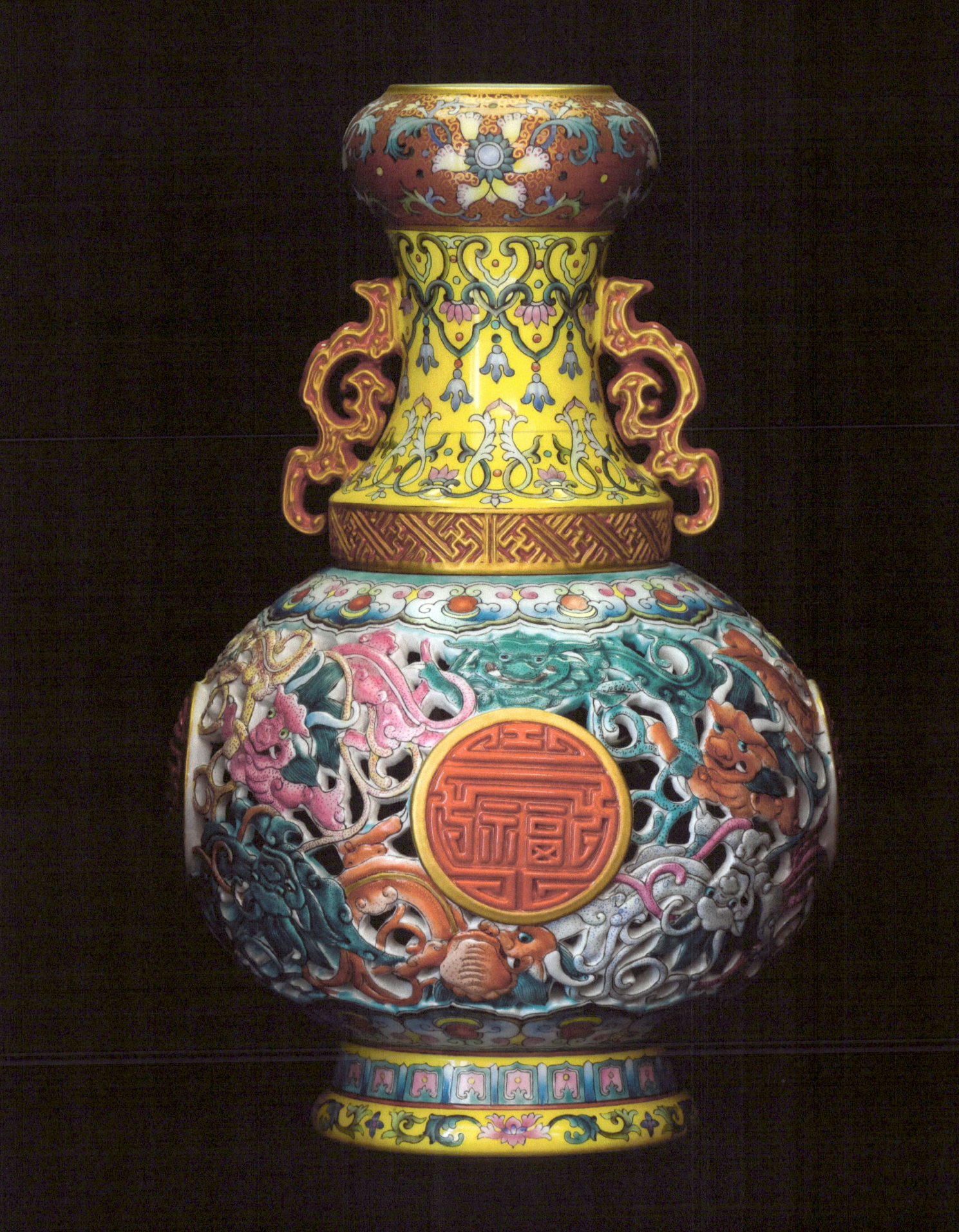

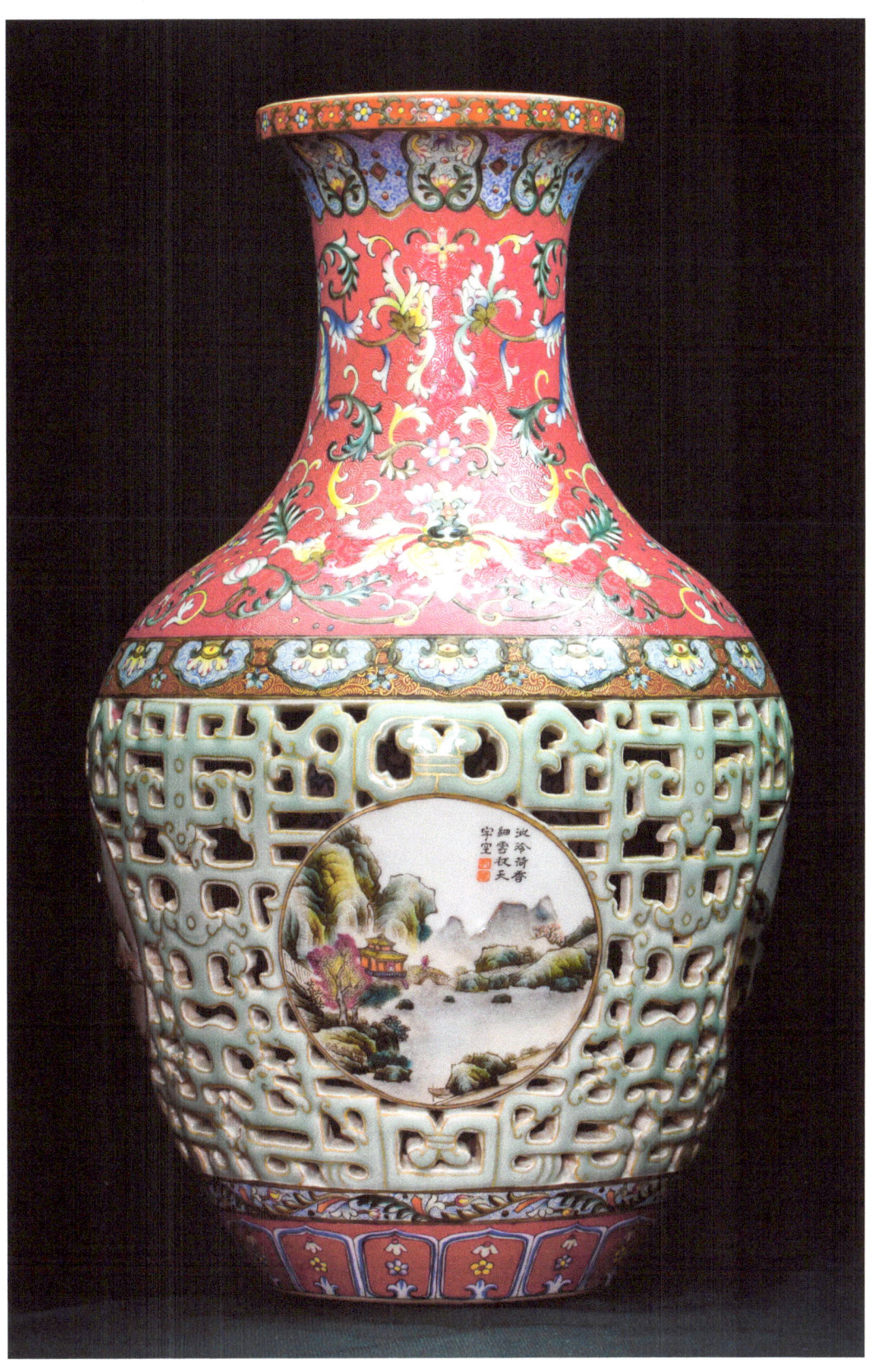

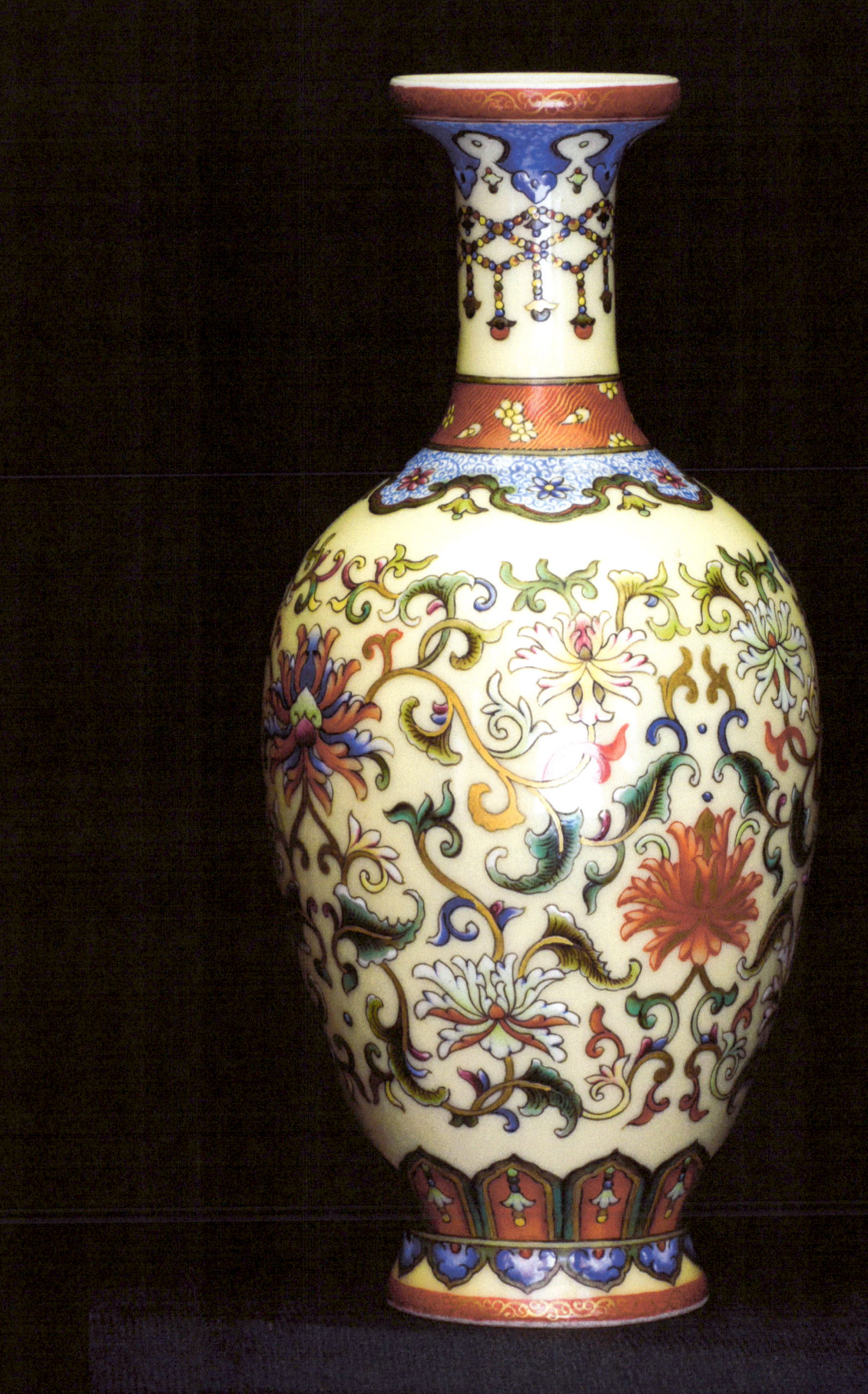

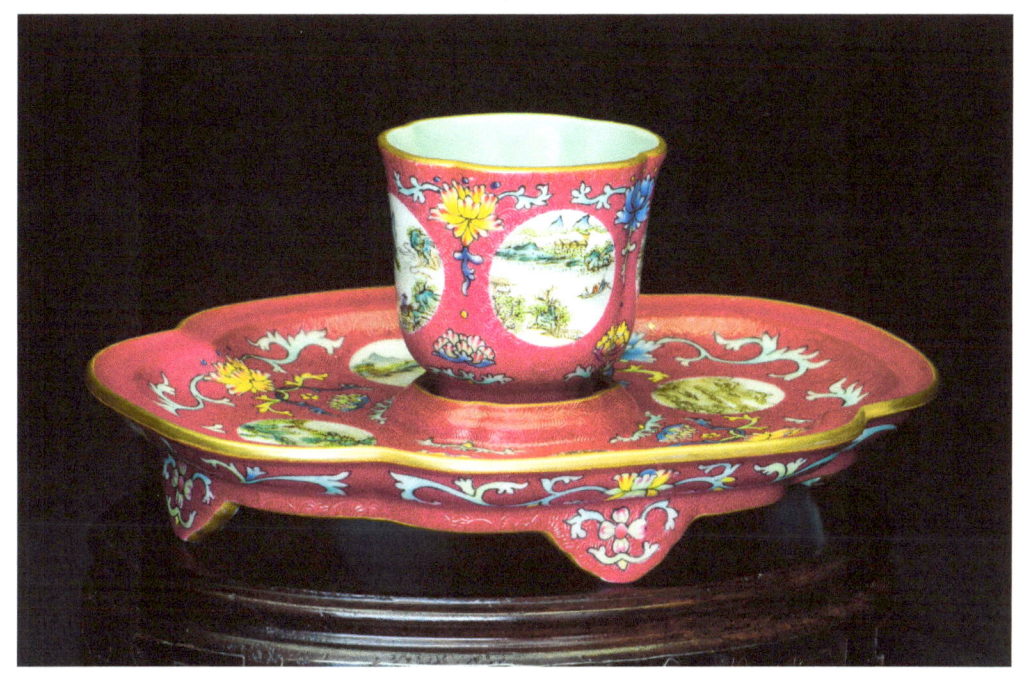

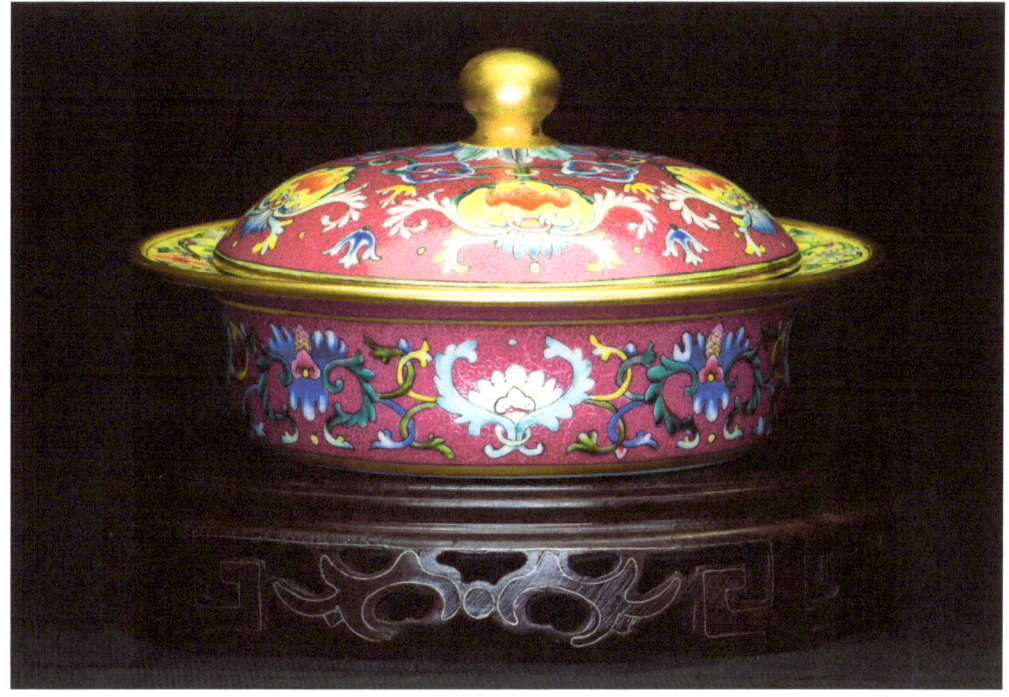

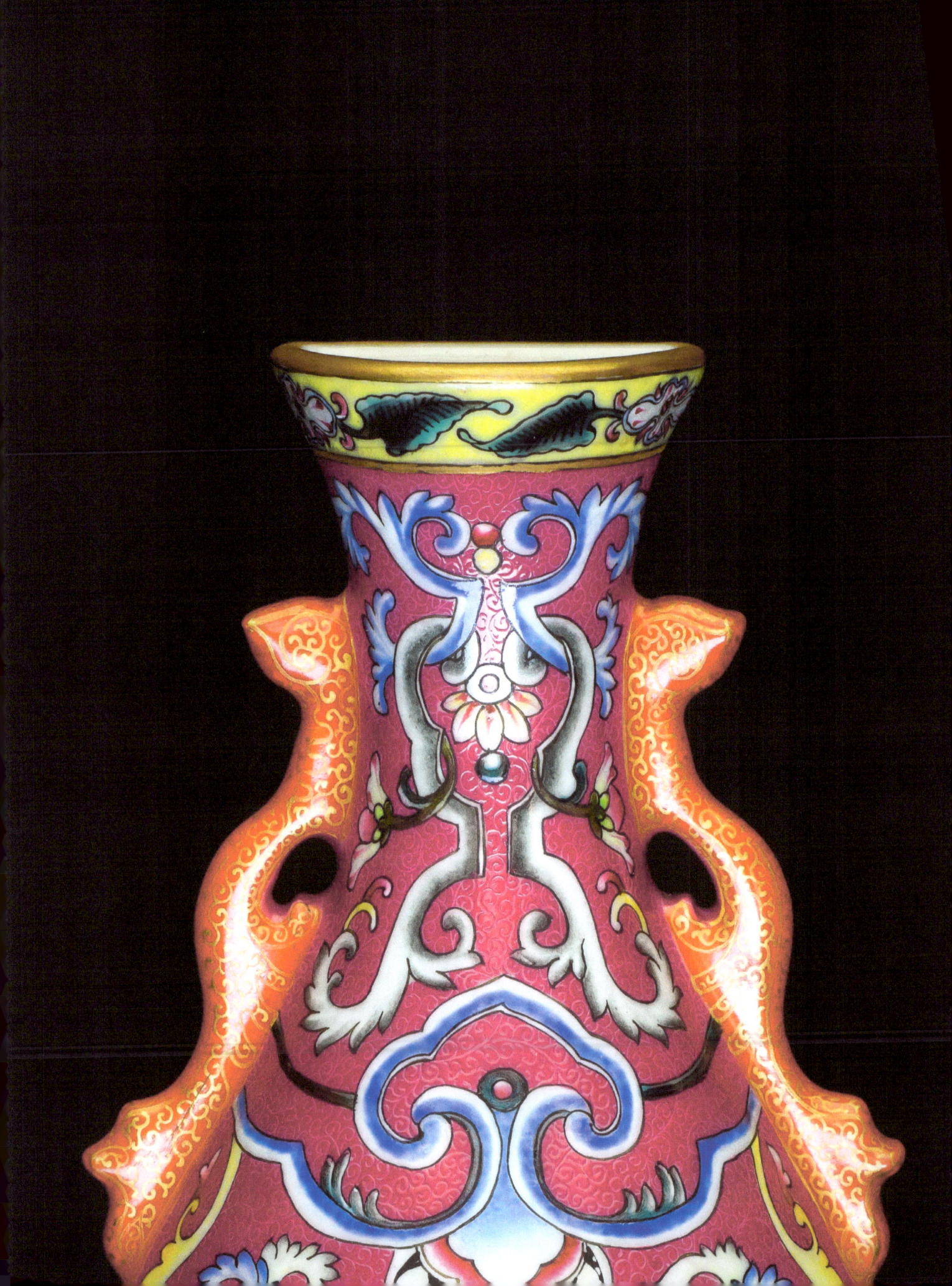

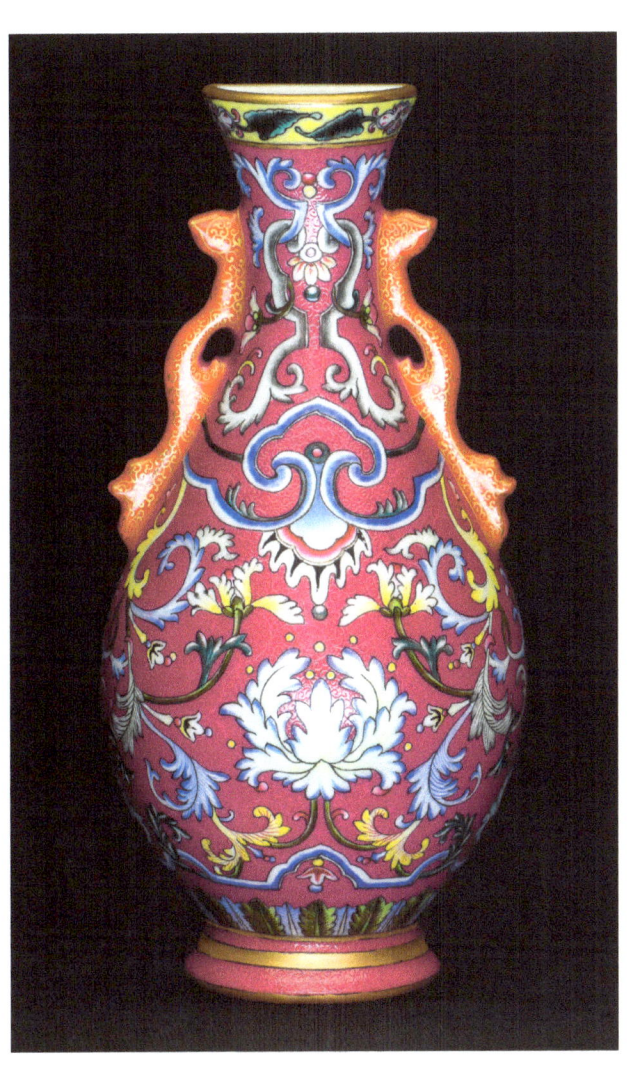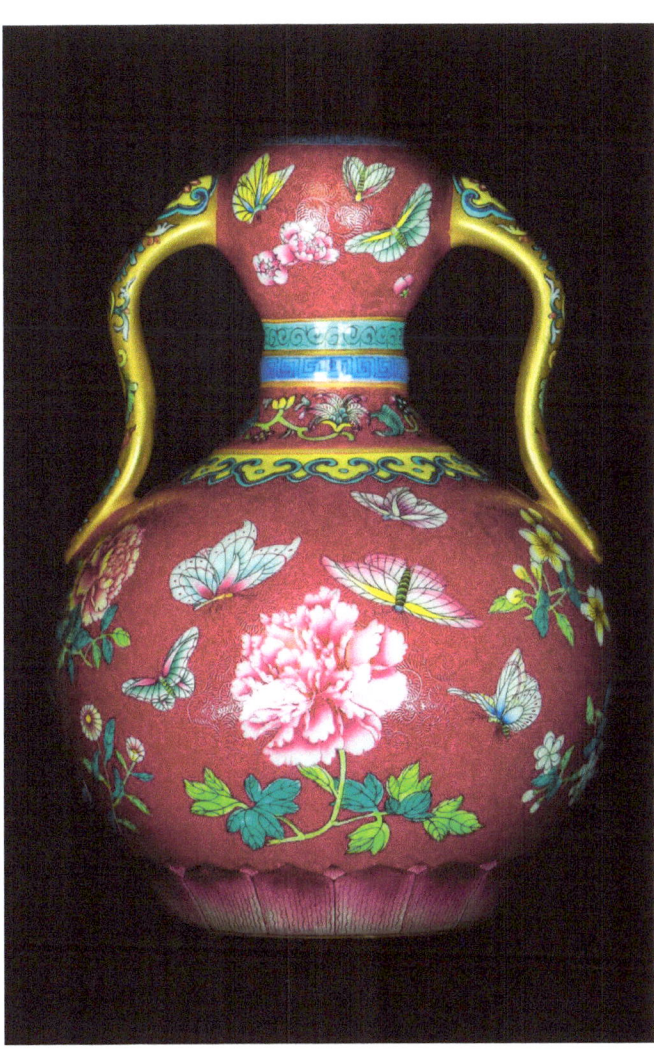

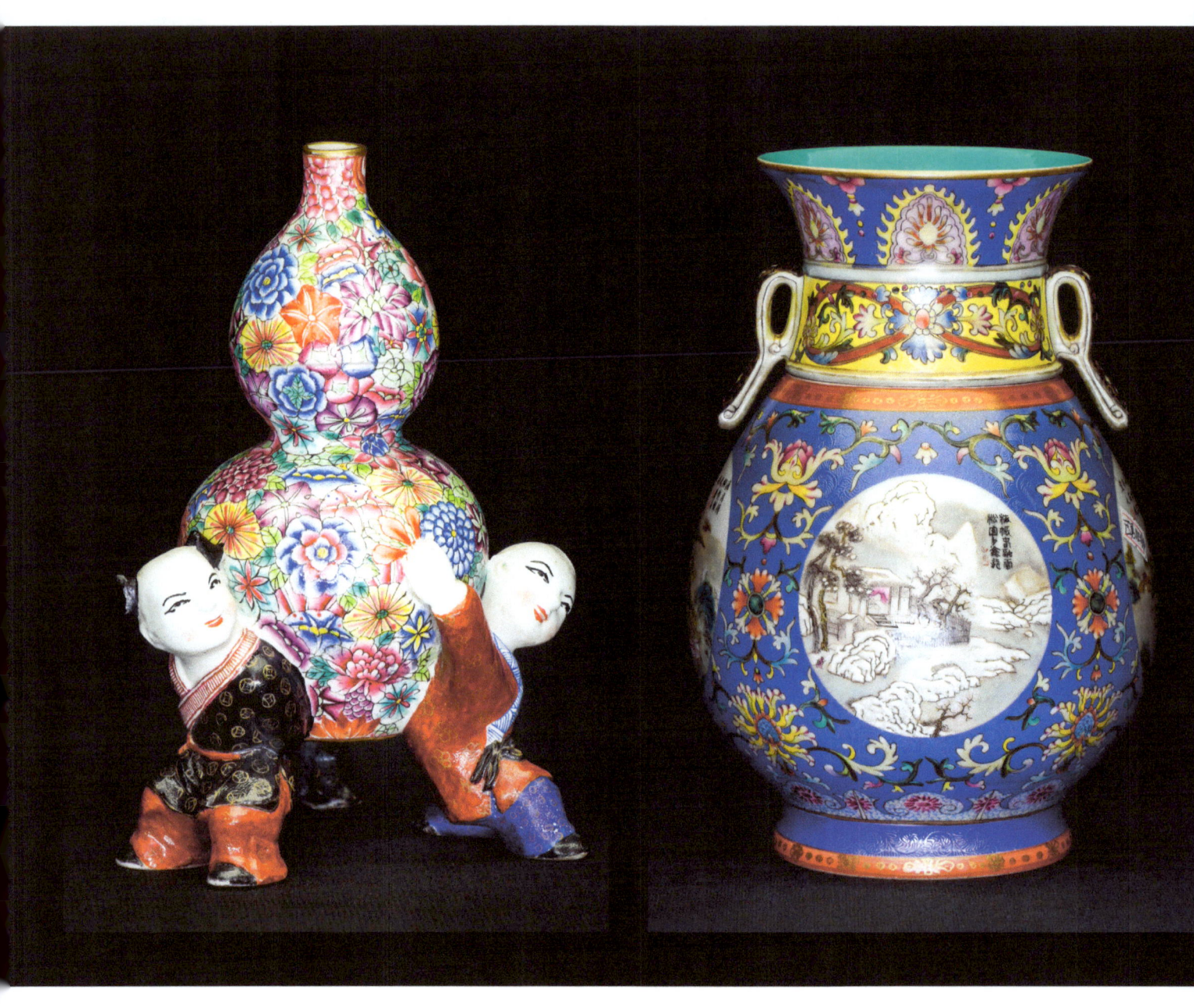

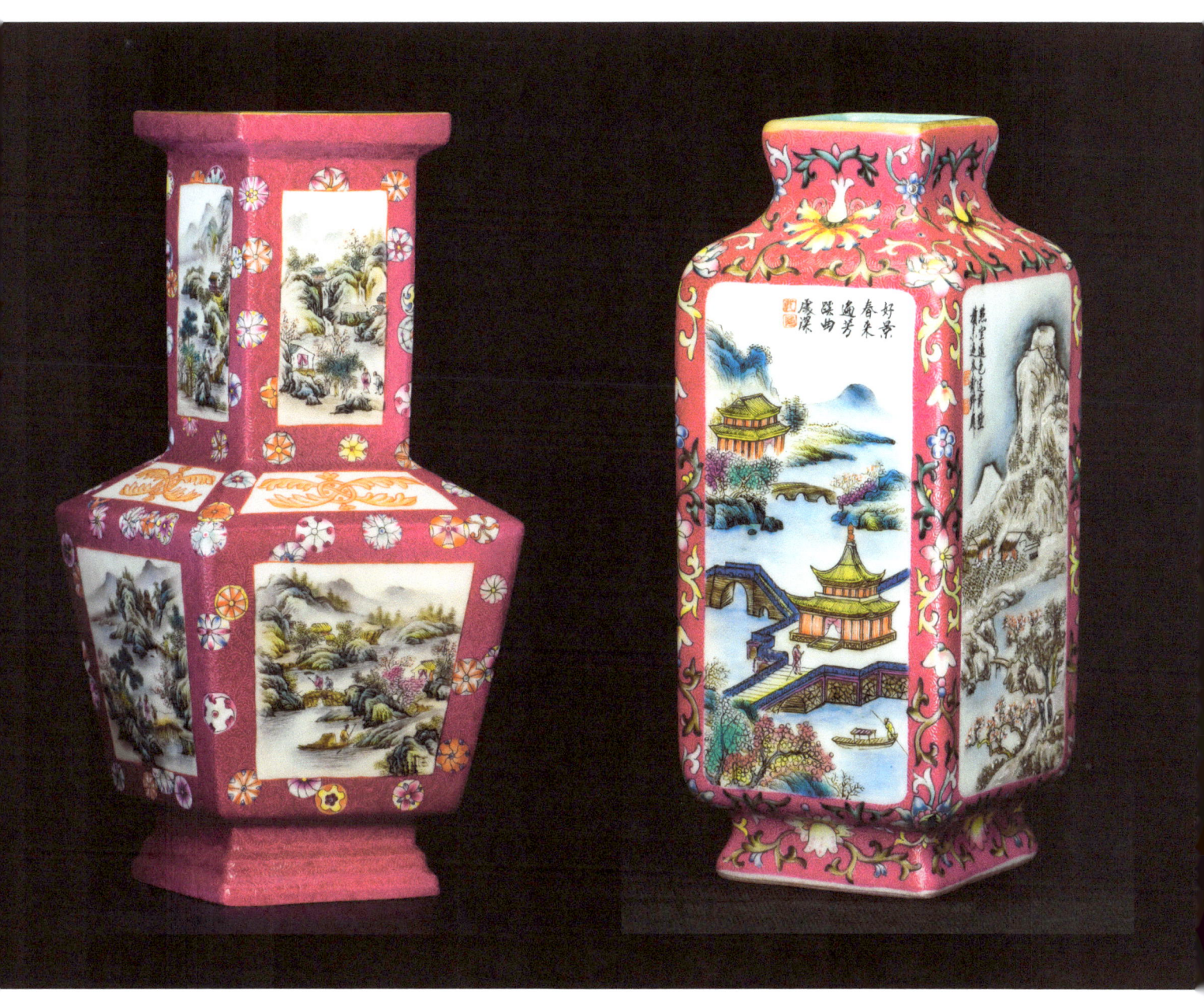

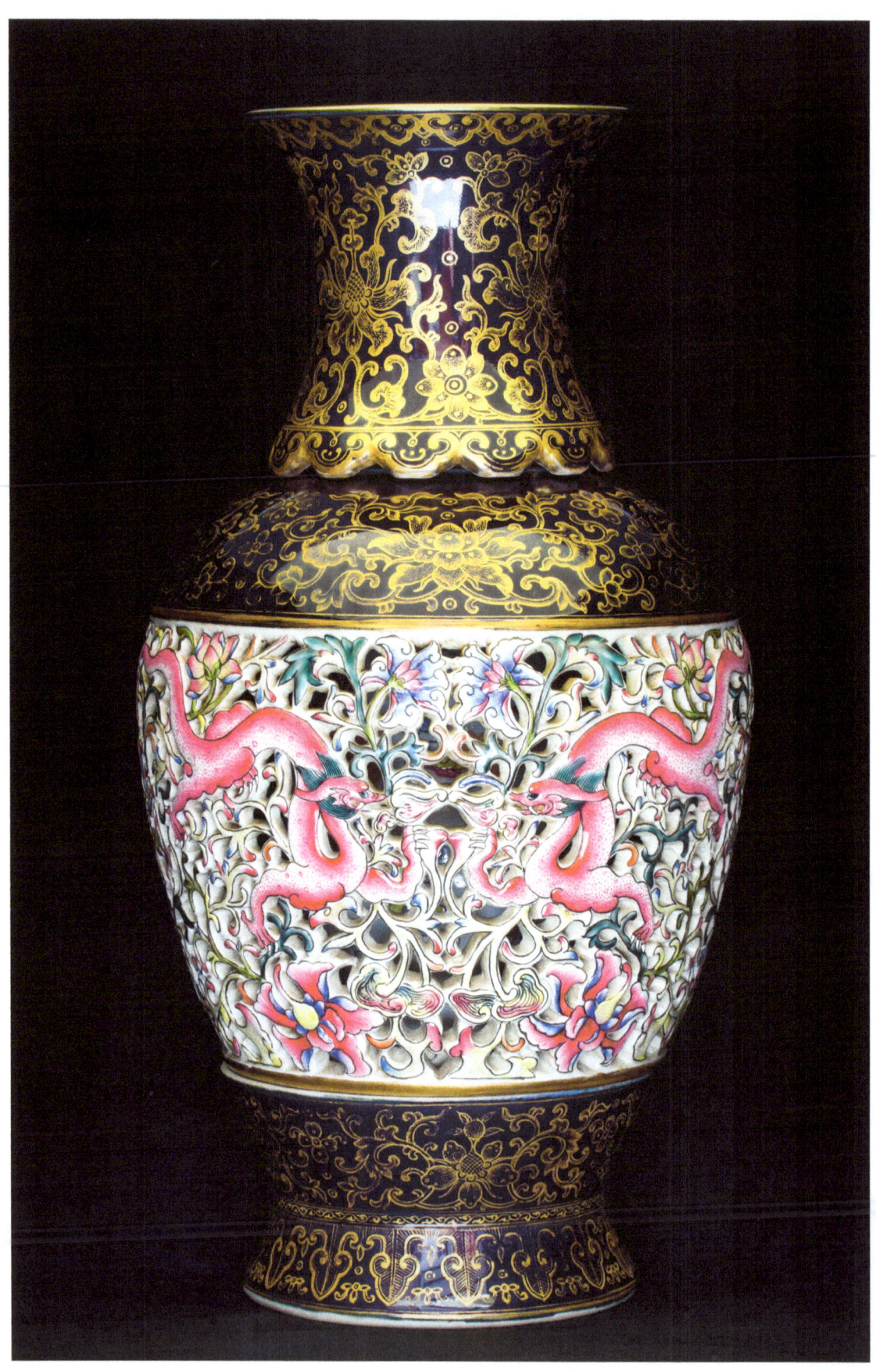

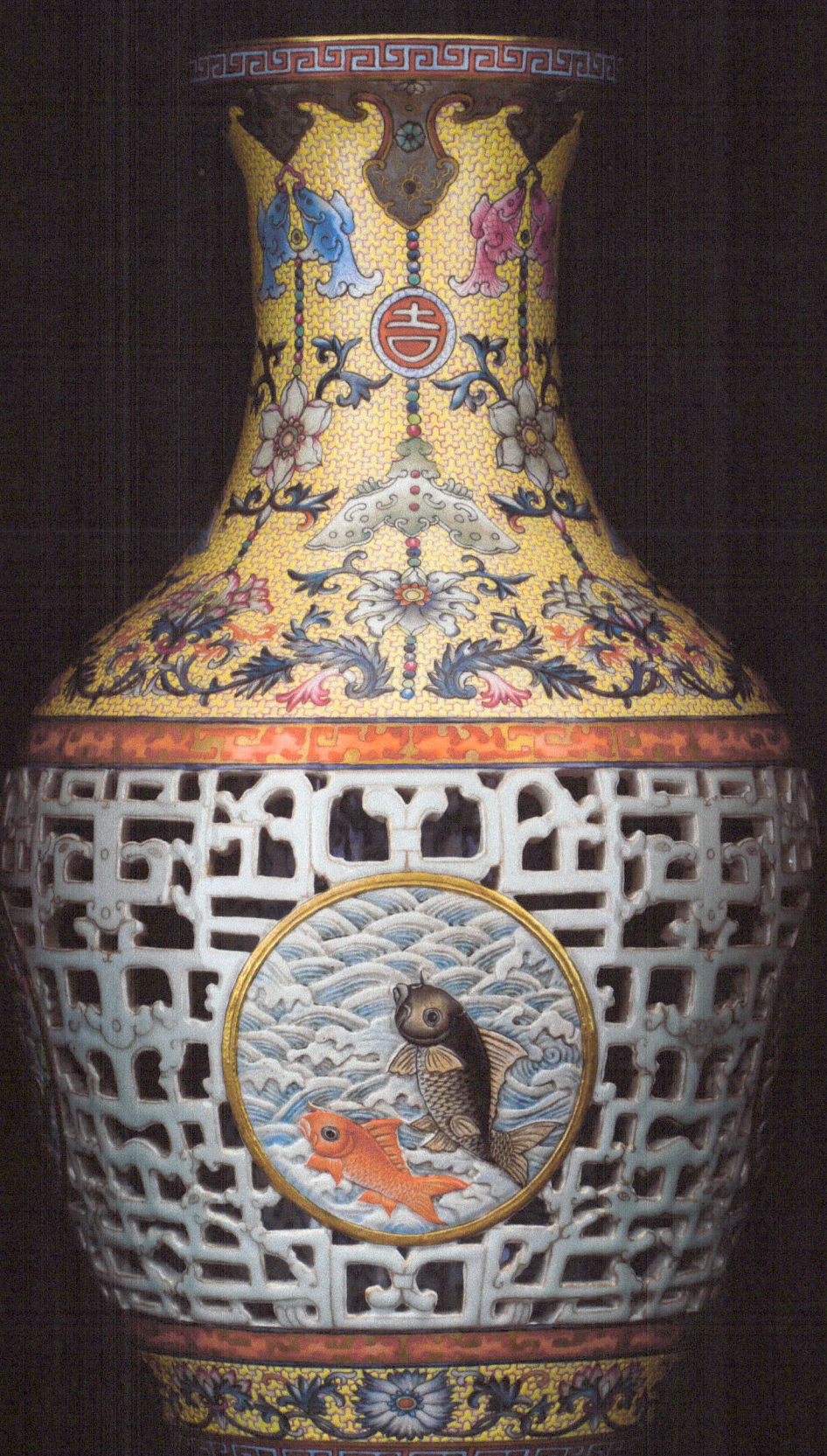

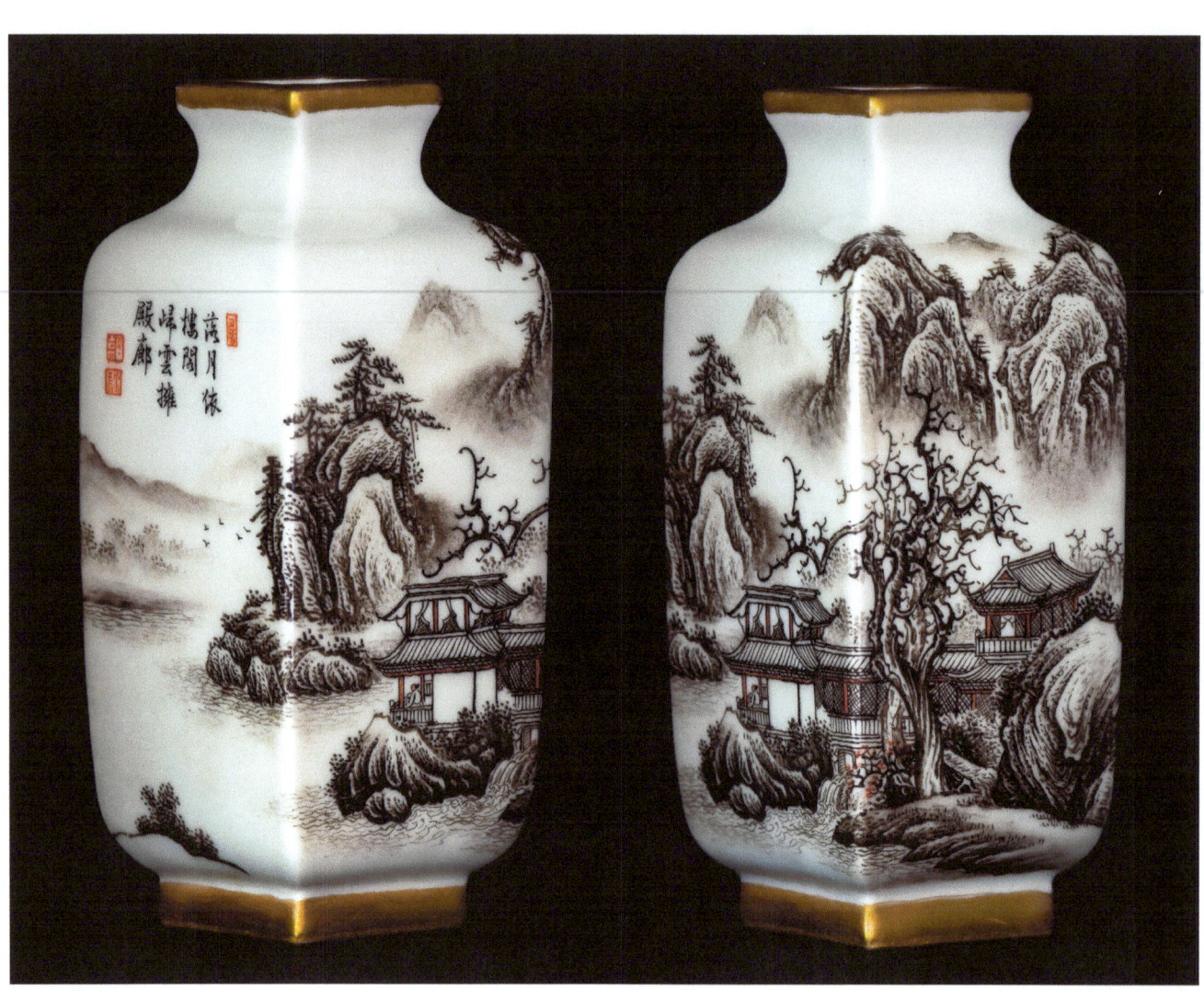

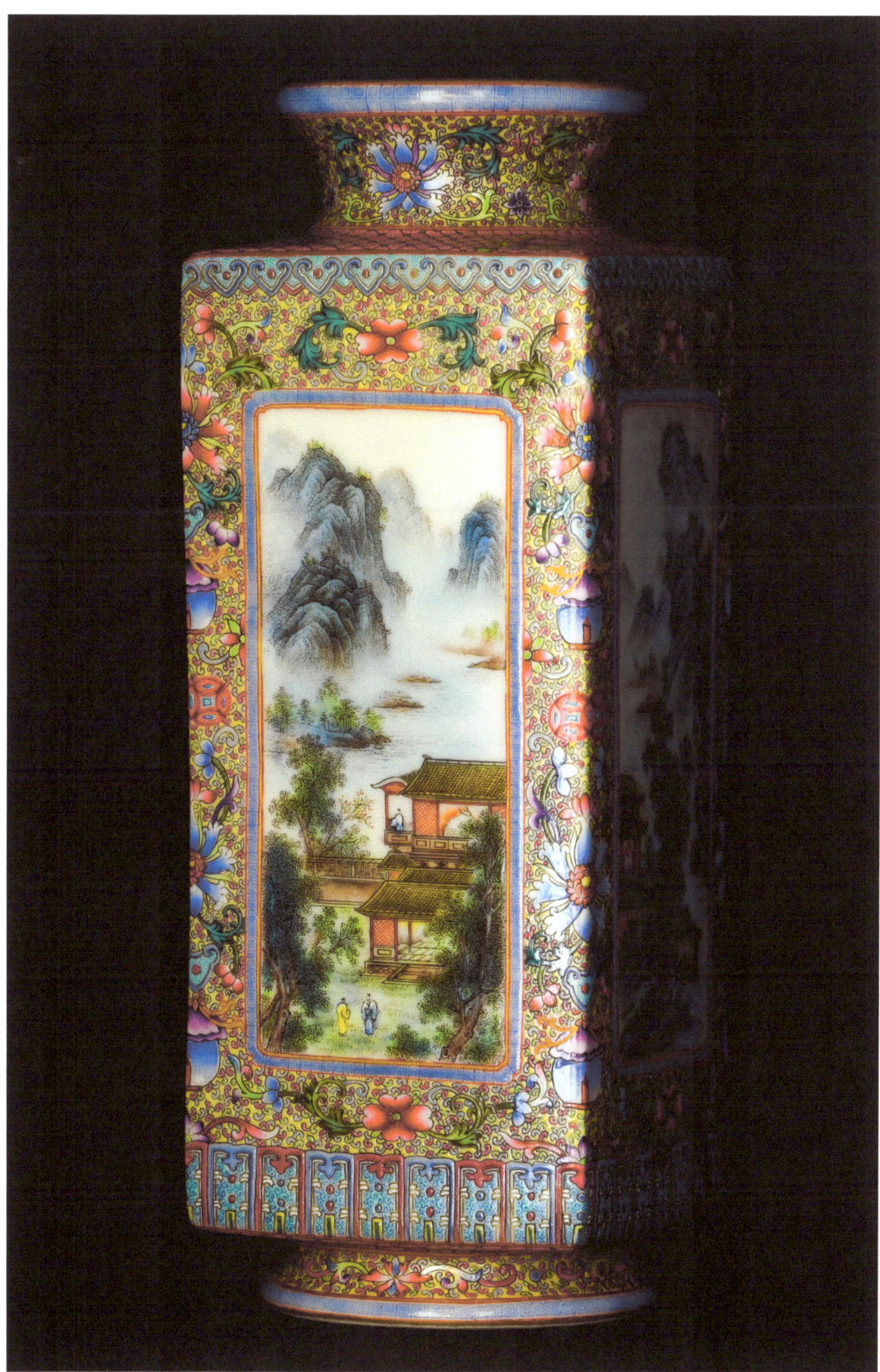

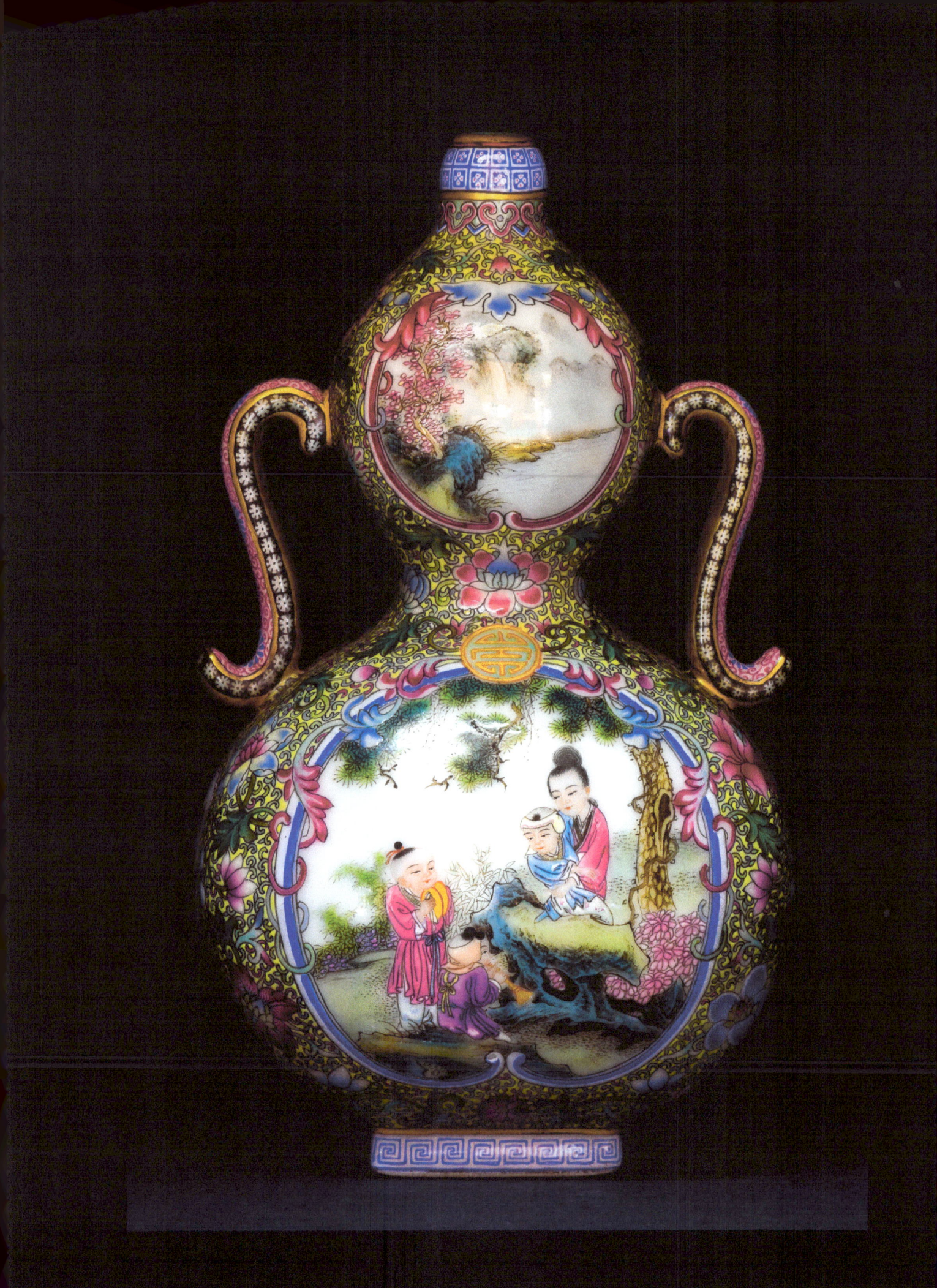

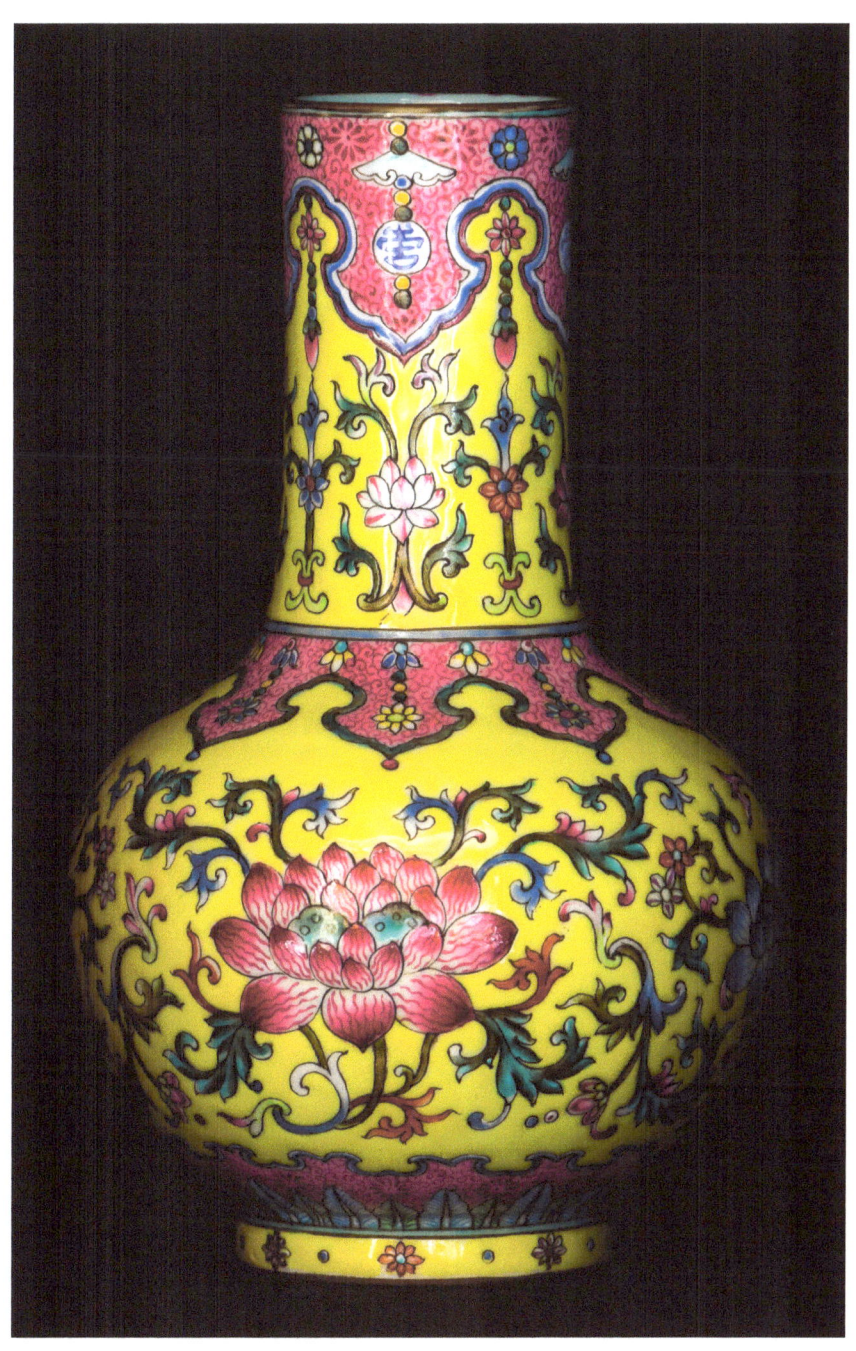

HONOURING THE UNKNOWN 55

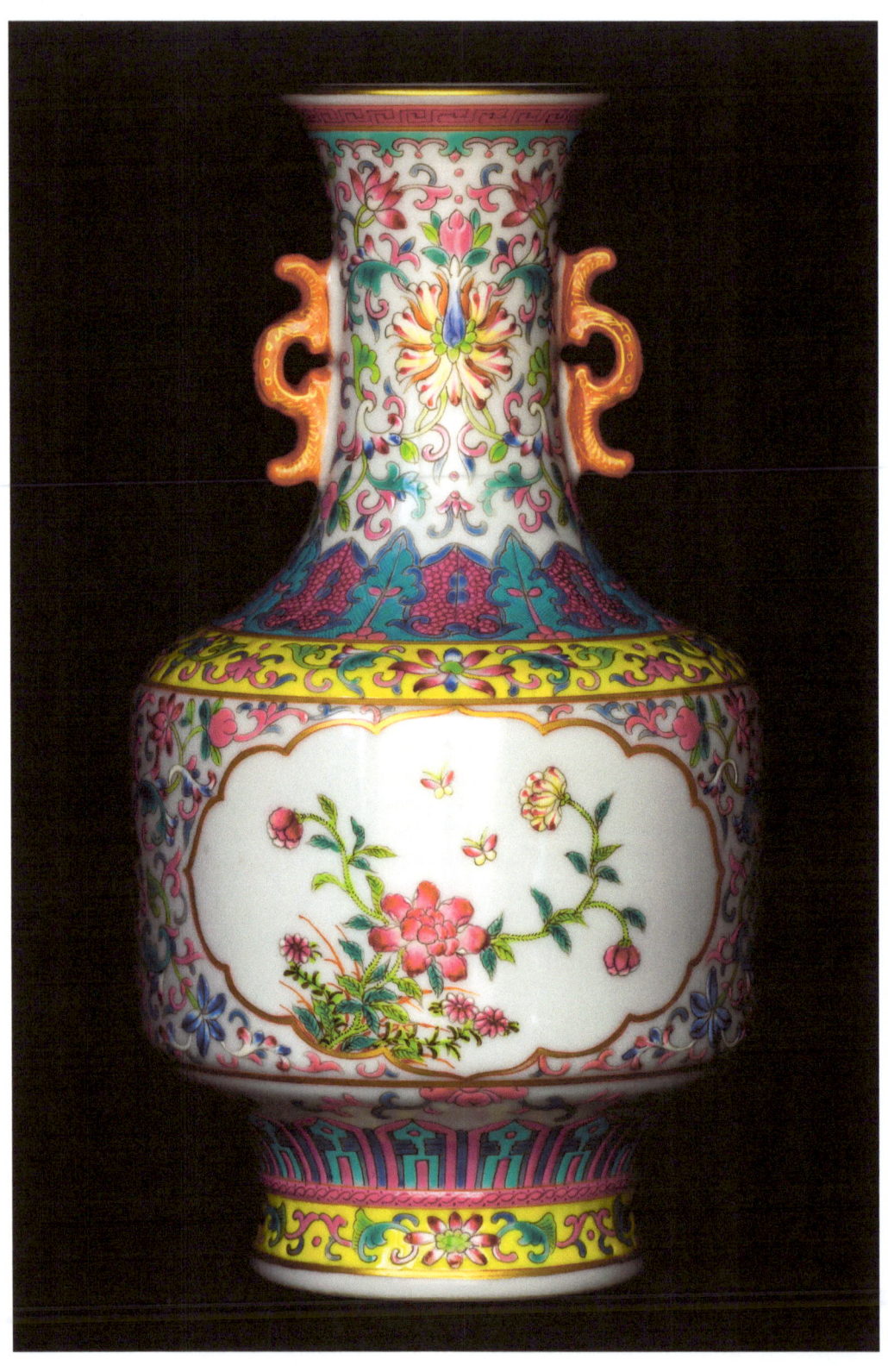

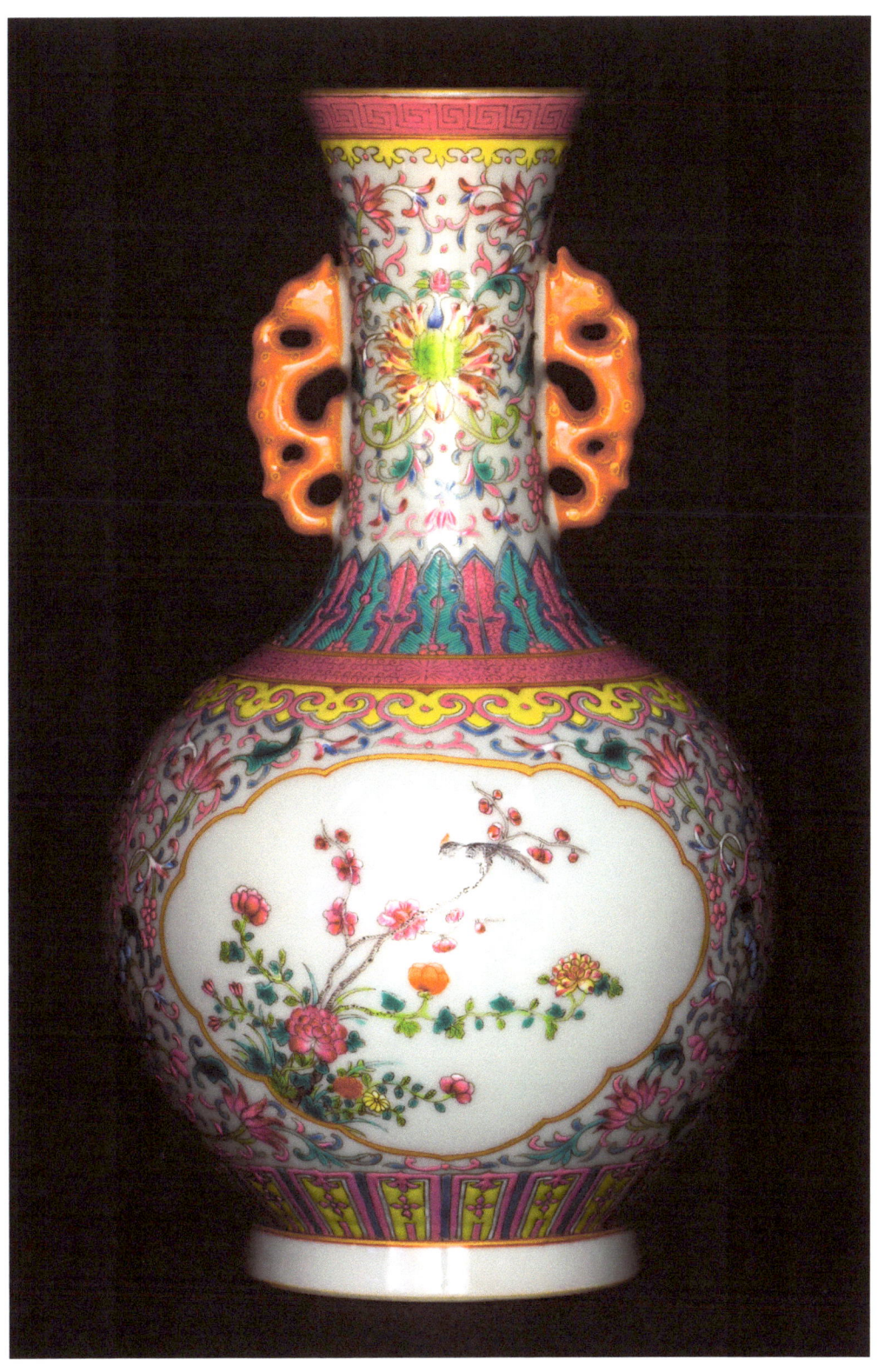

HONOURING THE UNKNOWN 57

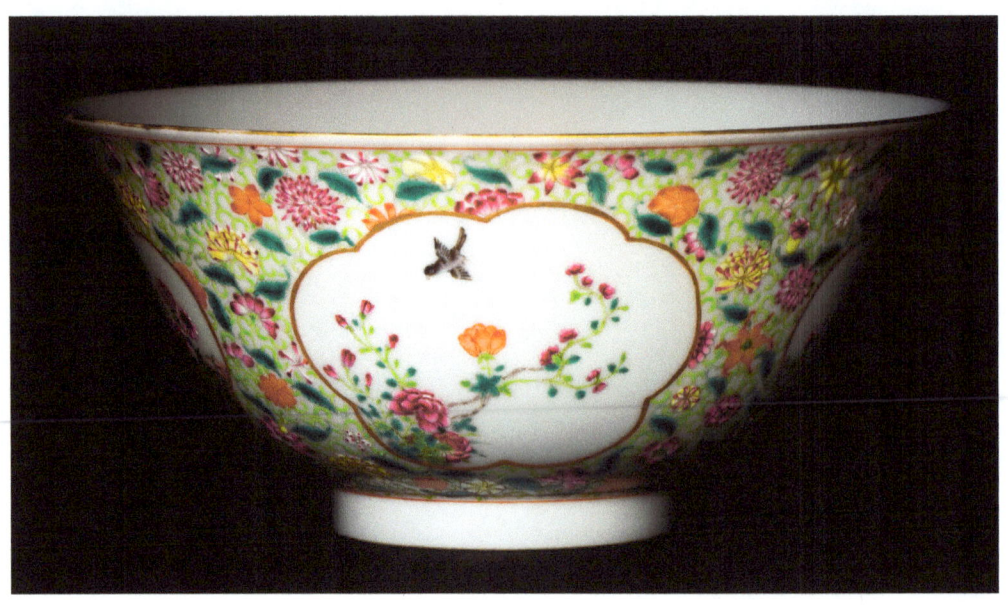

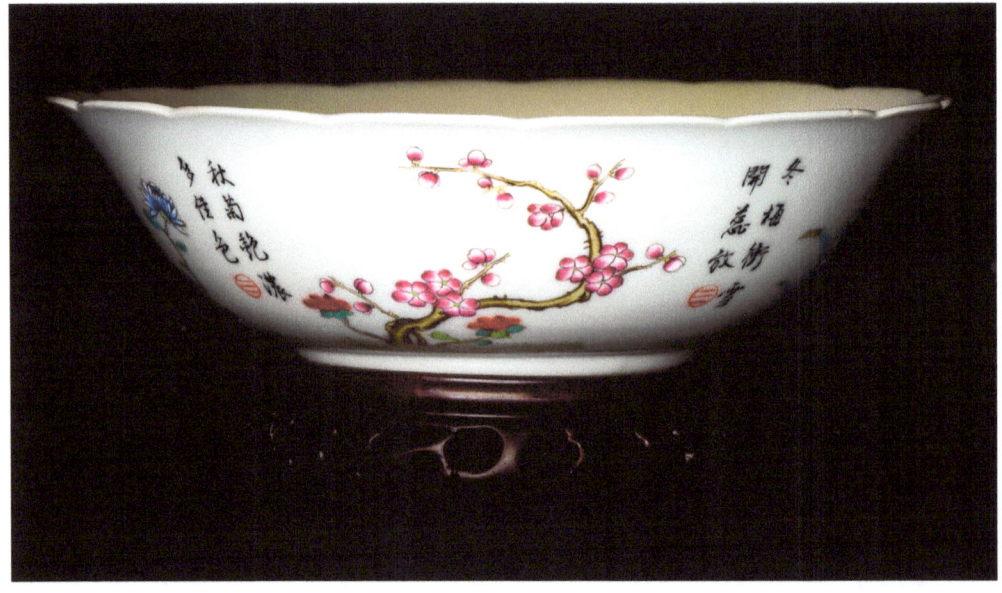

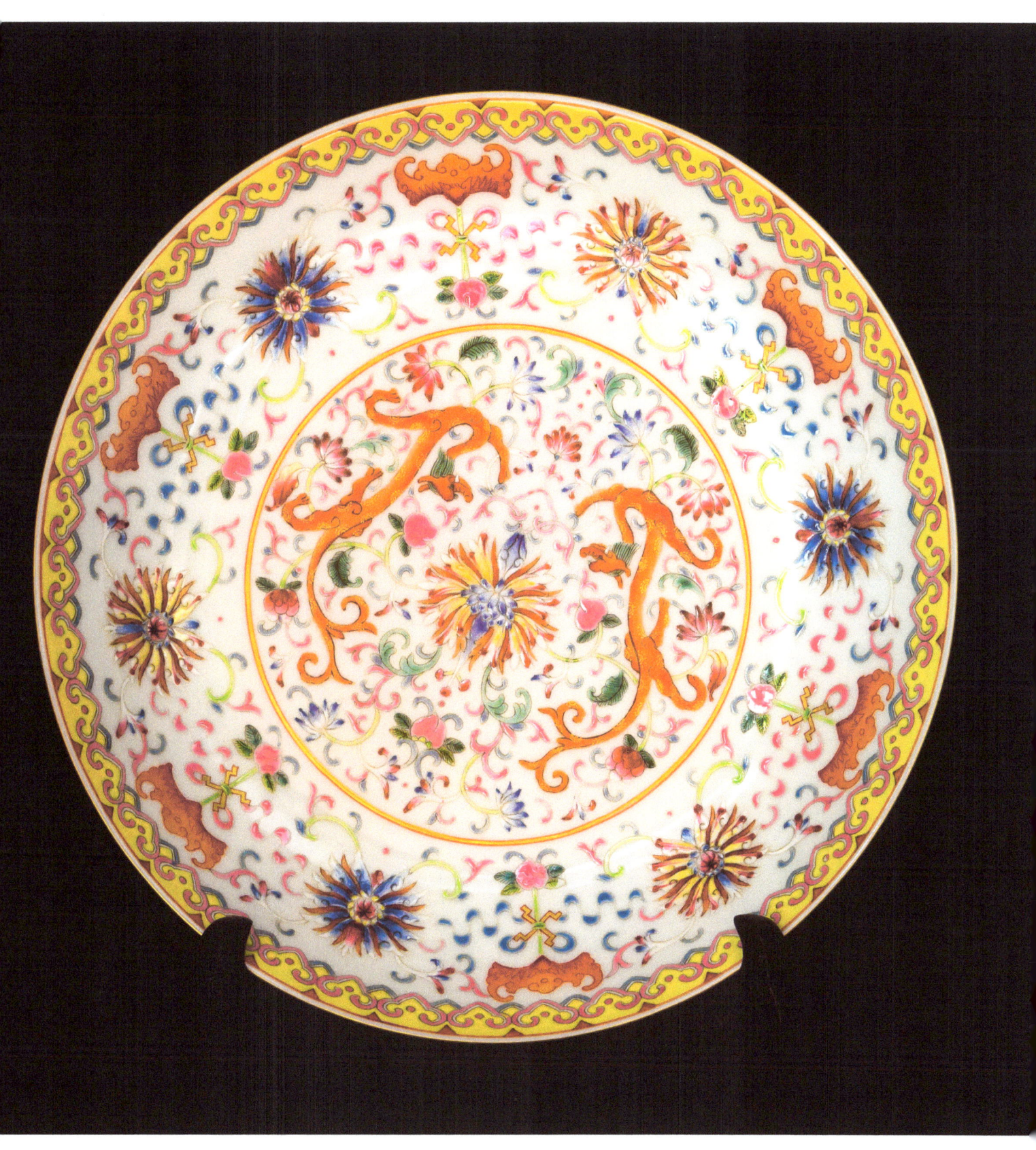

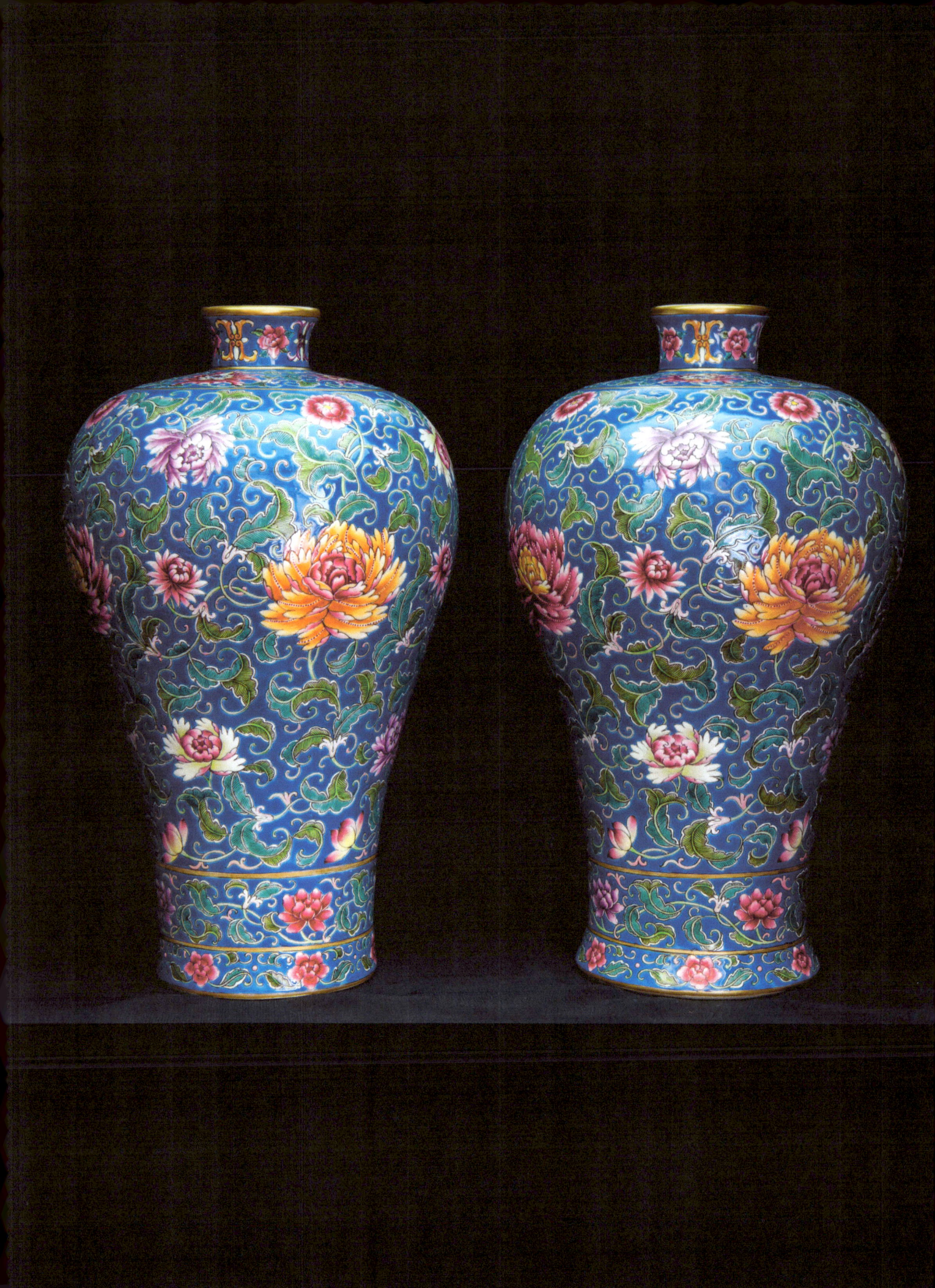

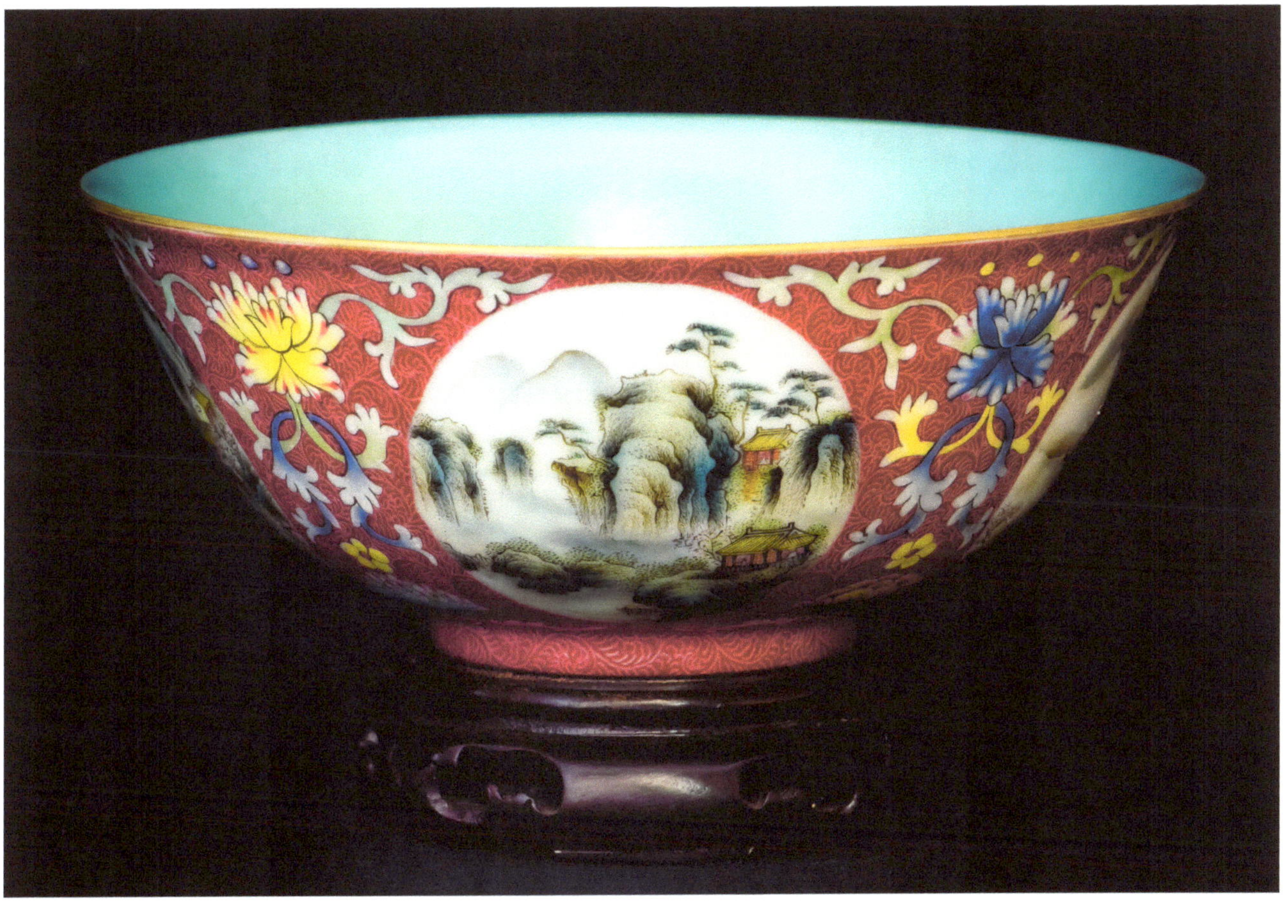

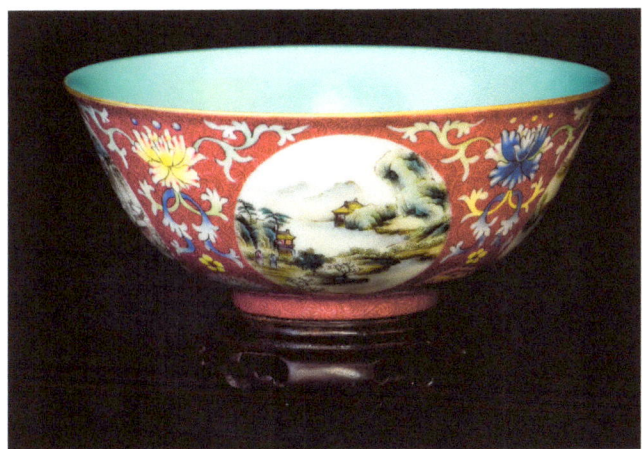
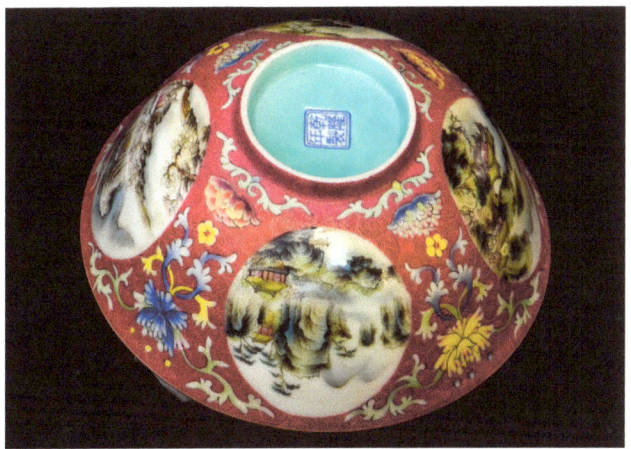

HONOURING THE UNKNOWN 61

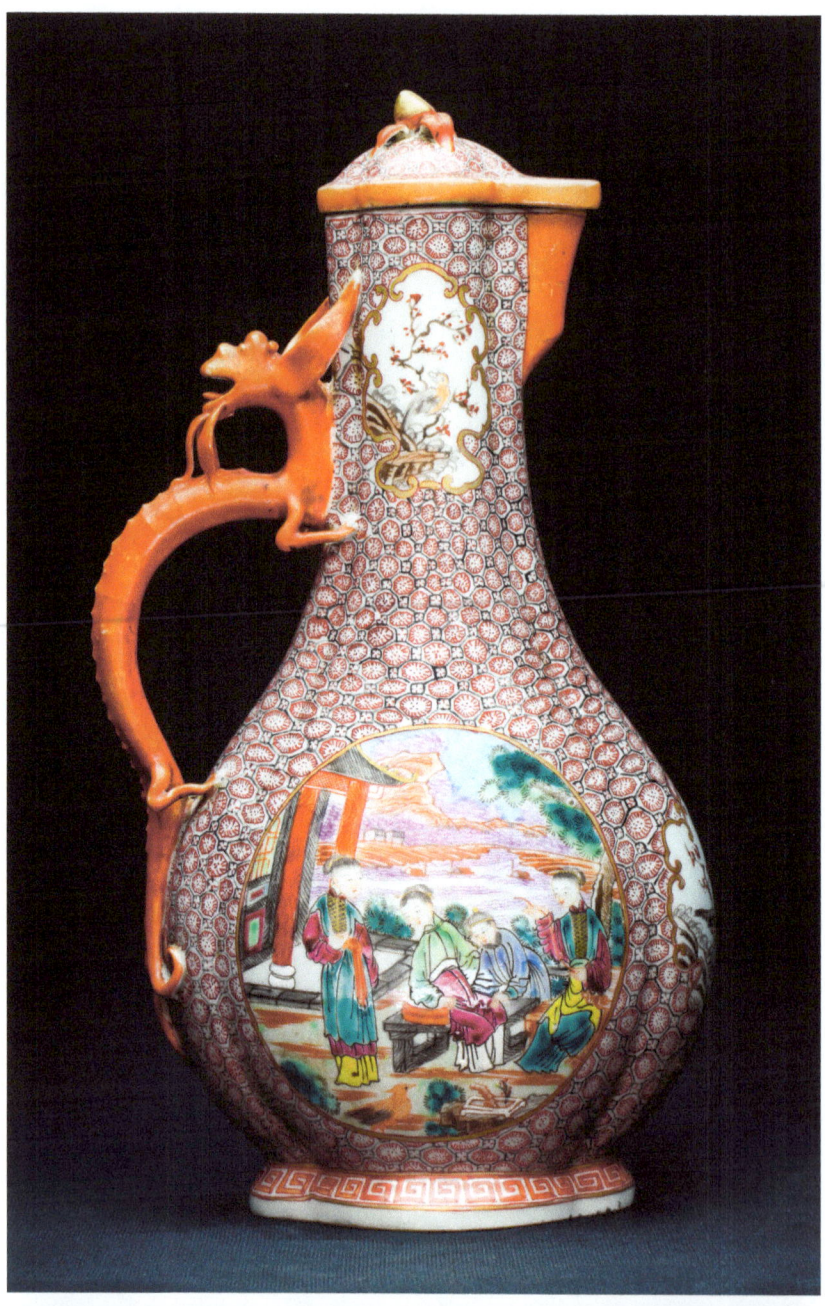
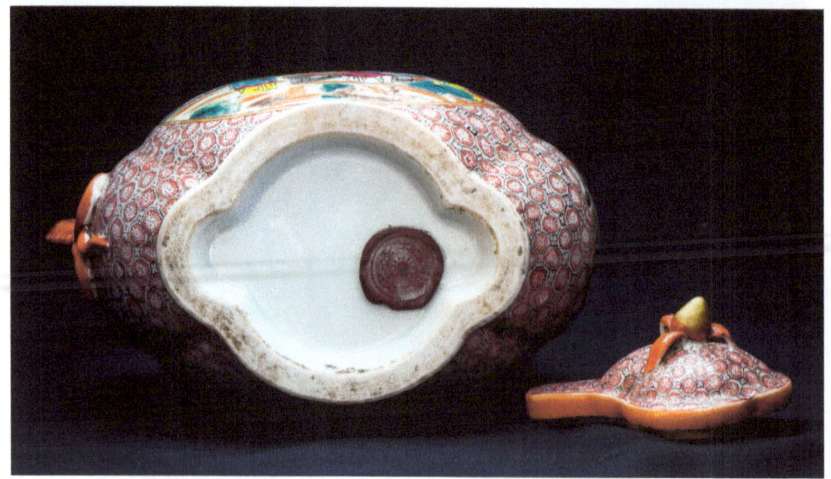

62 FORBIDDEN REPLICAS

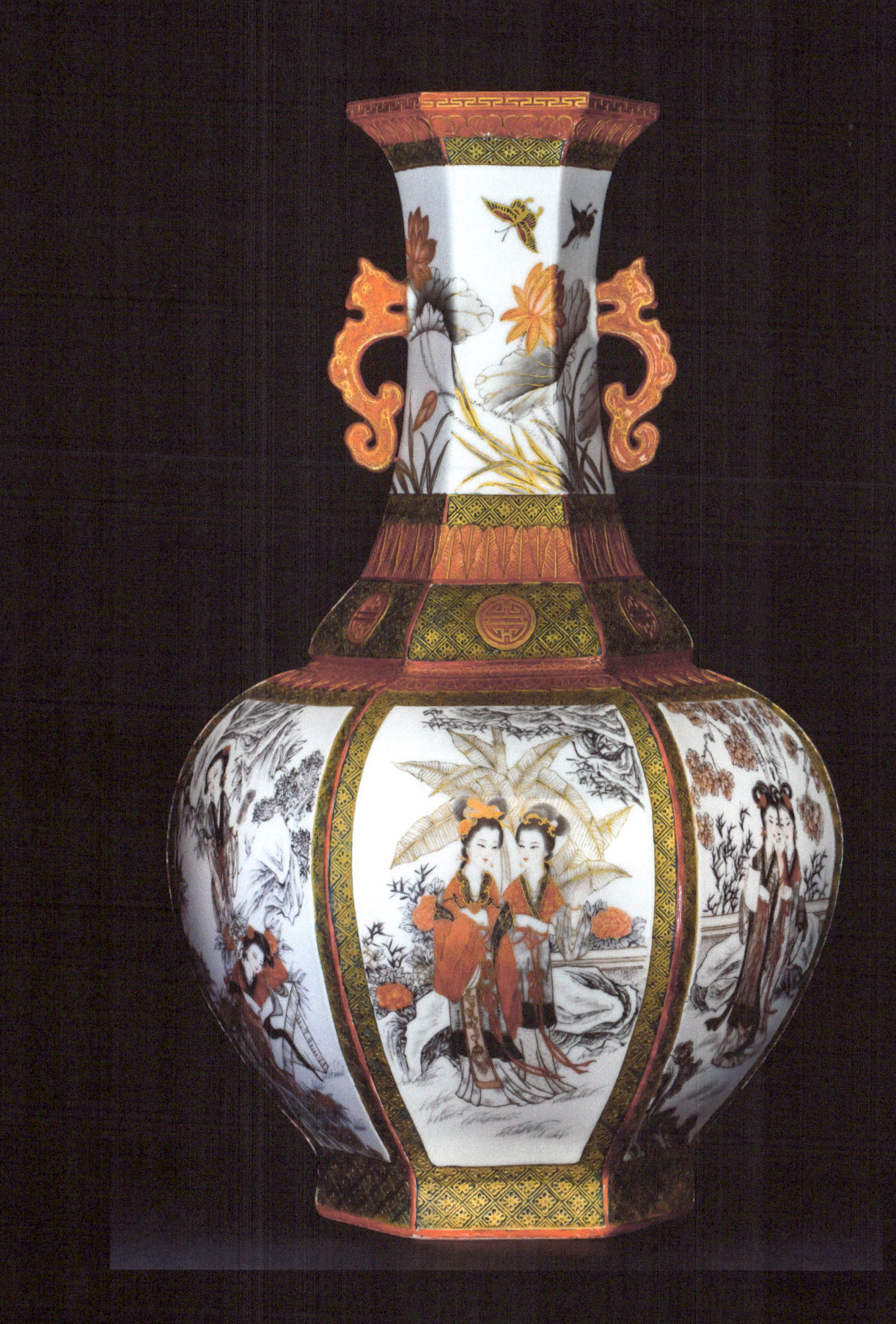

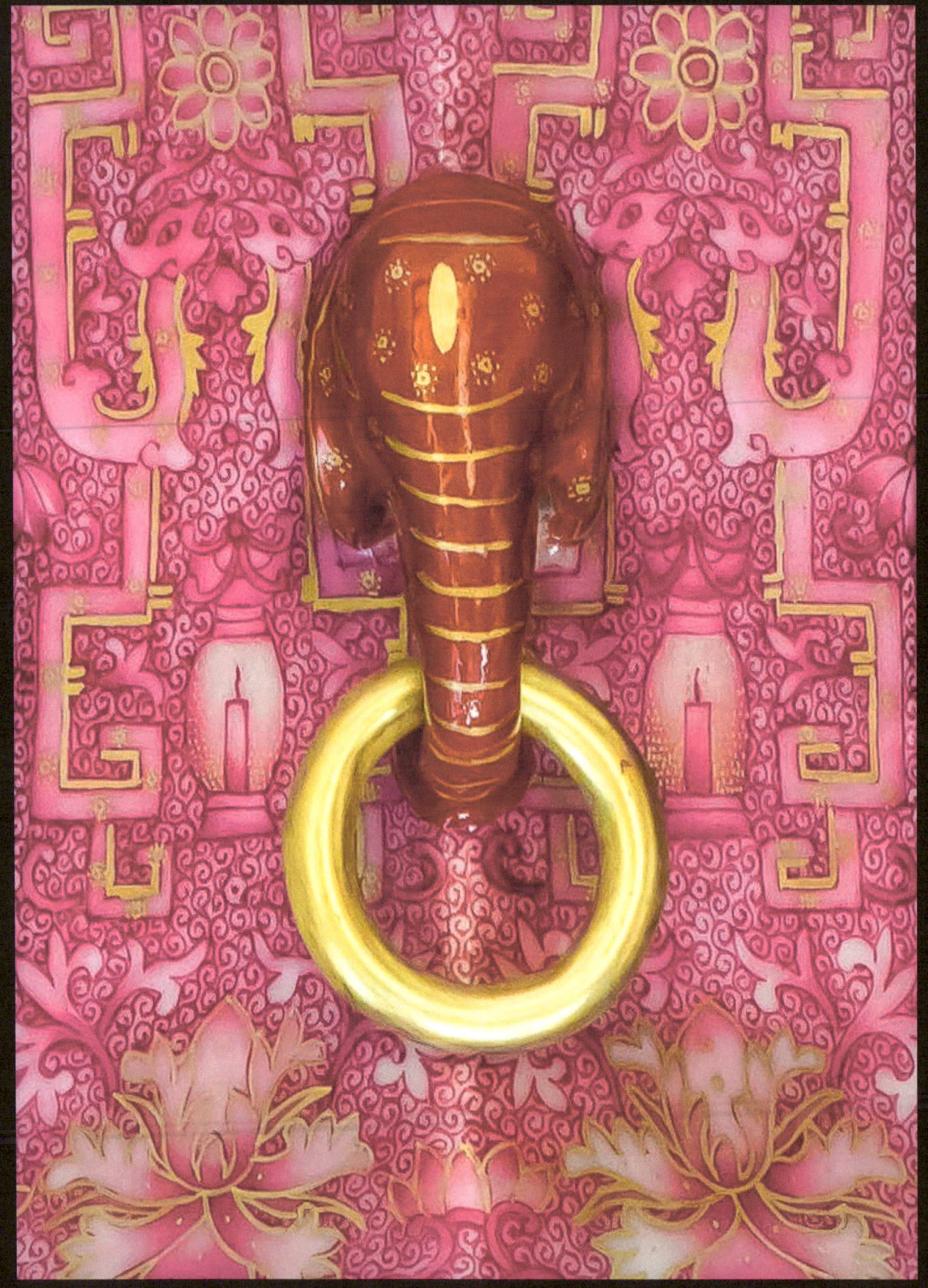

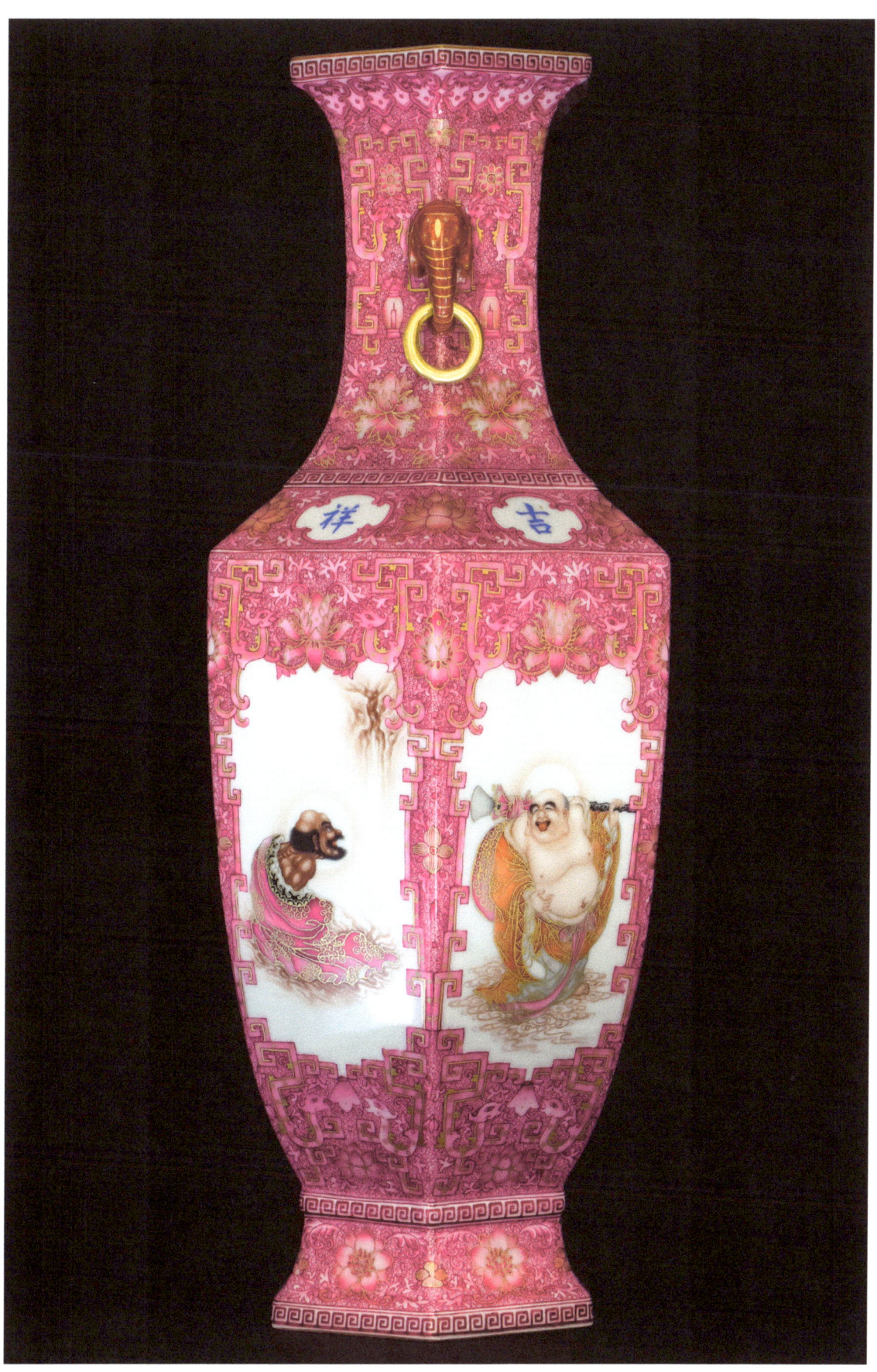

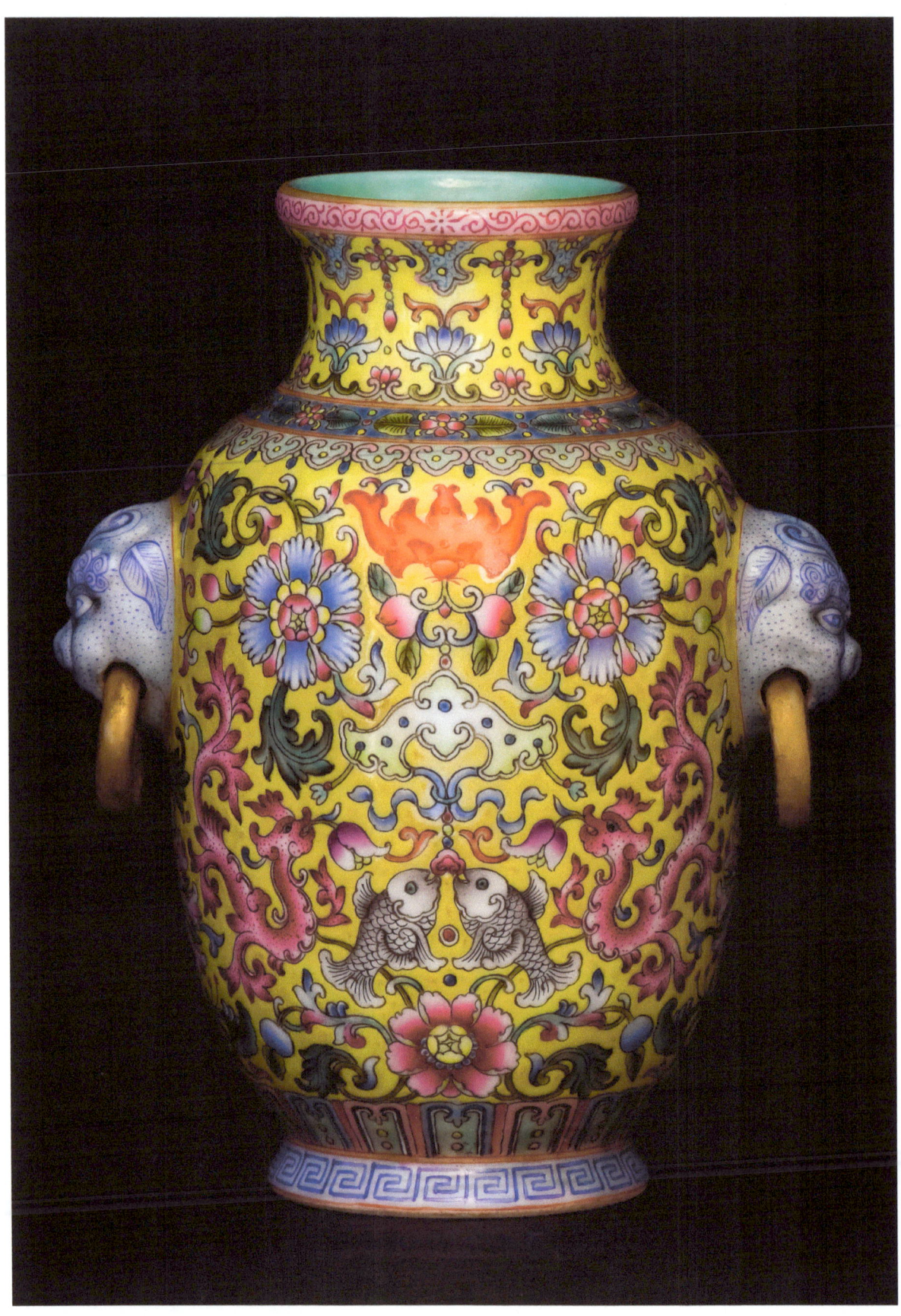

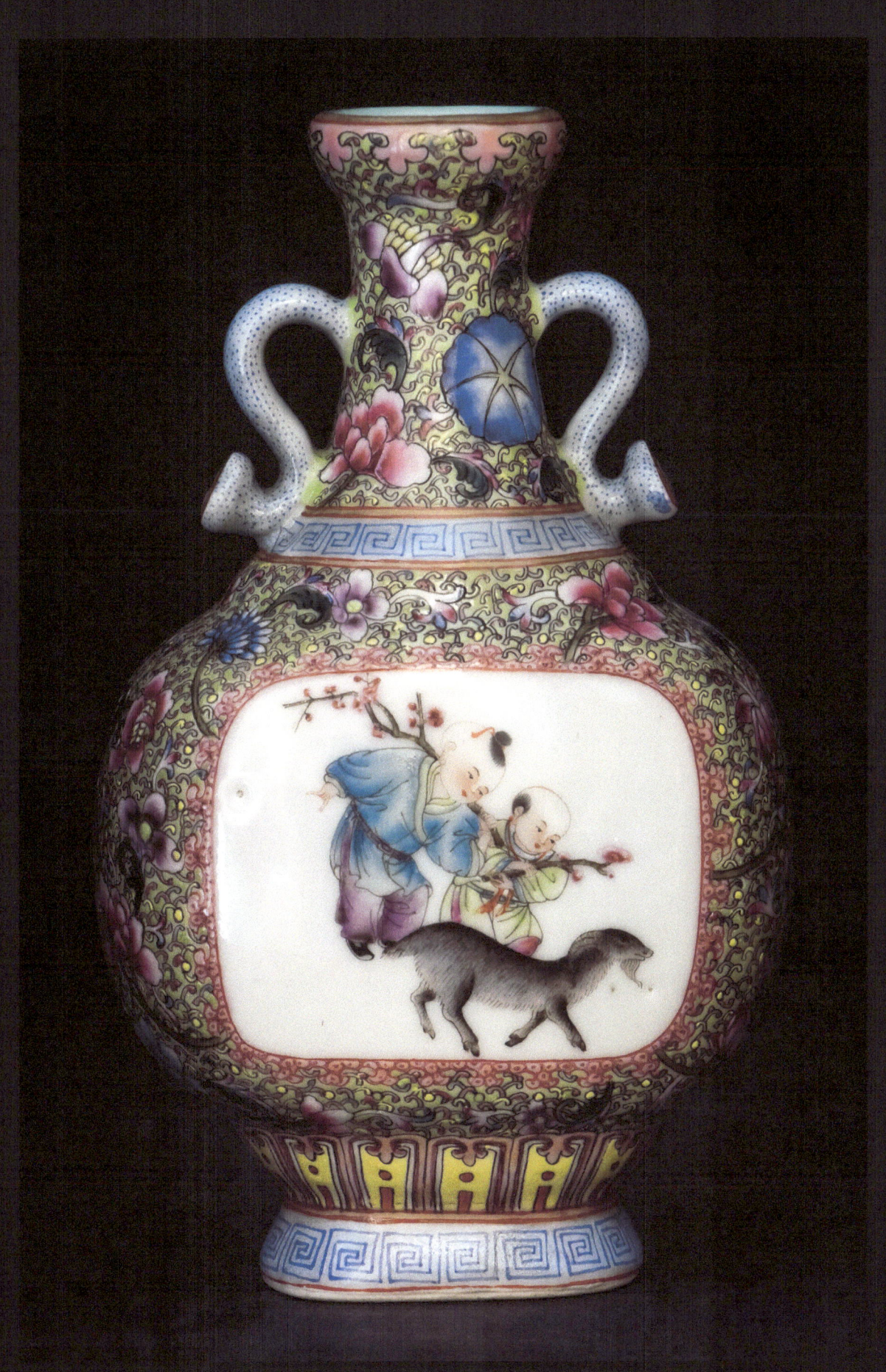

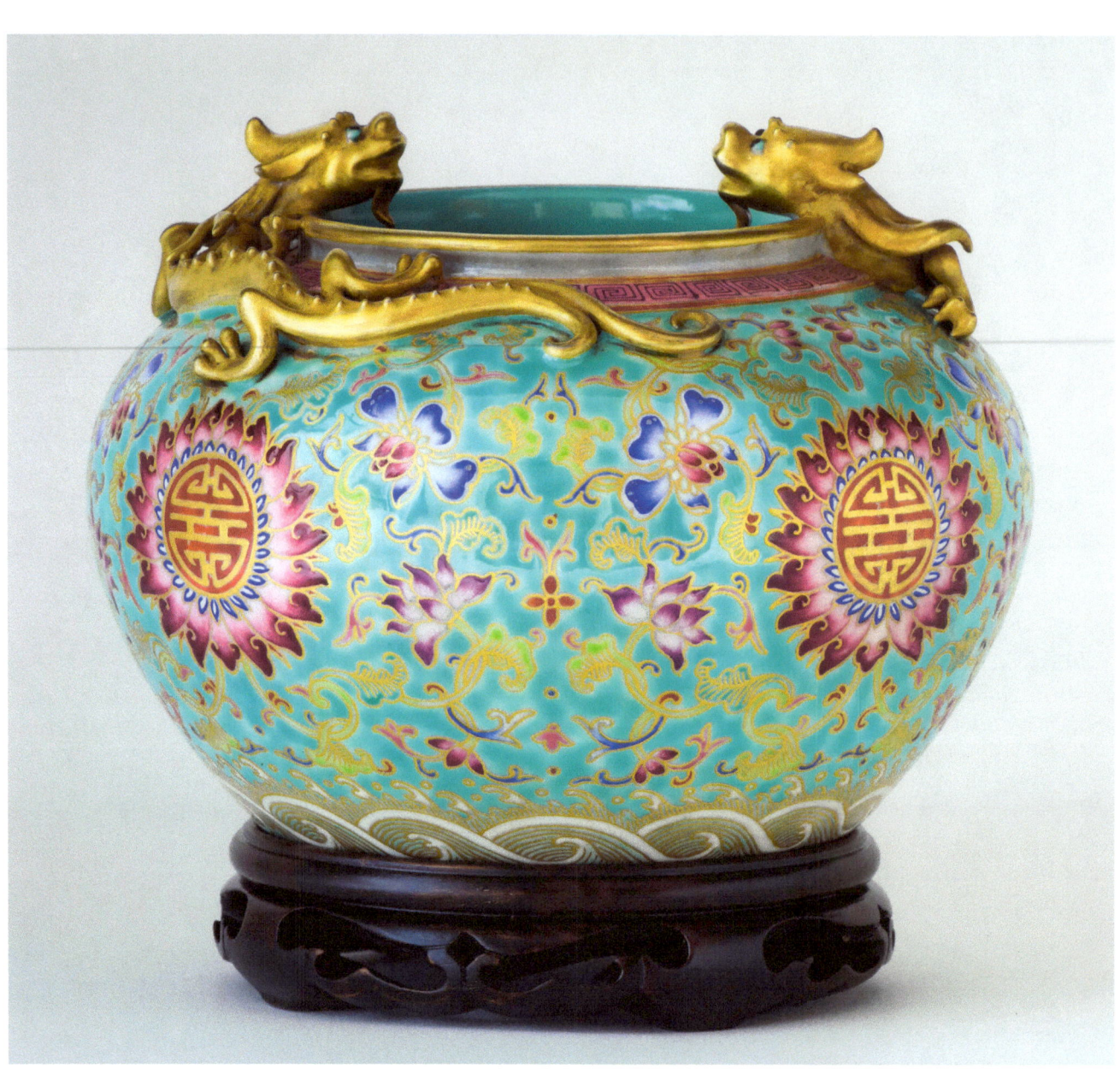

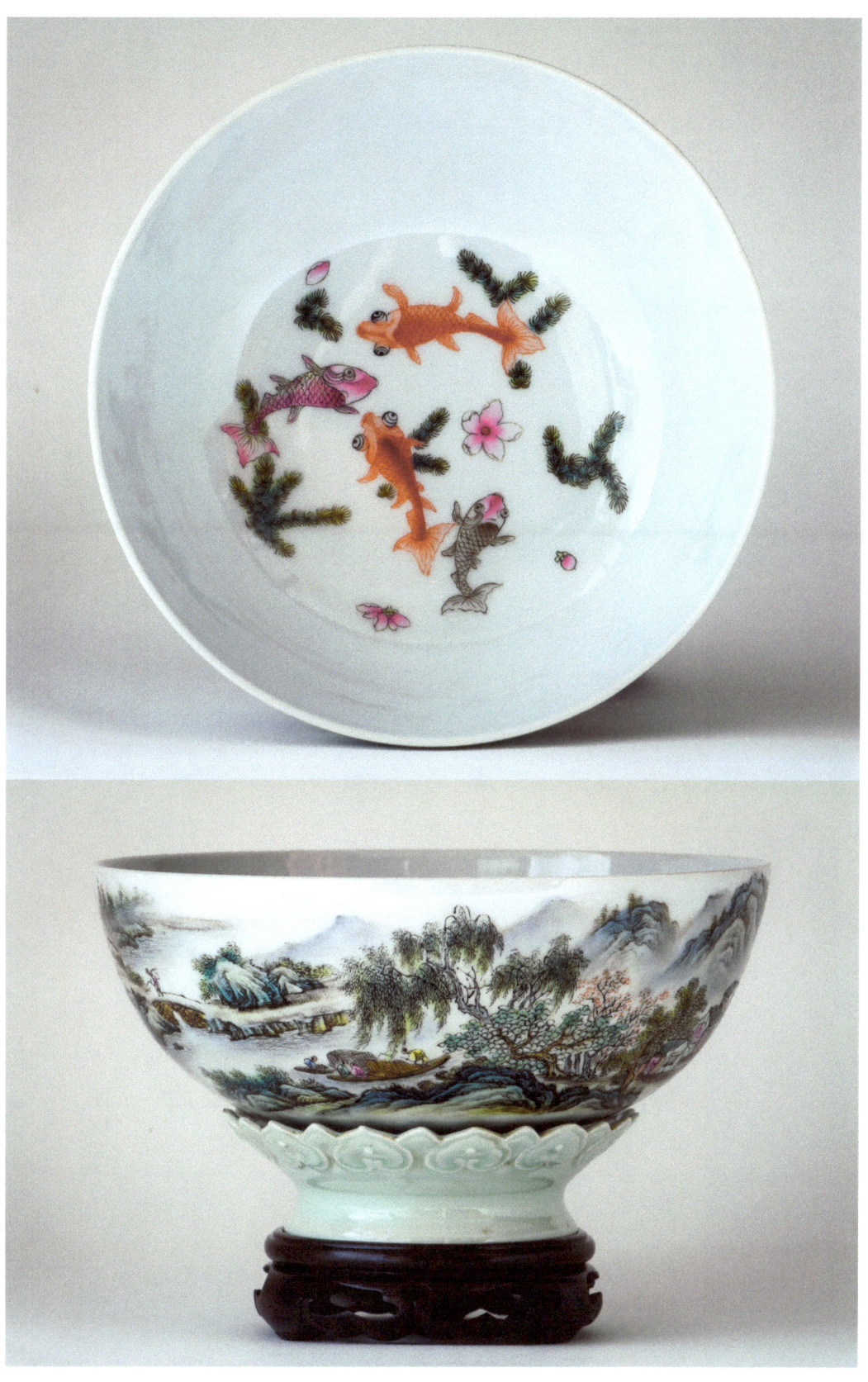

HONOURING THE UNKNOWN 69

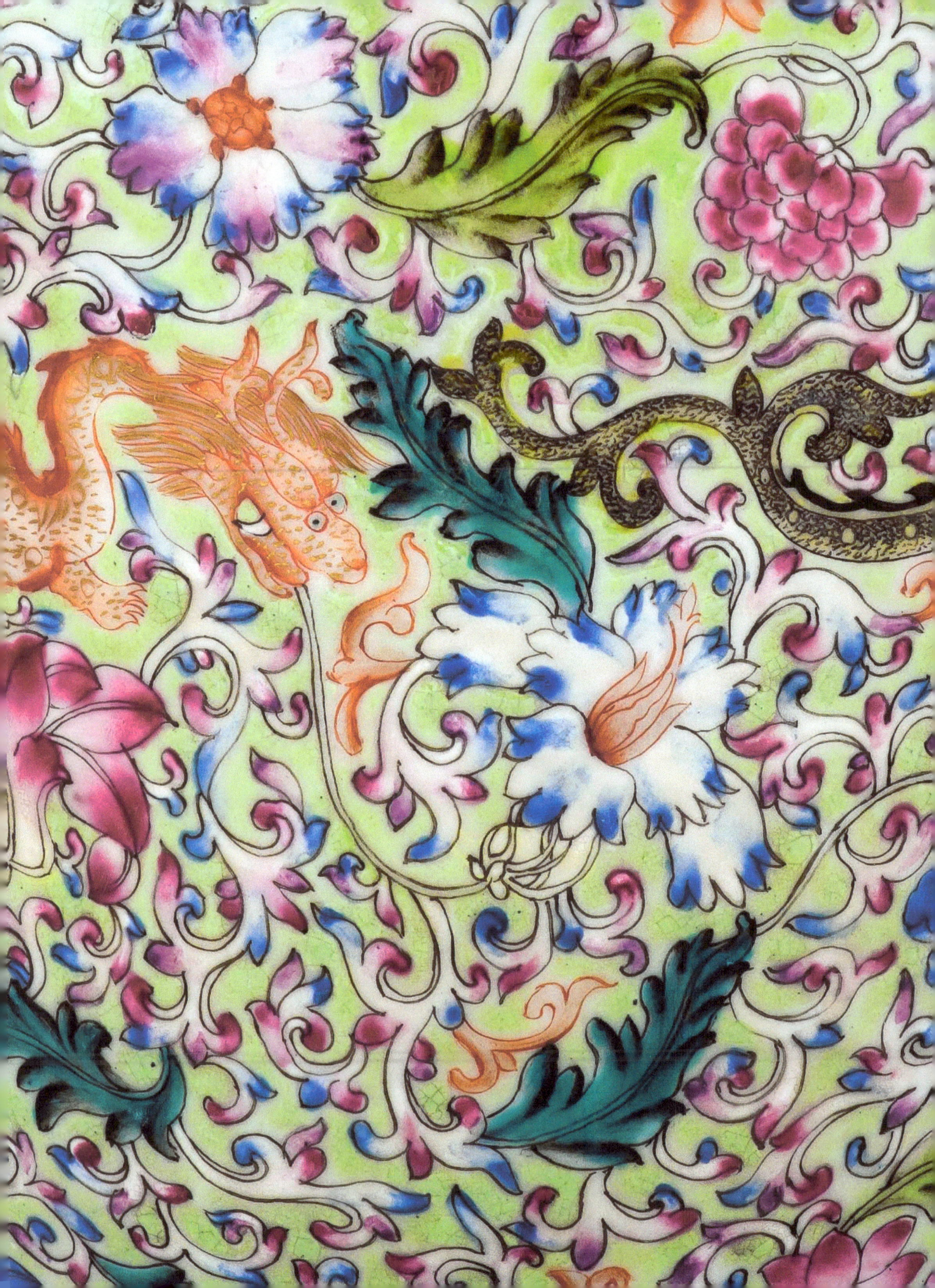

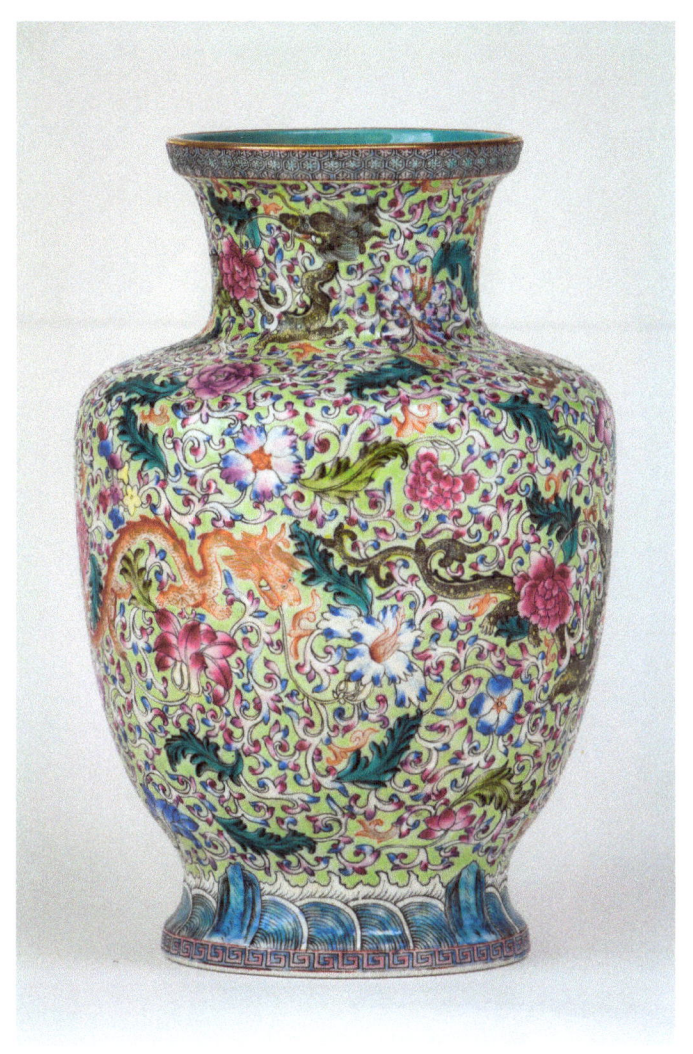
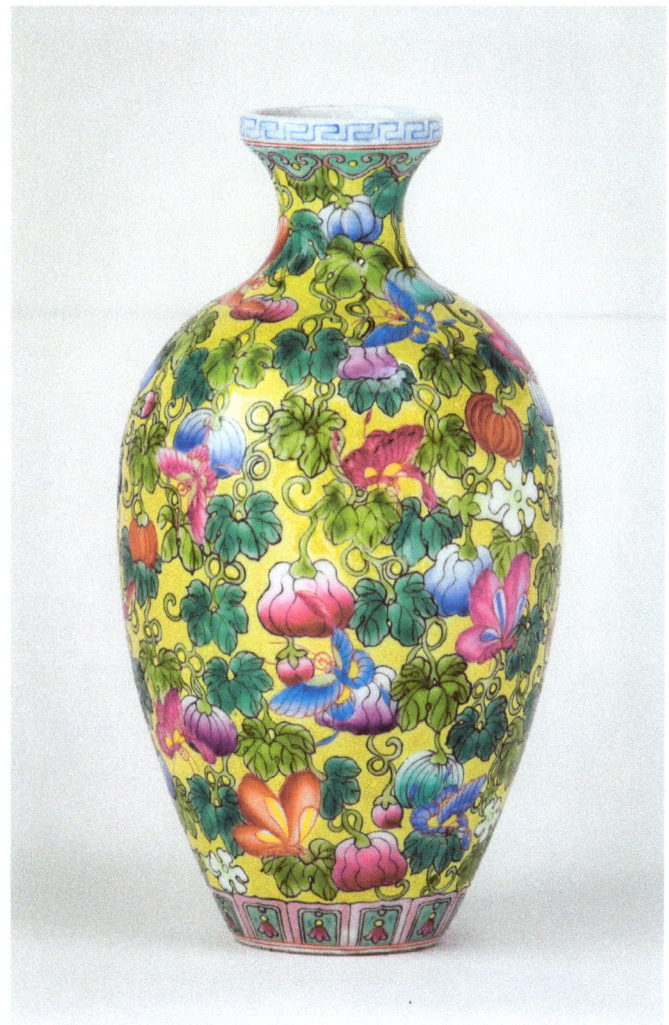

HONOURING THE UNKNOWN 71

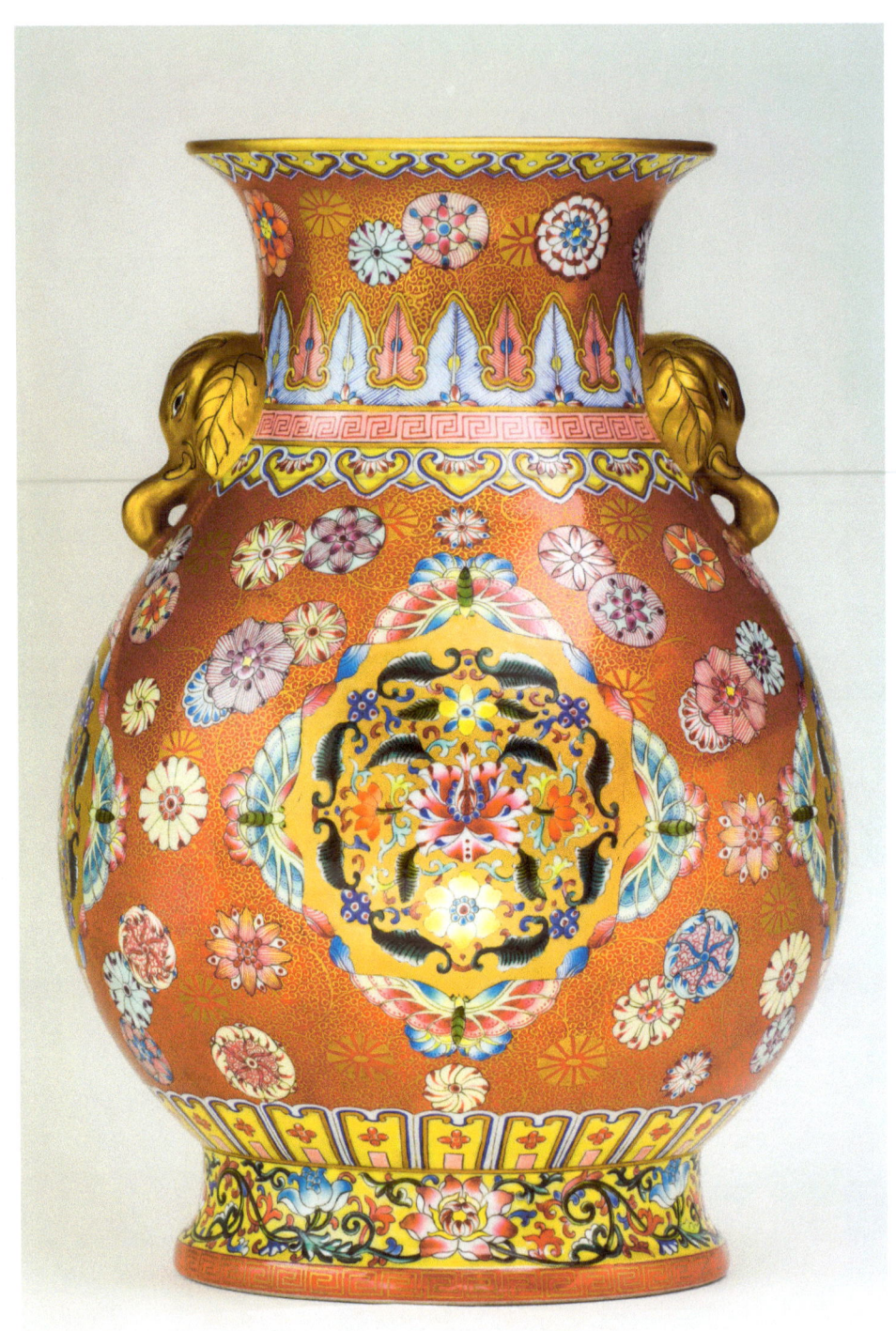

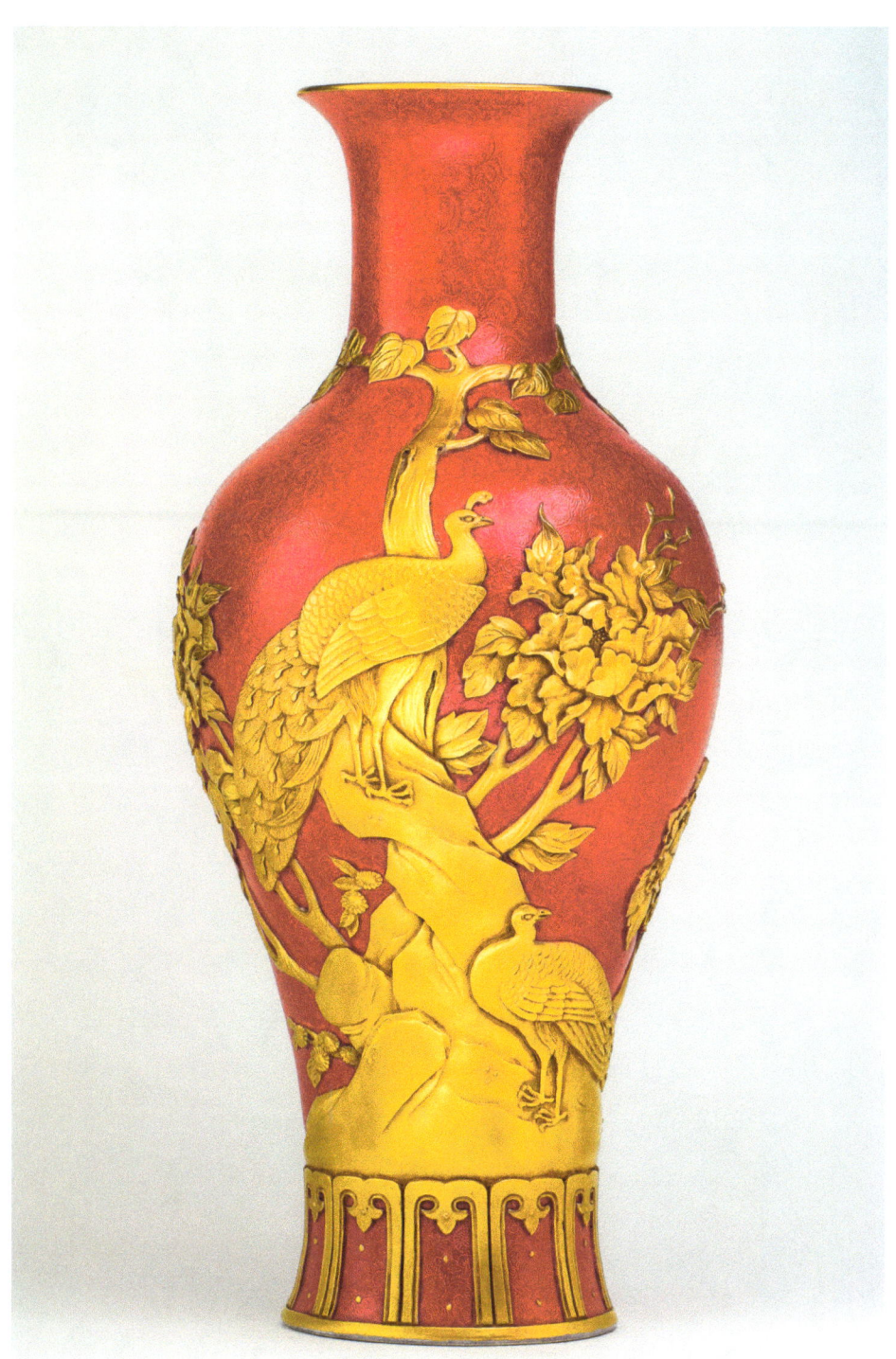

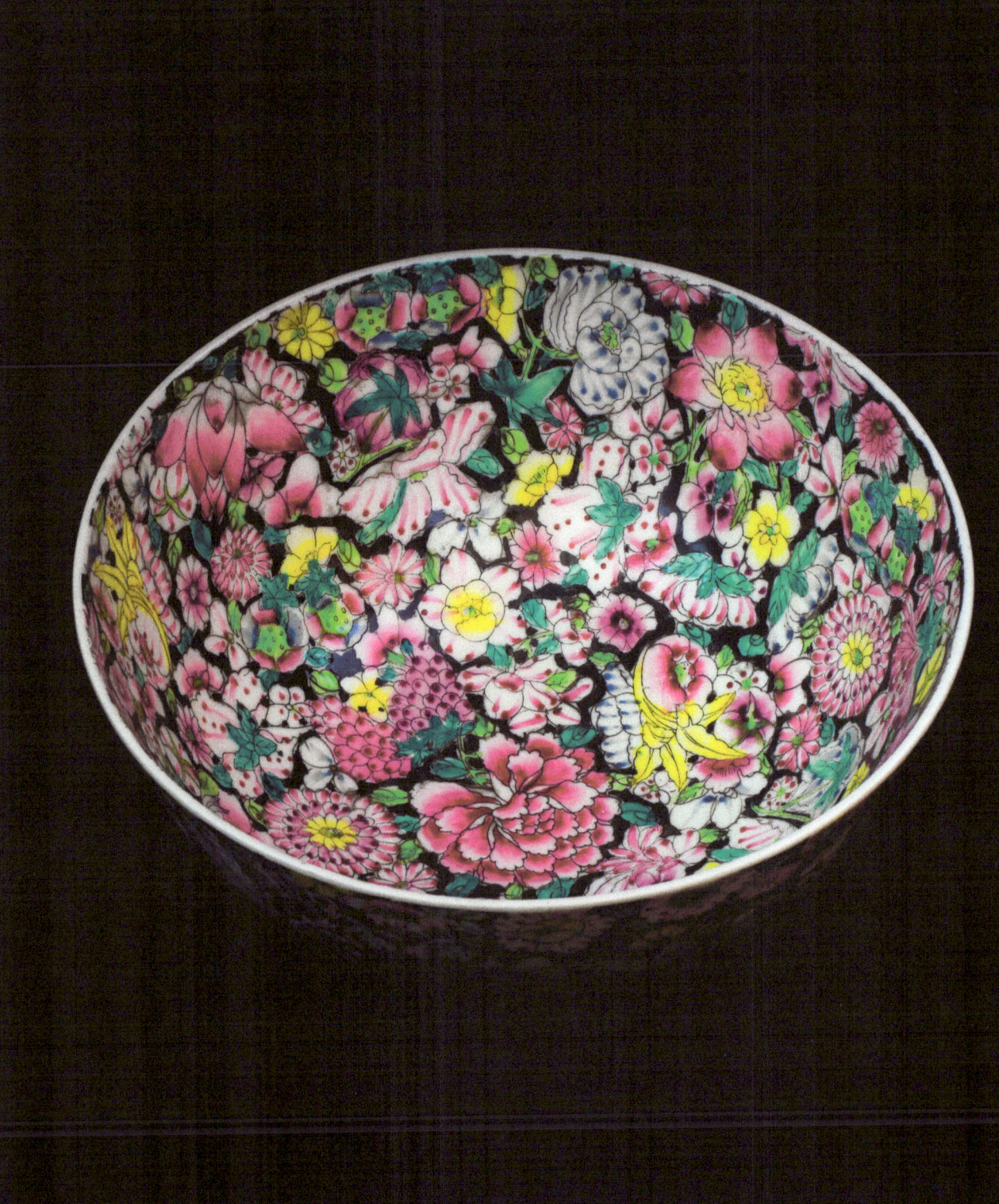

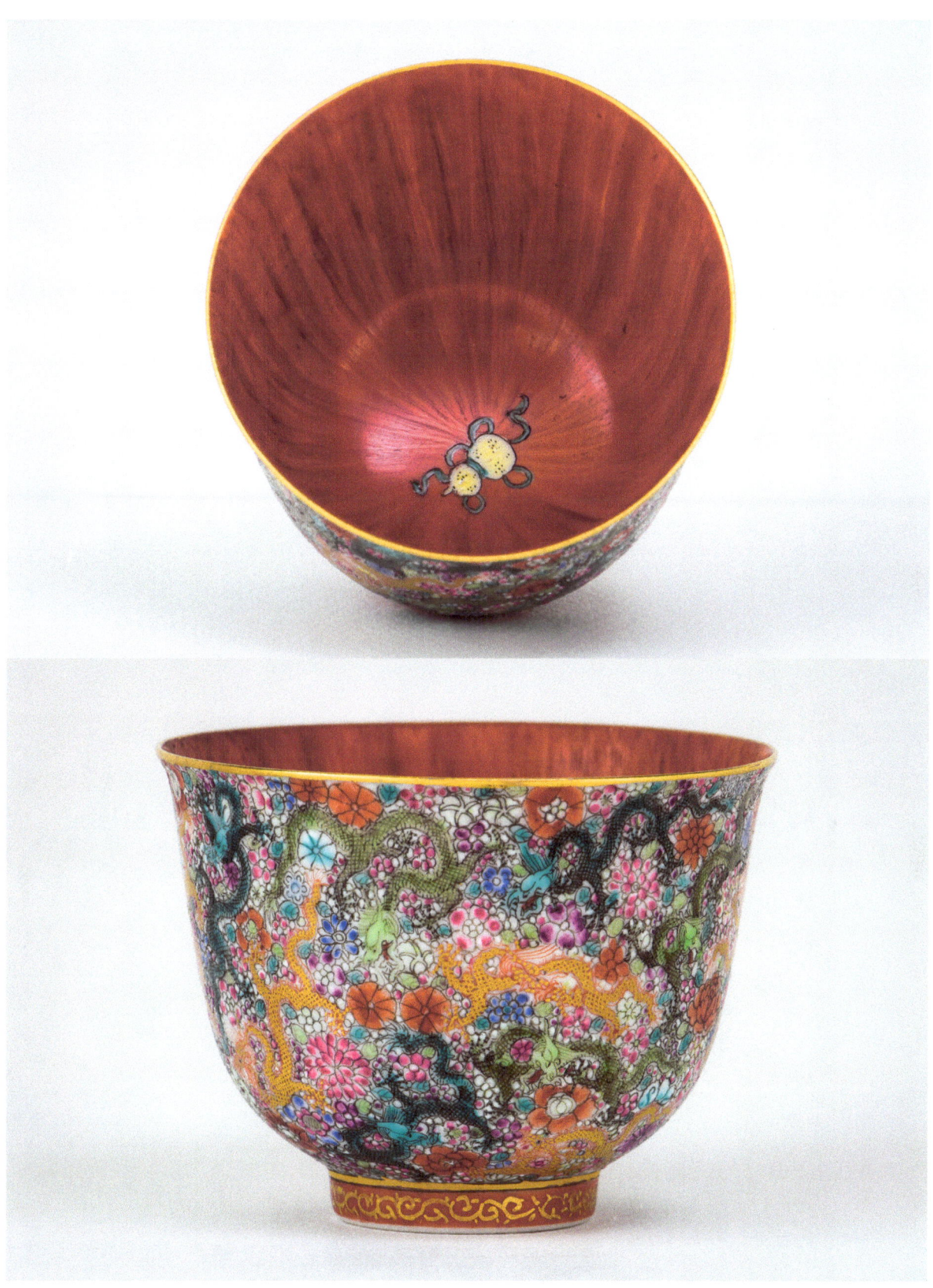

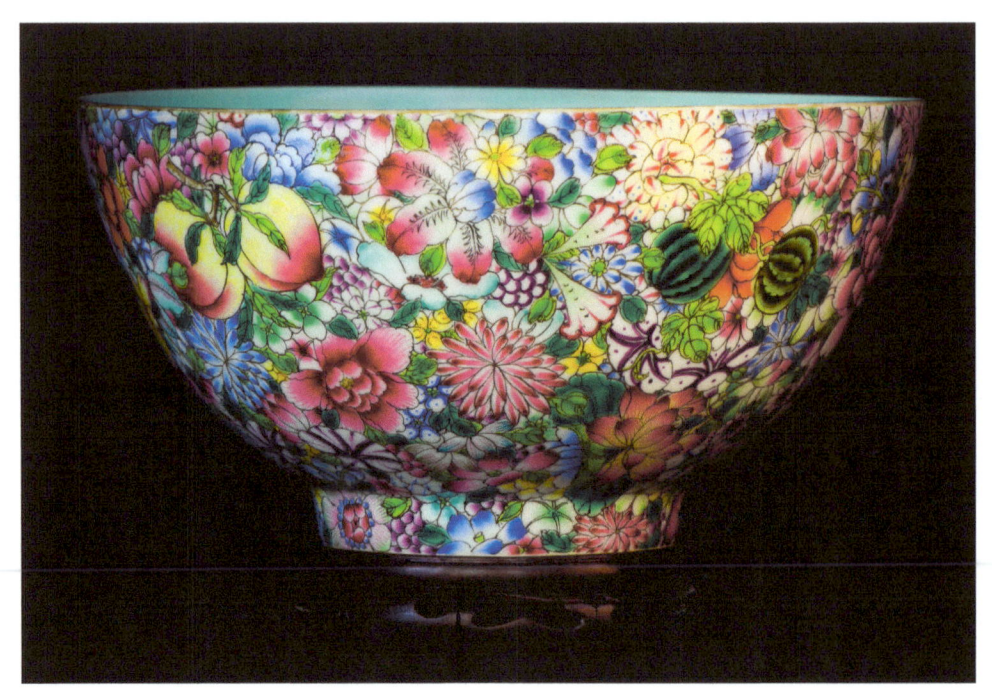

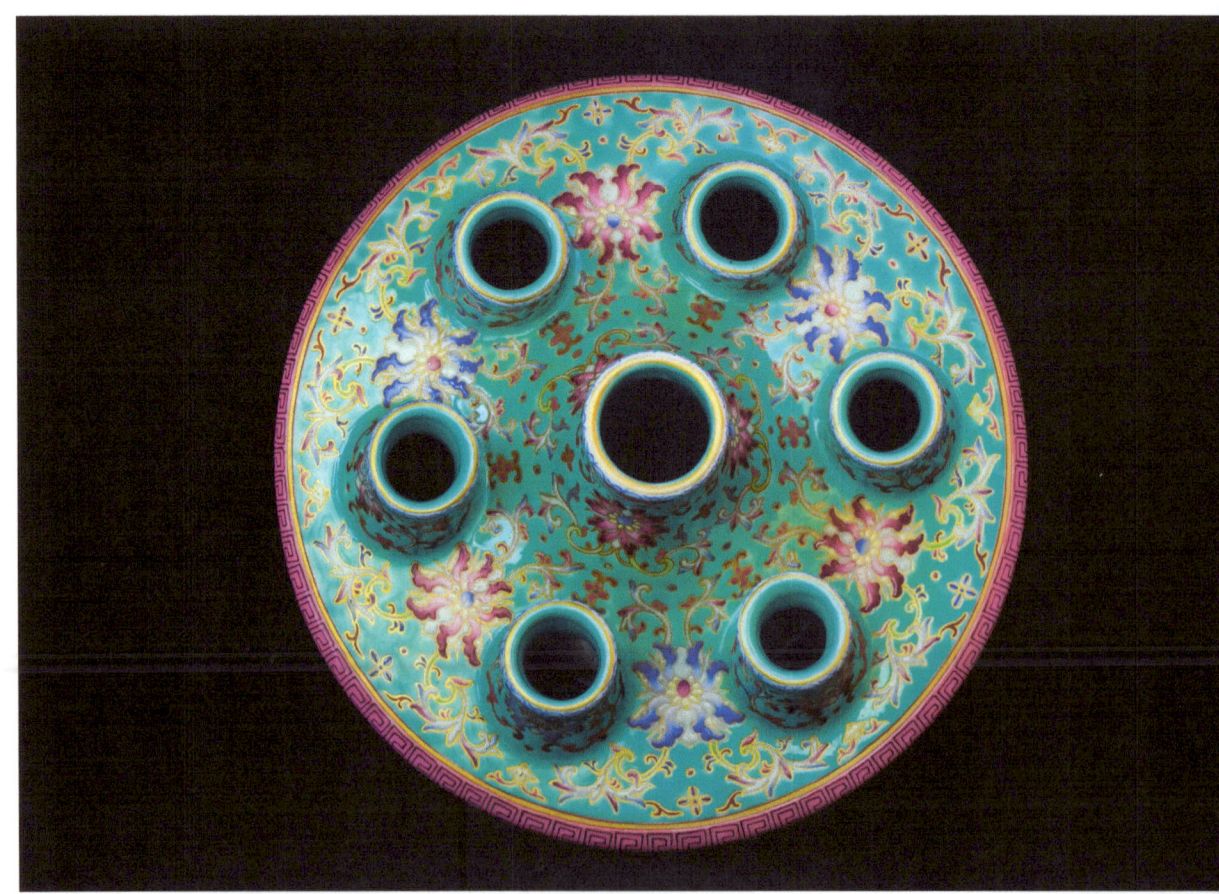

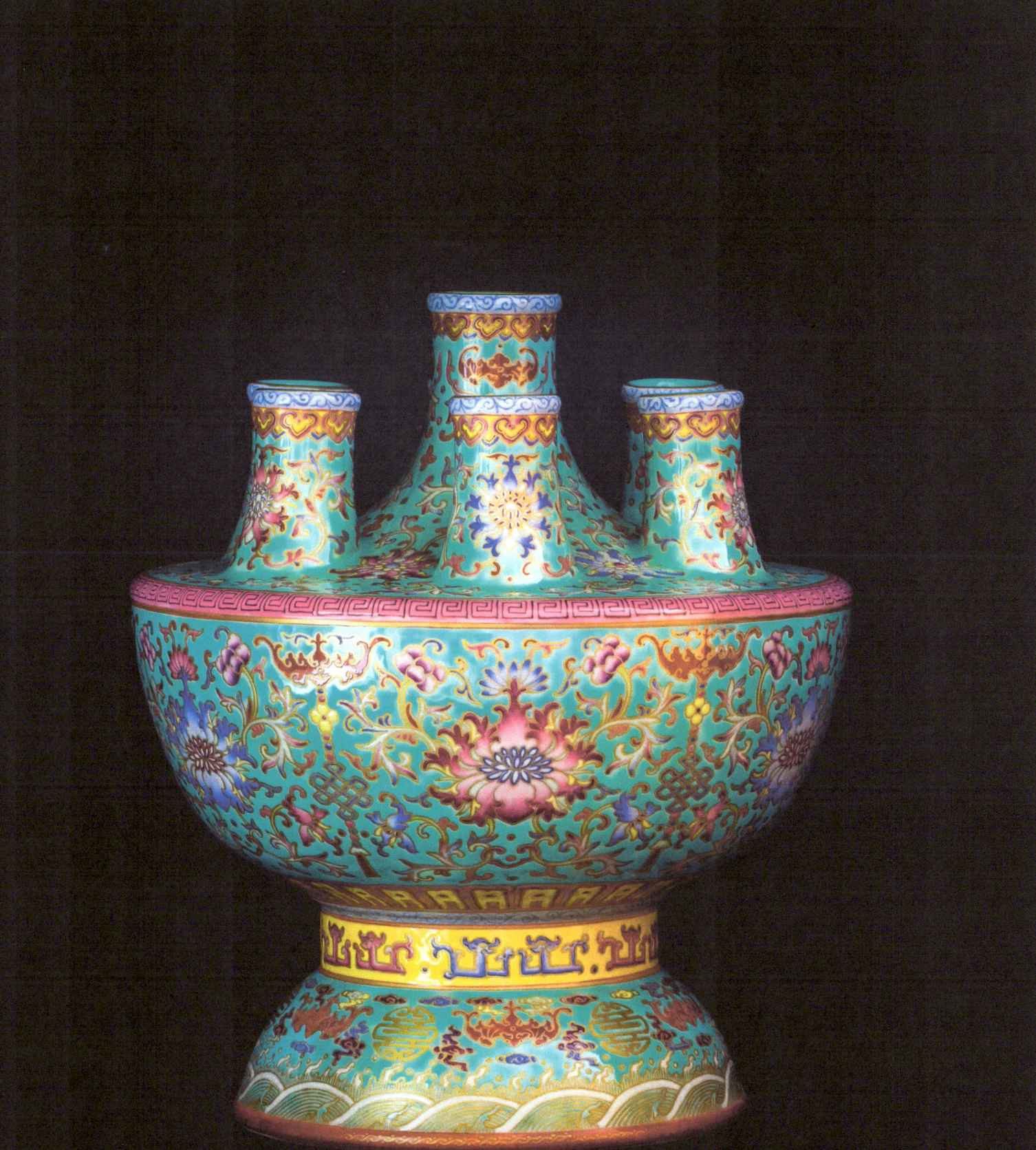

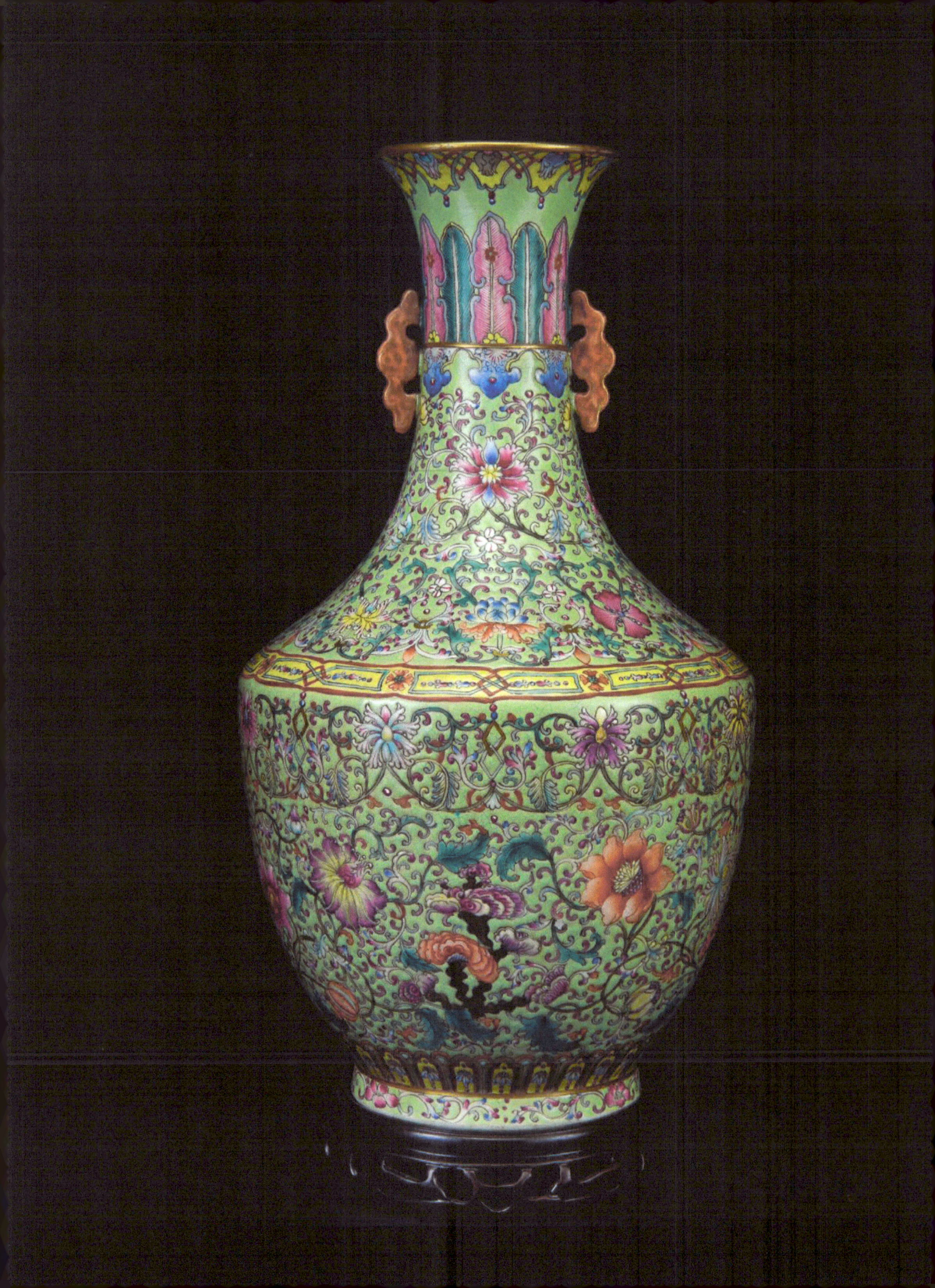

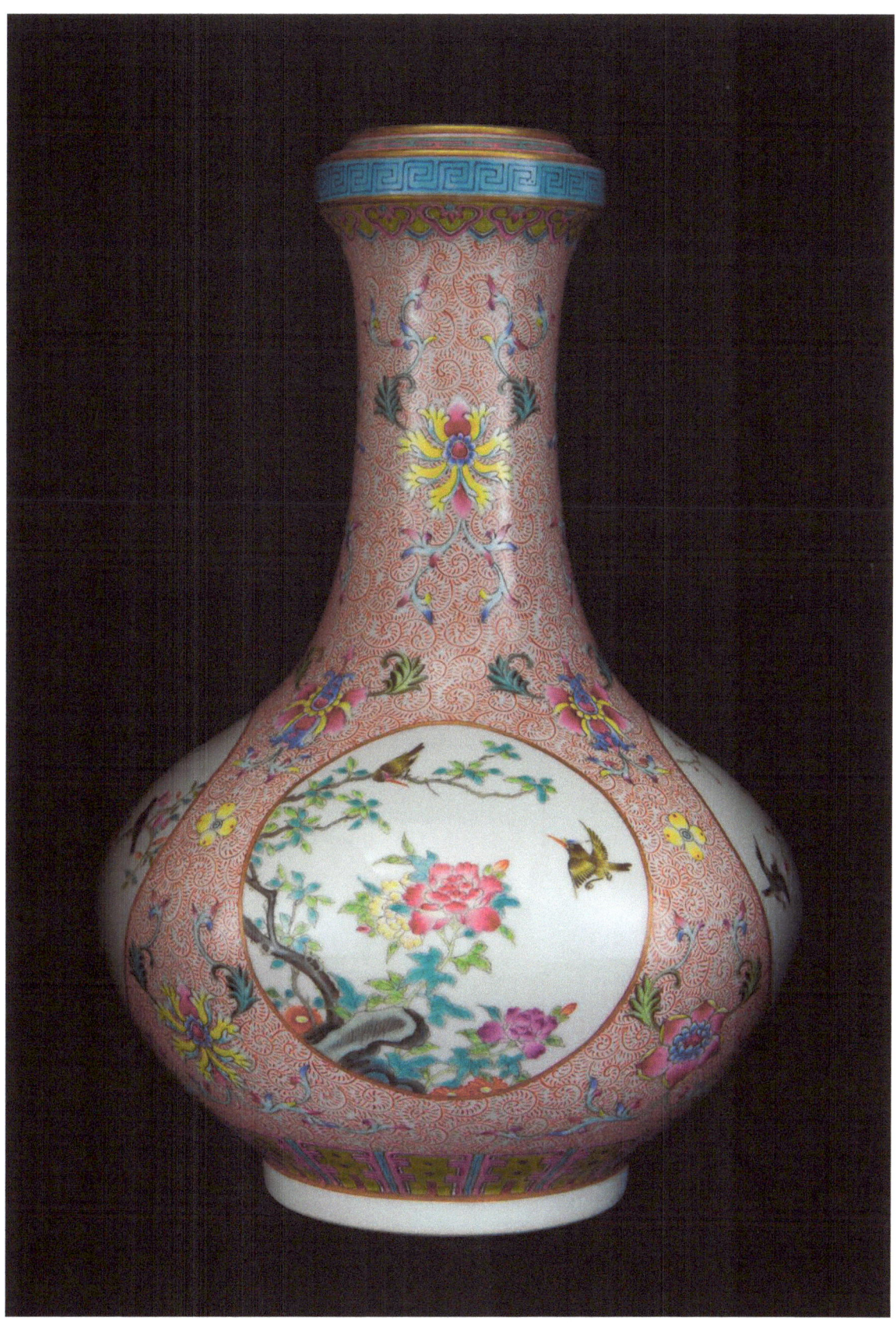

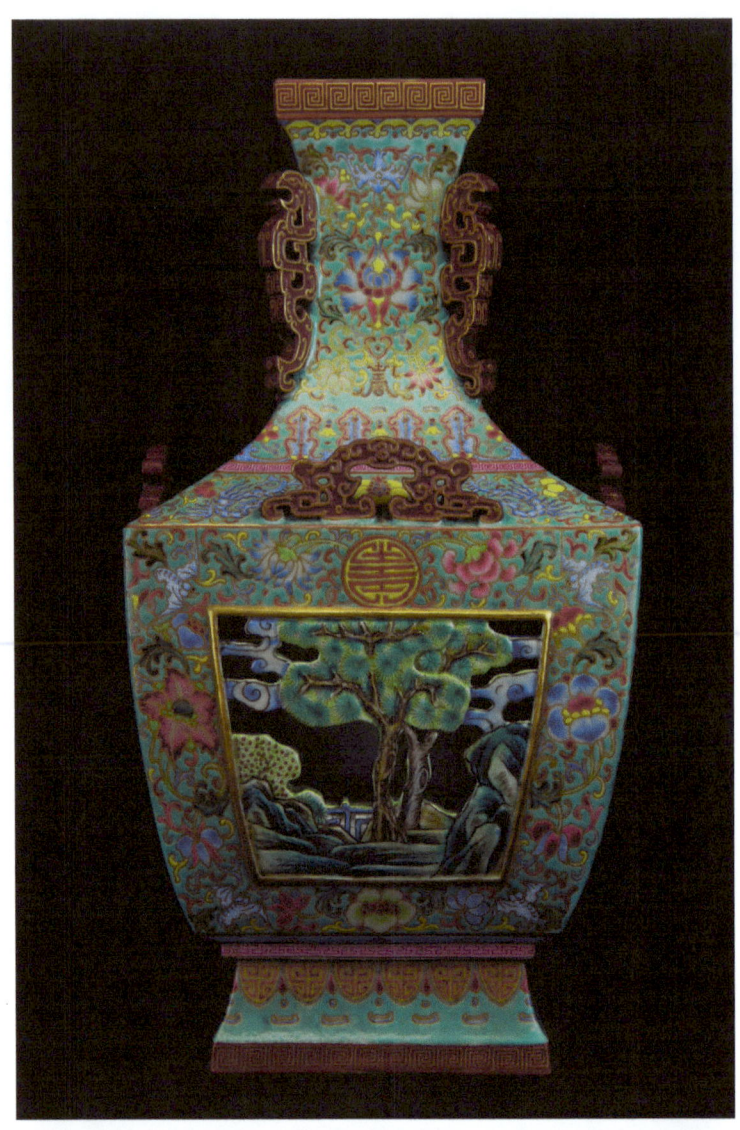
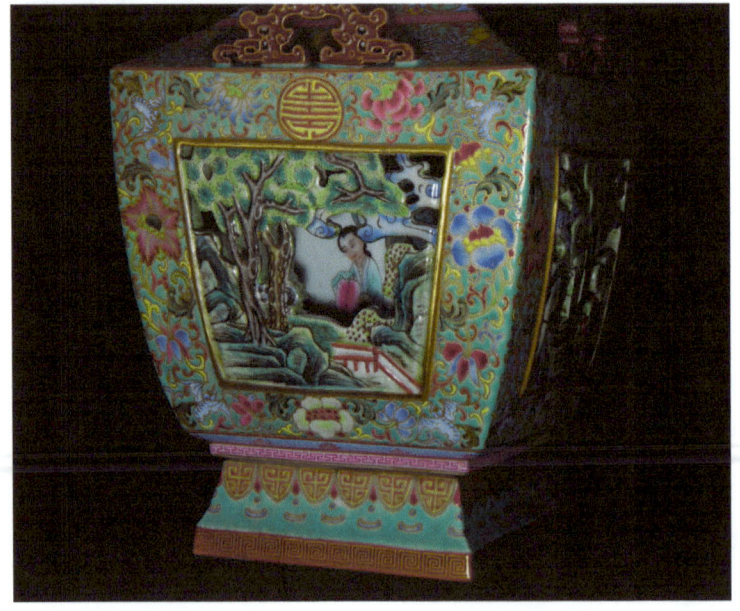

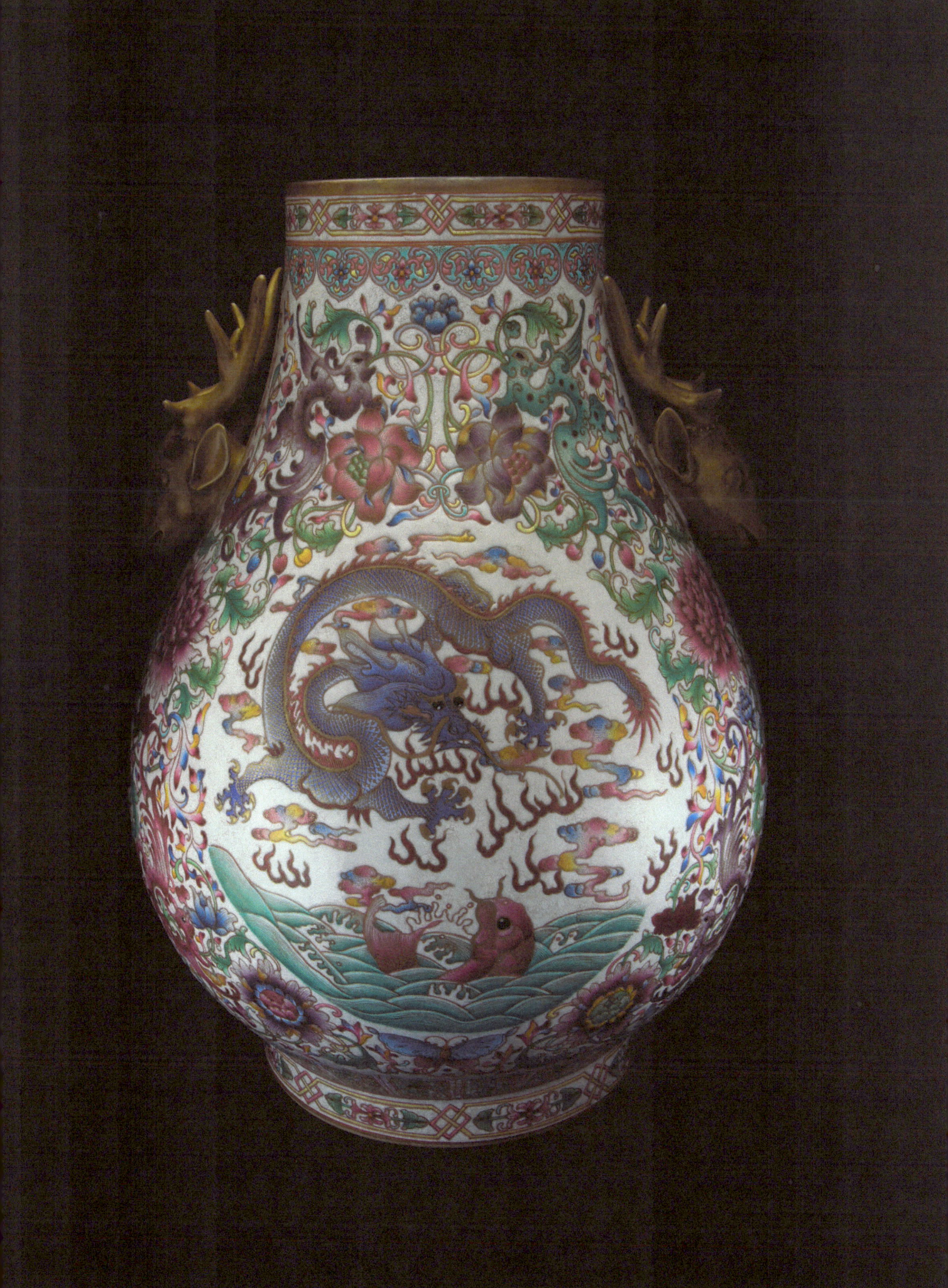

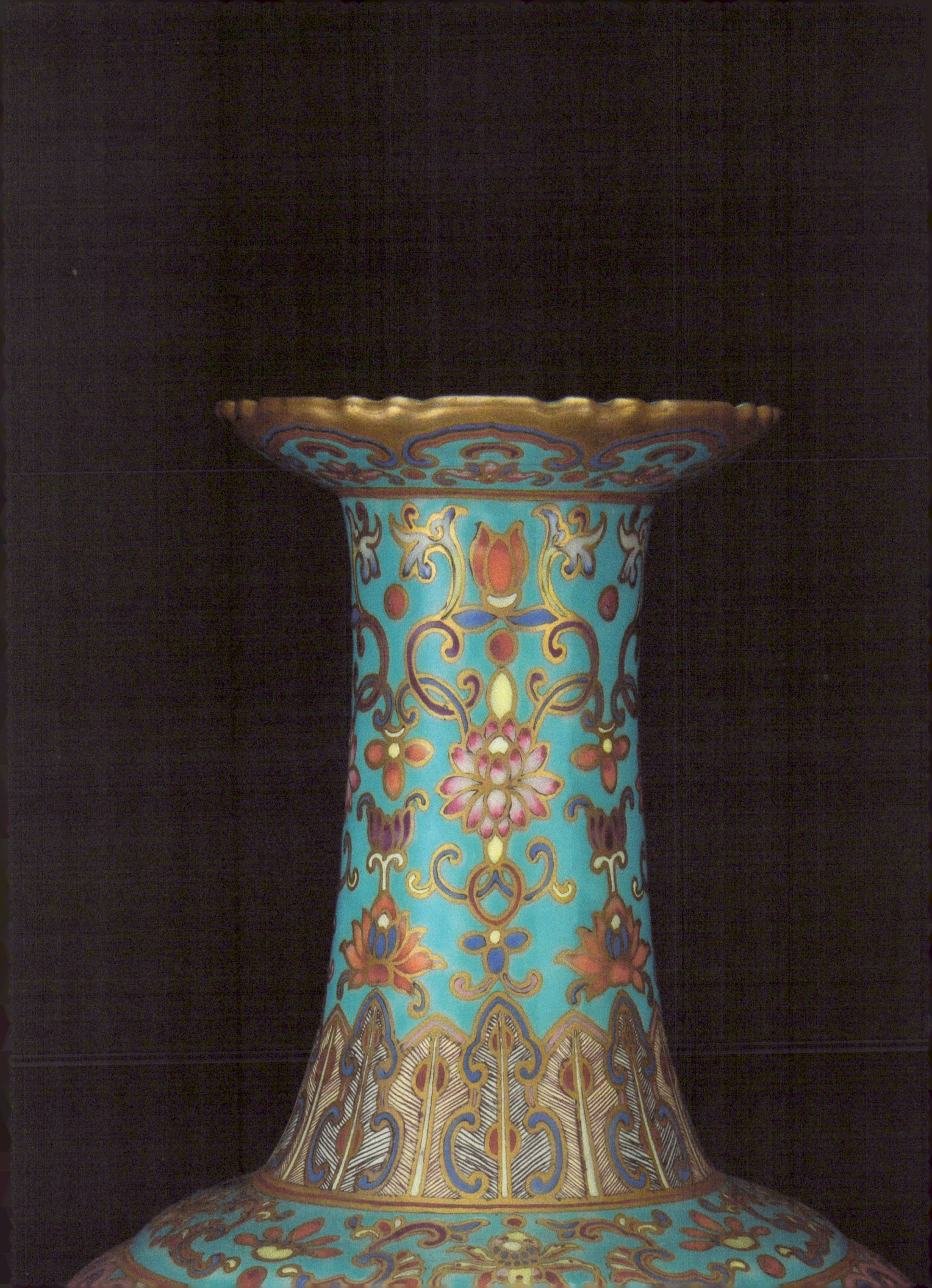

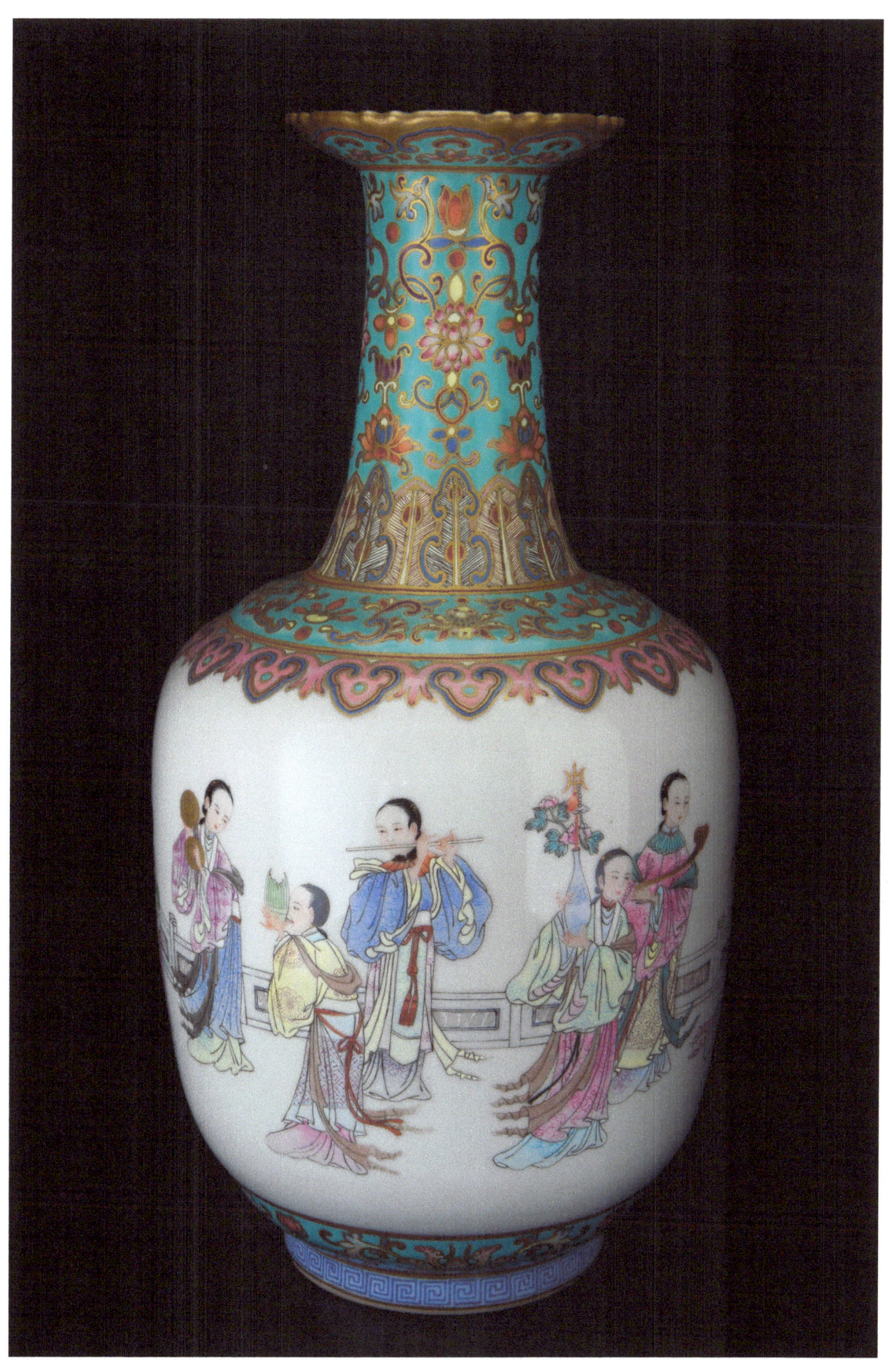

HONOURING THE UNKNOWN 83

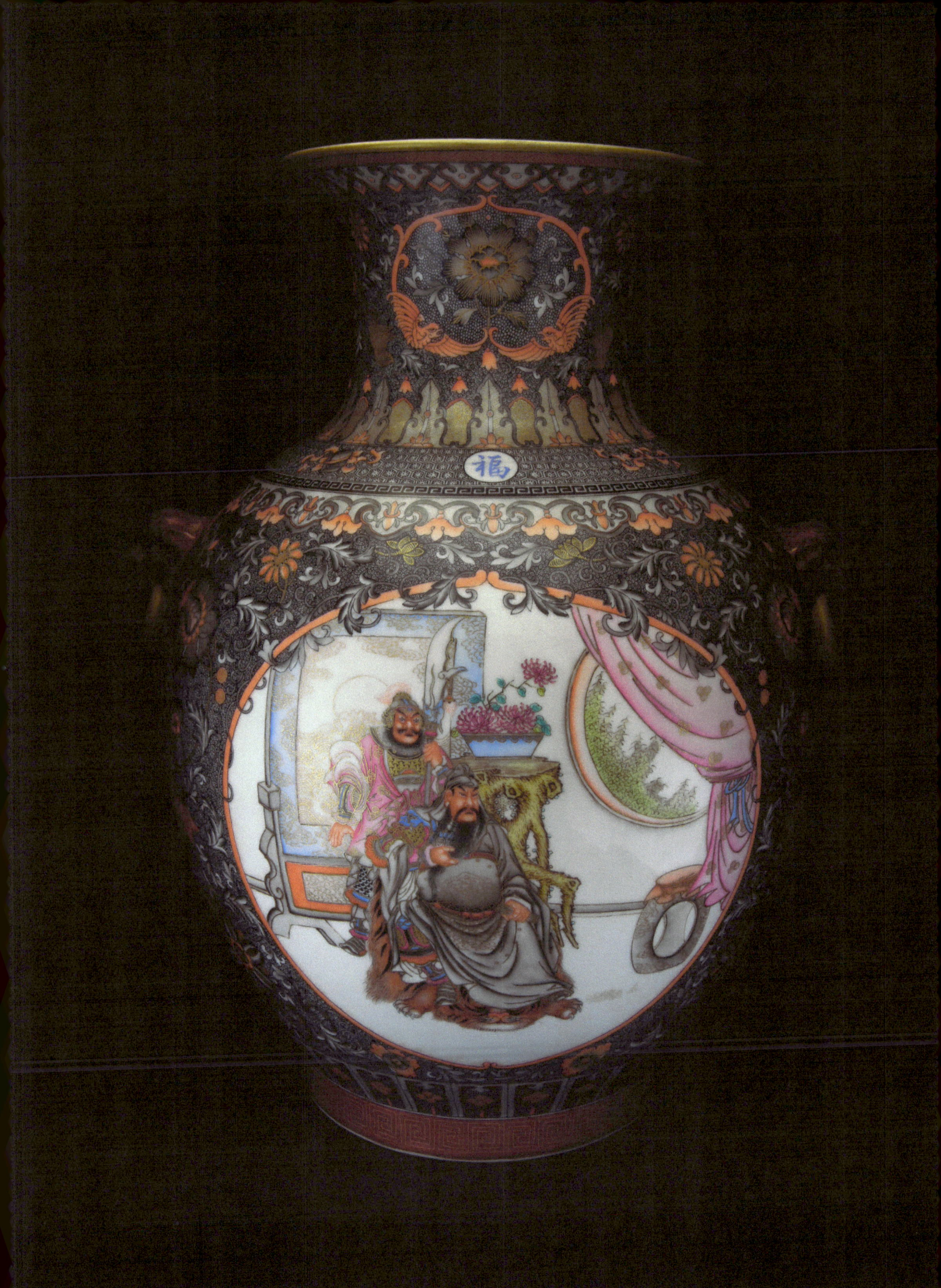

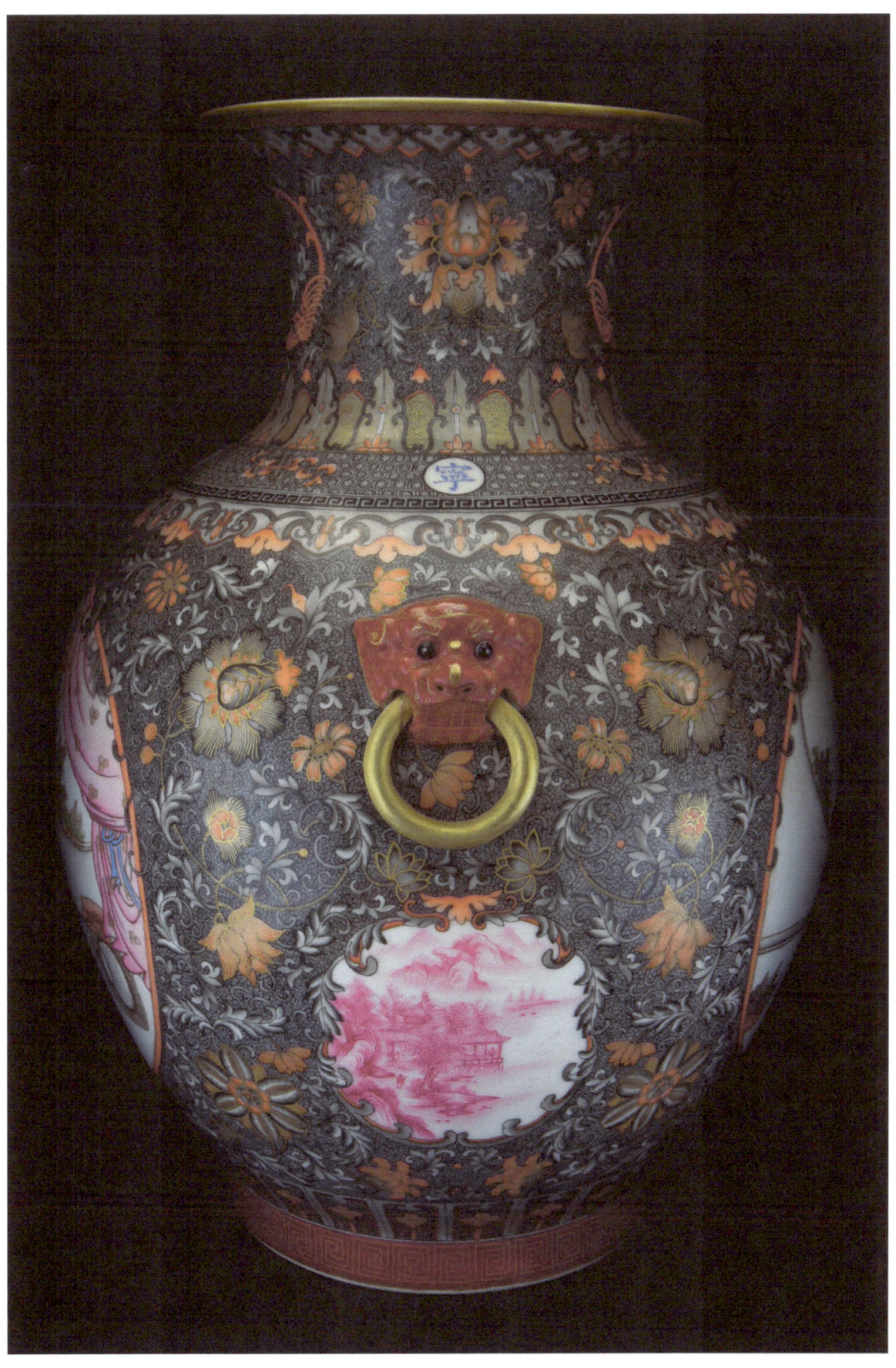

HONOURING THE UNKNOWN 85

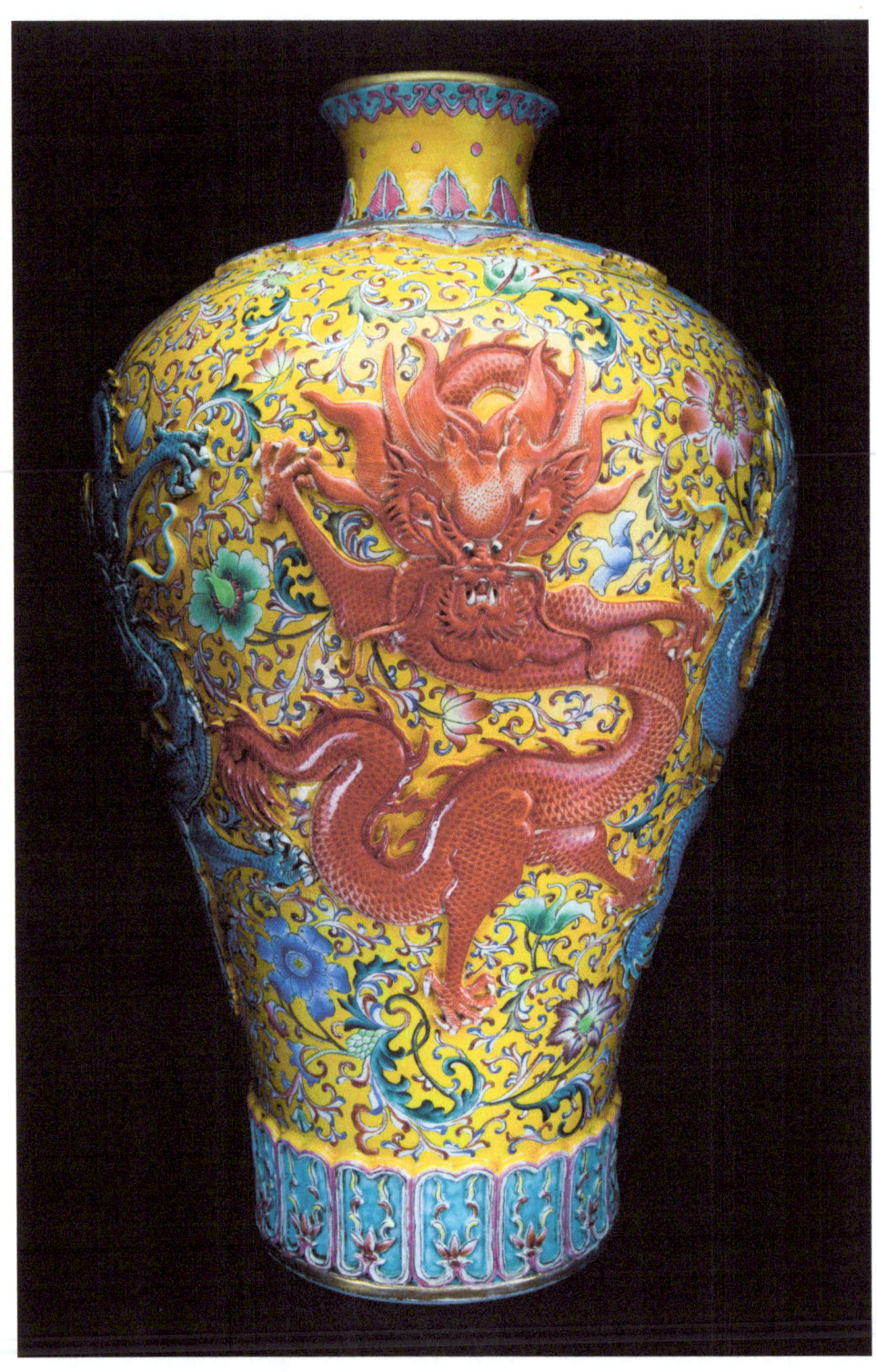

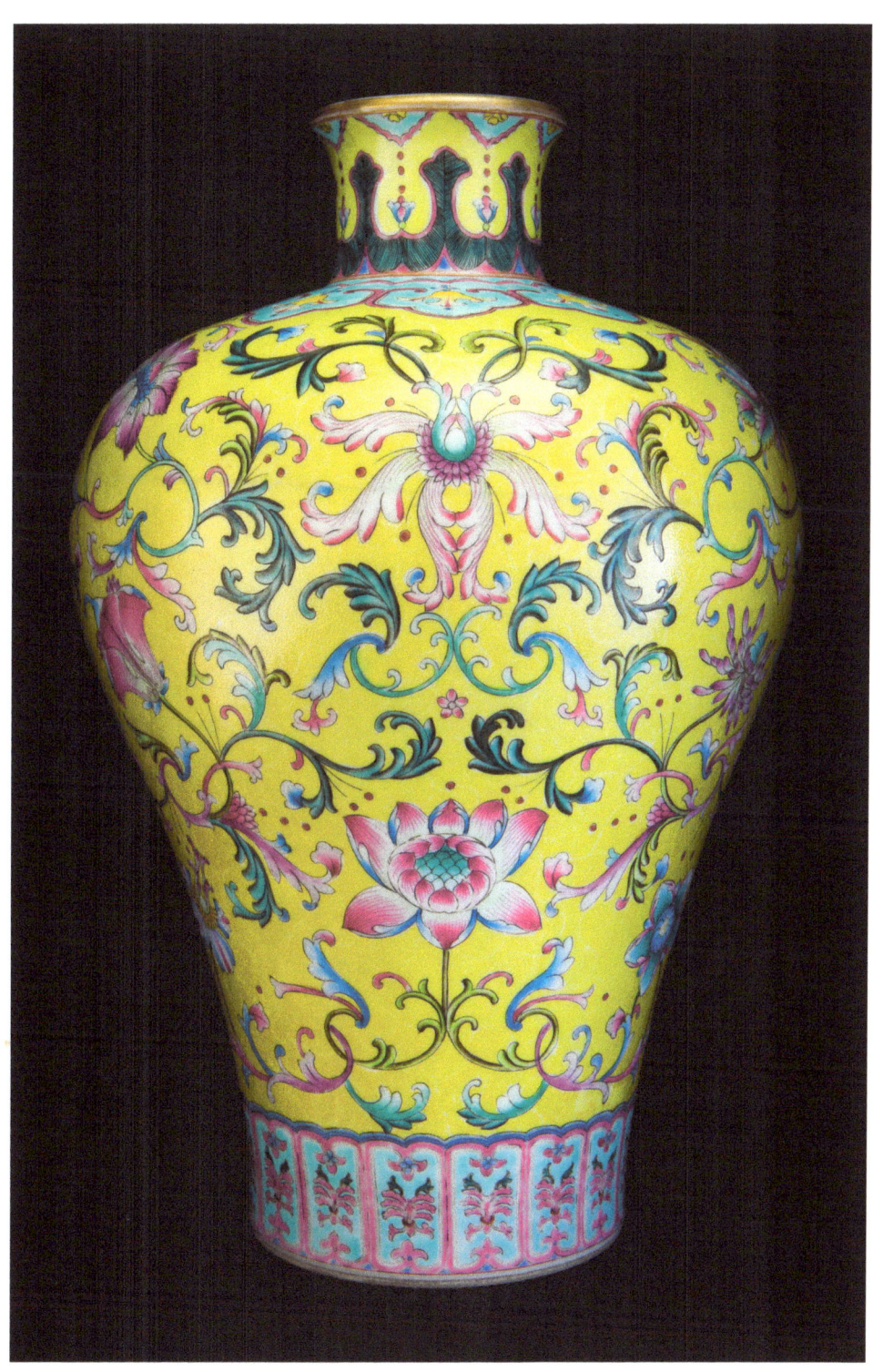

HONOURING THE UNKNOWN **87**

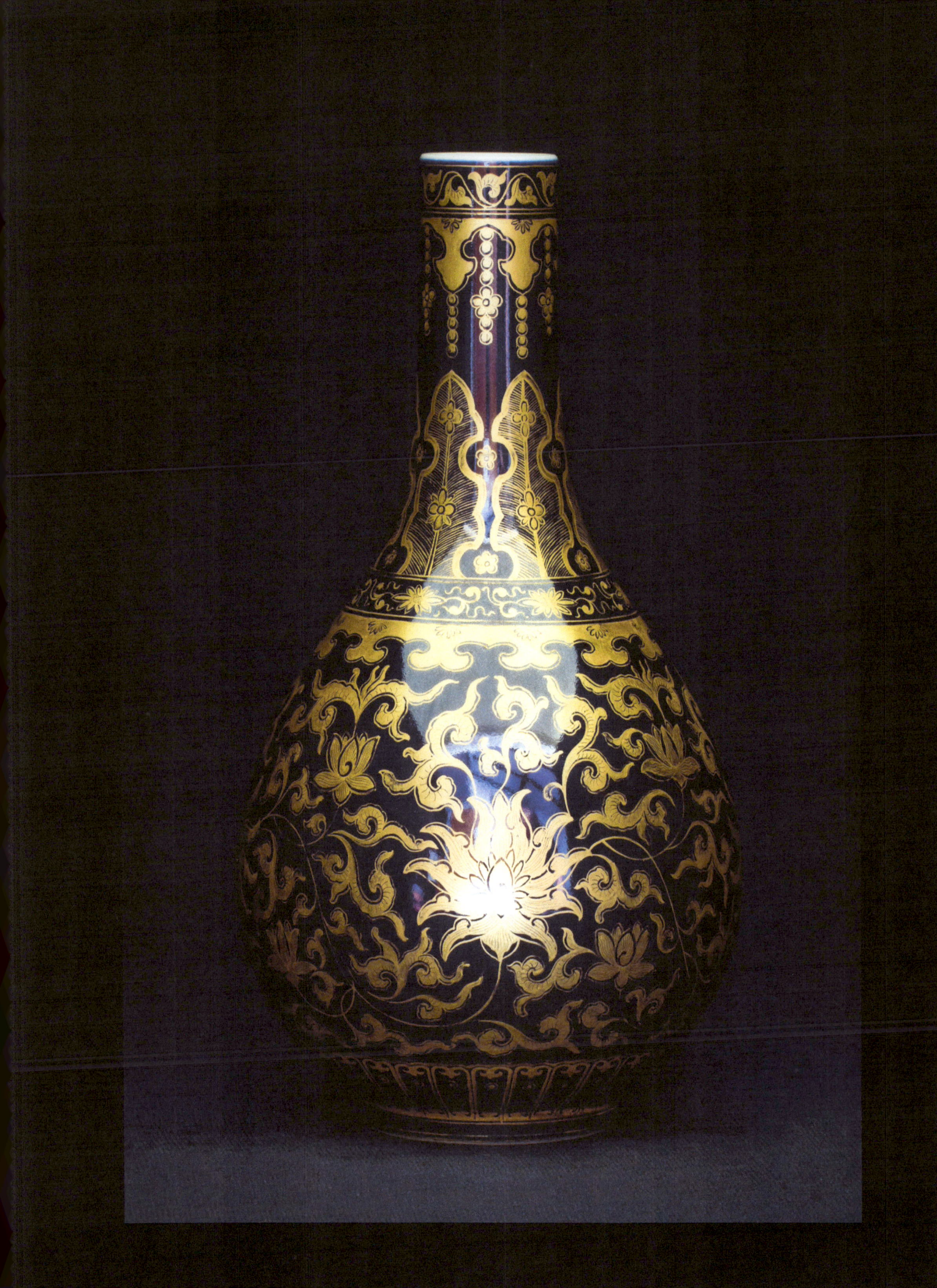

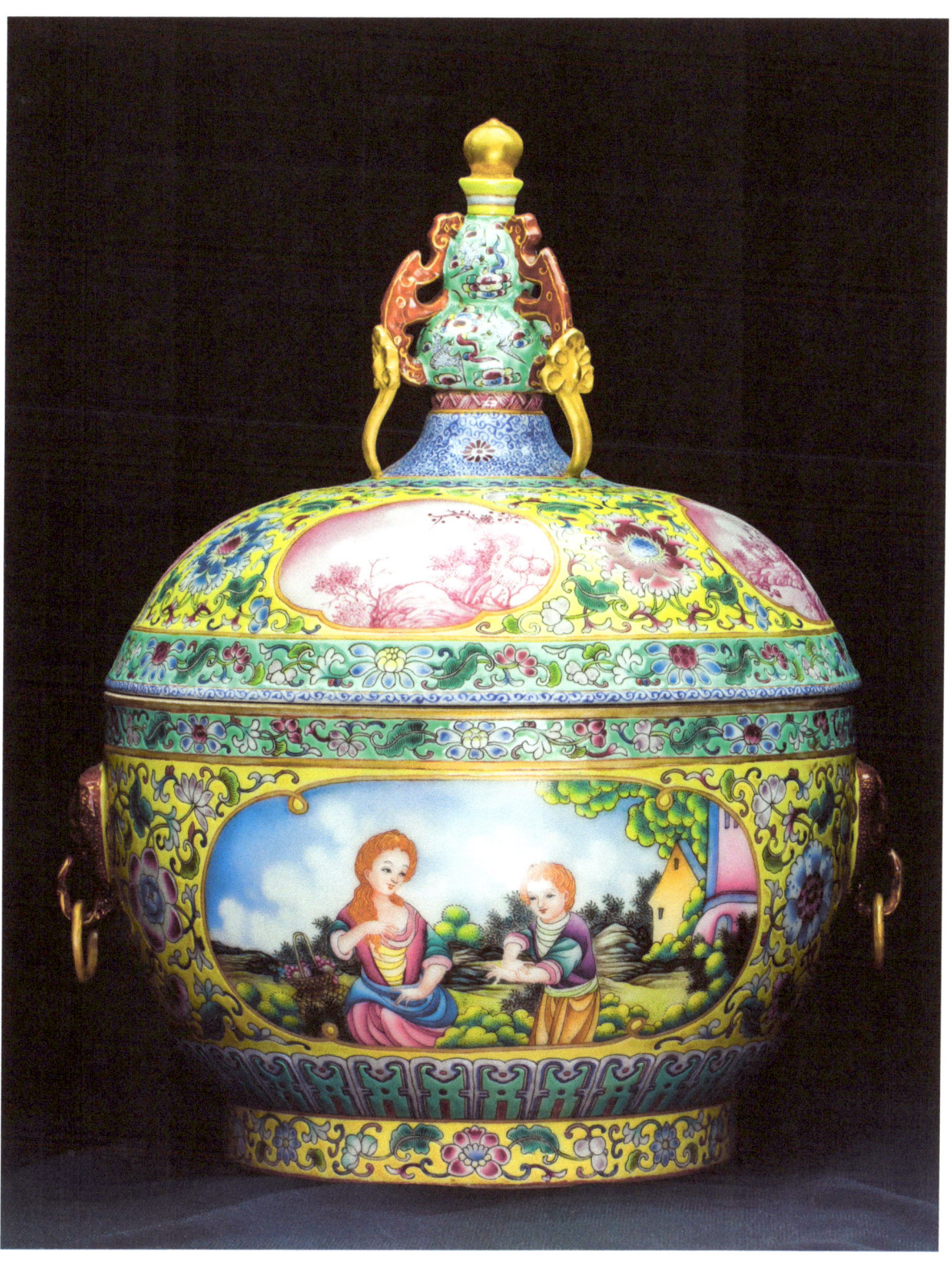

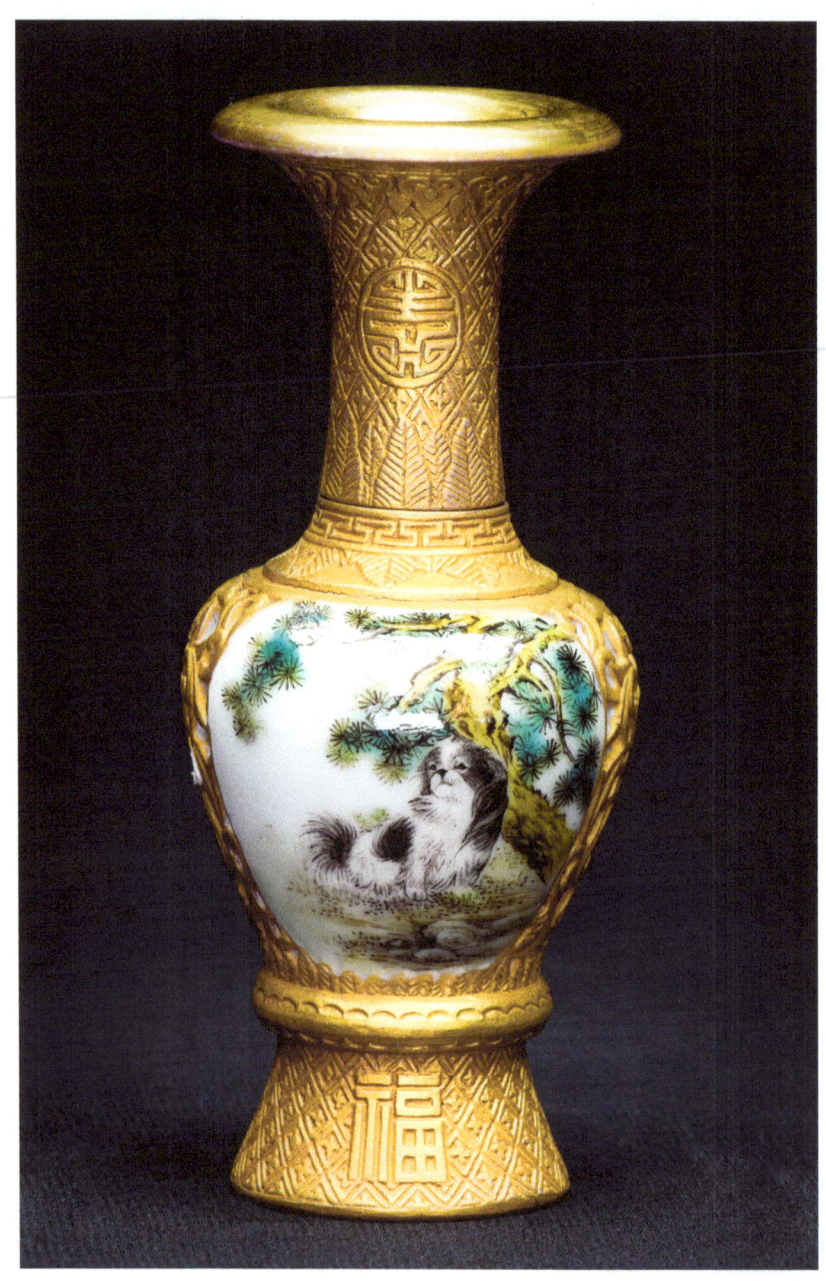

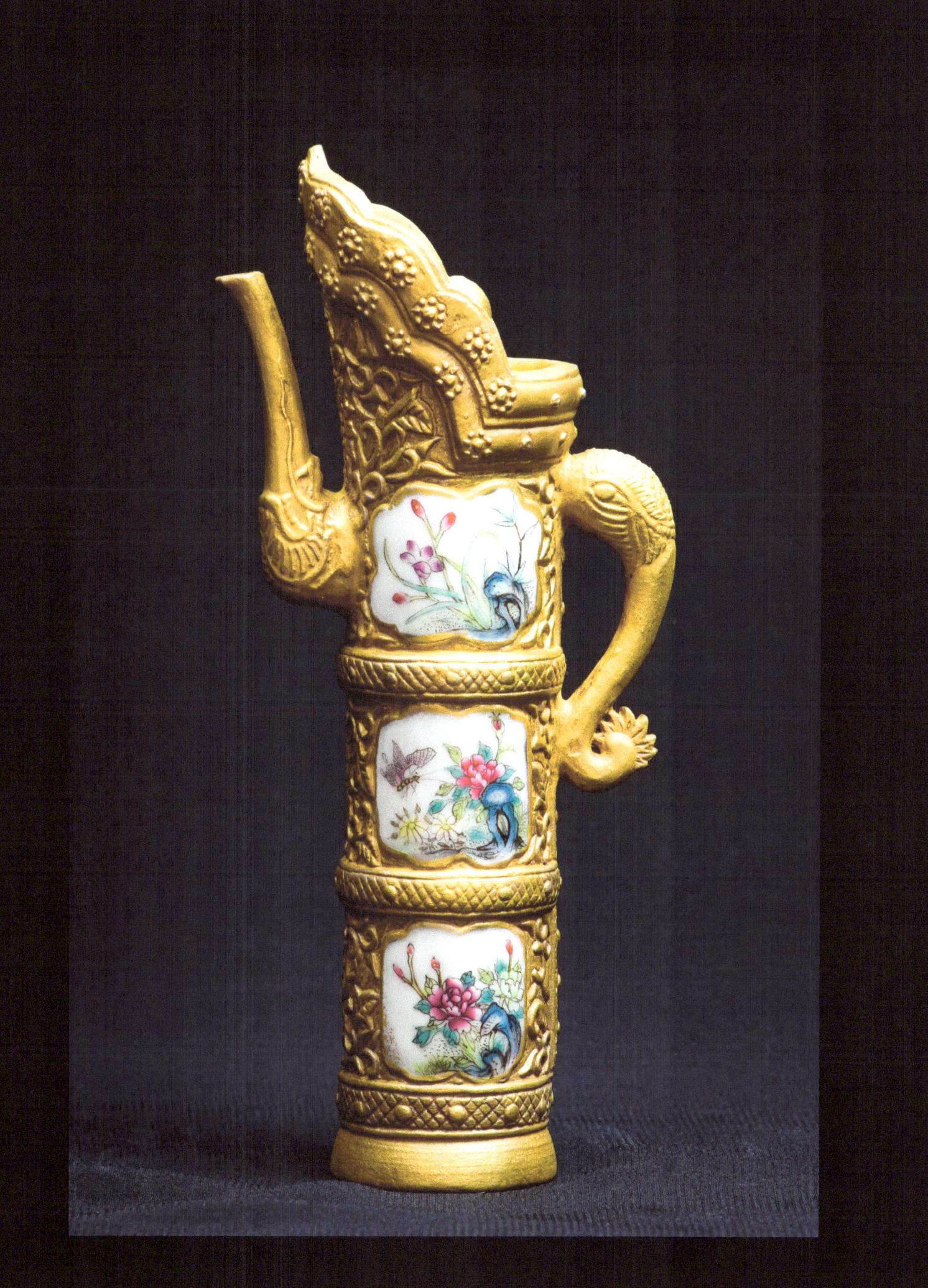

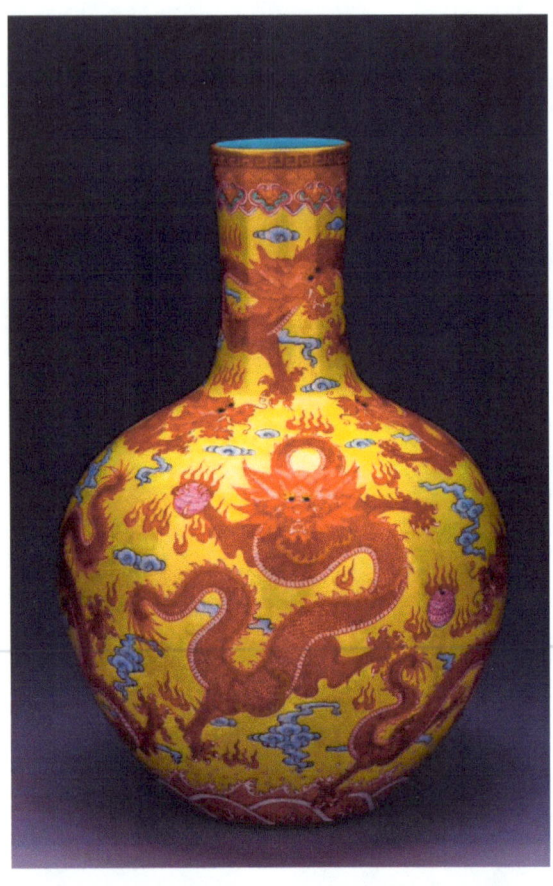
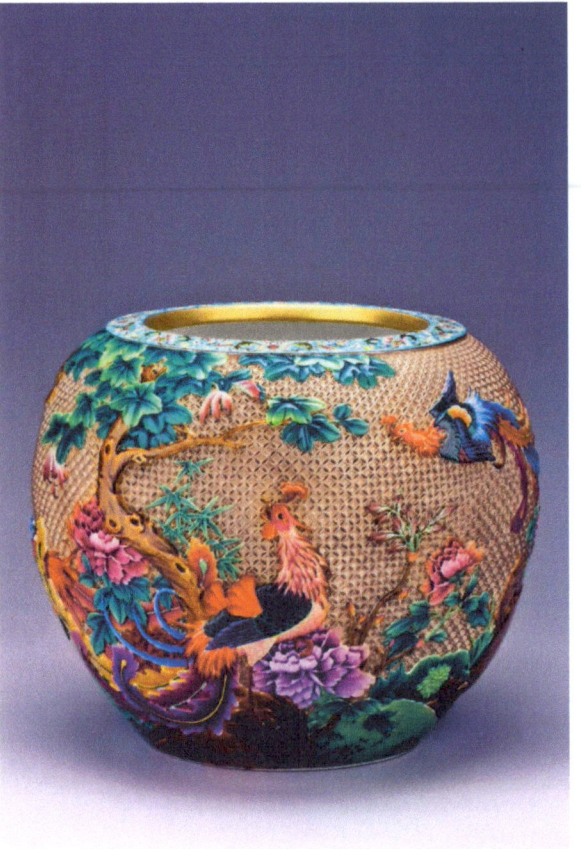
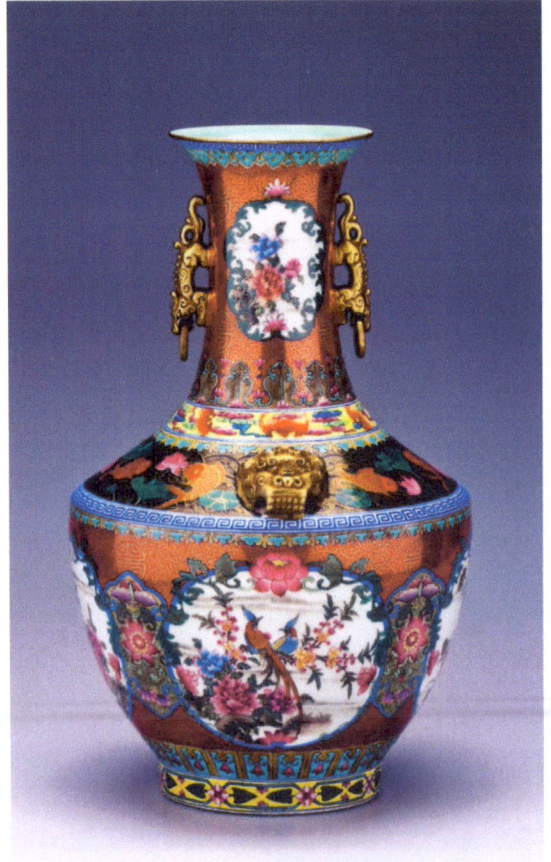

92 FORBIDDEN REPLICAS

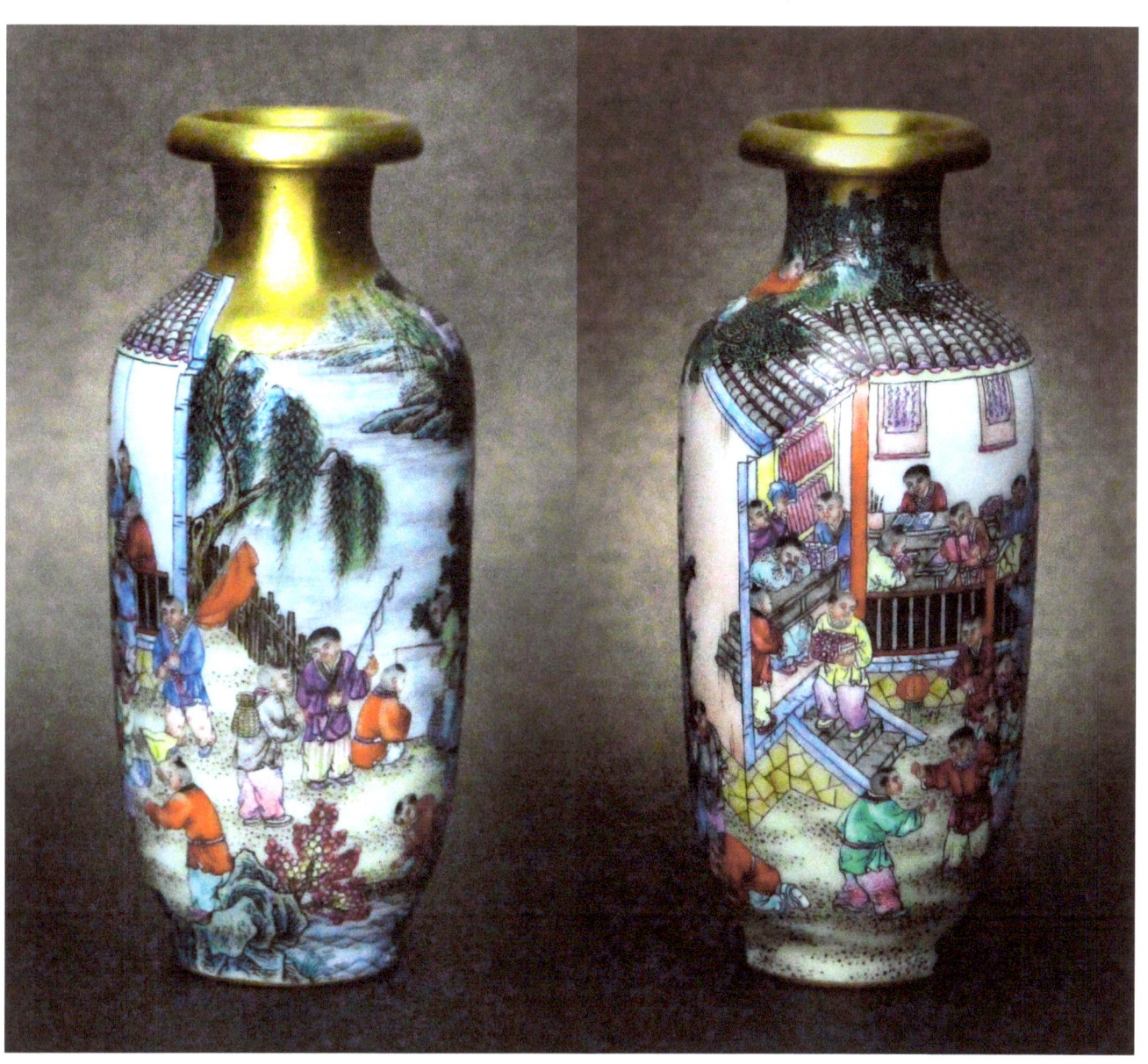

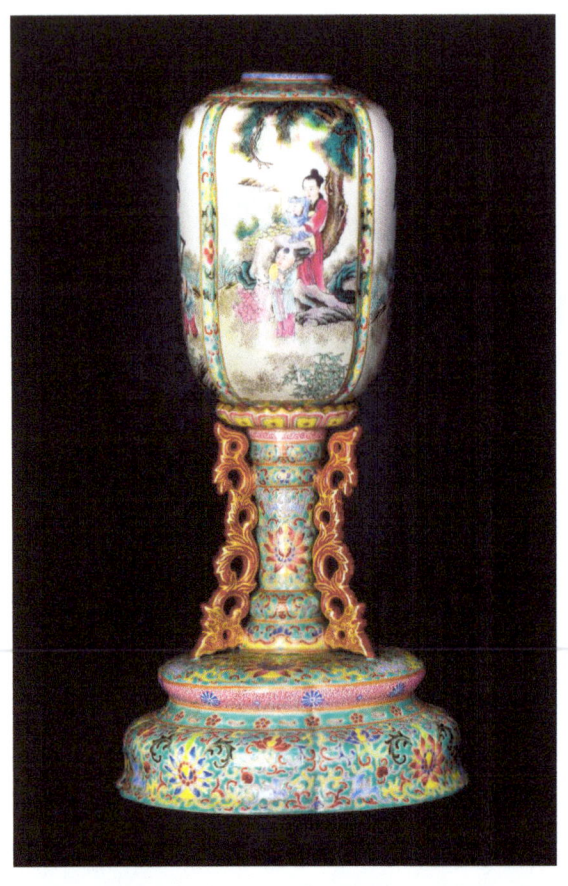
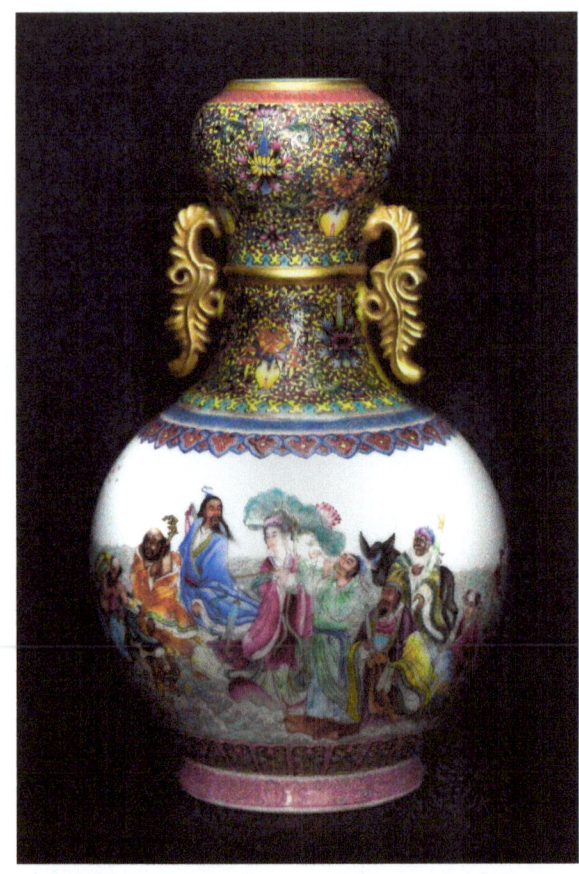
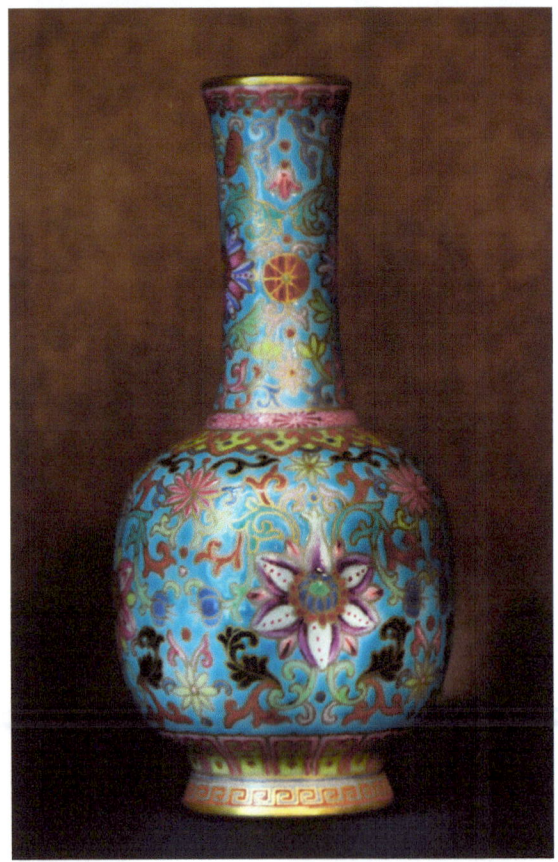
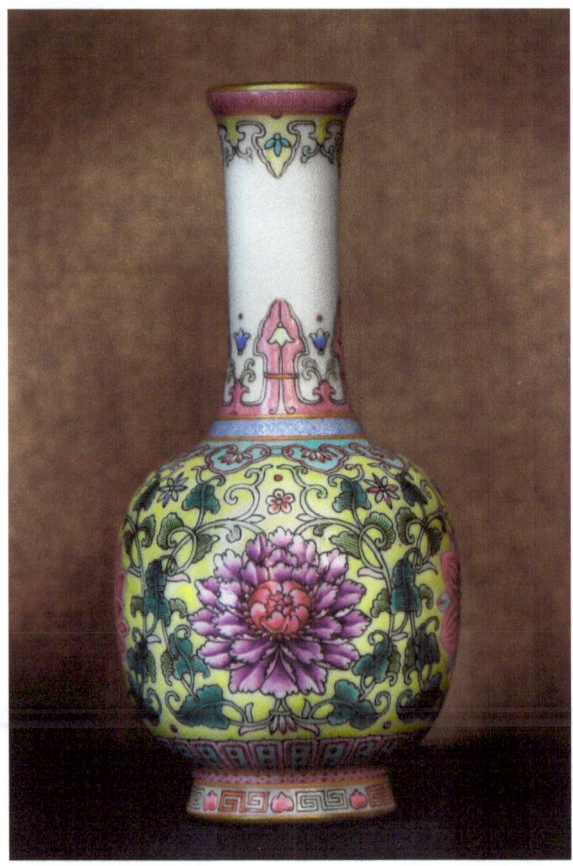

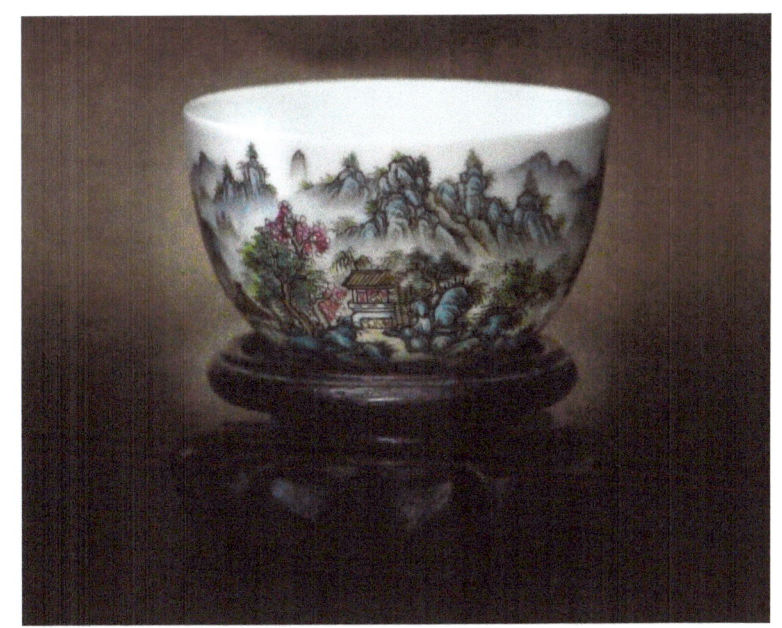
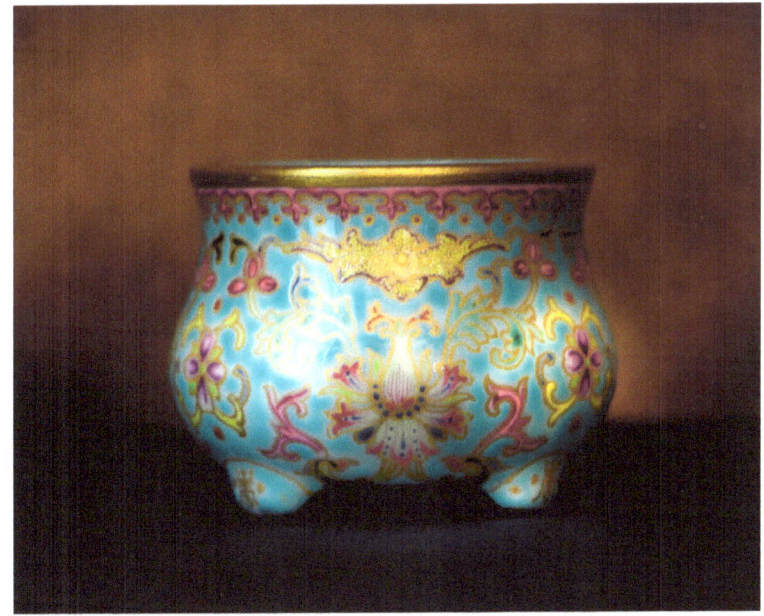
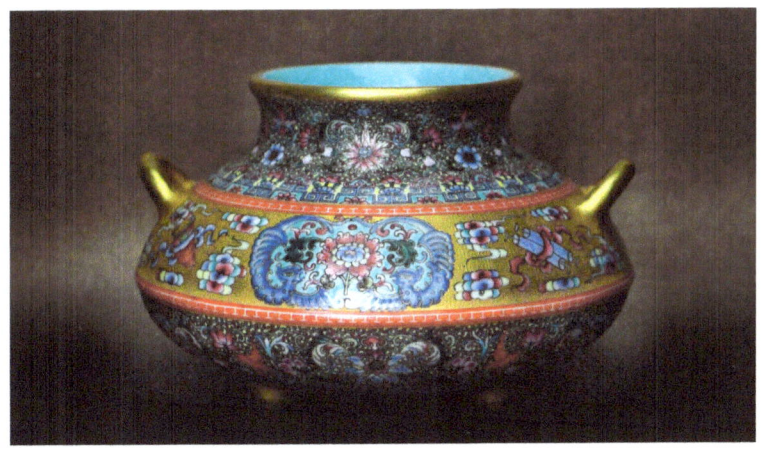

HONOURING THE UNKNOWN

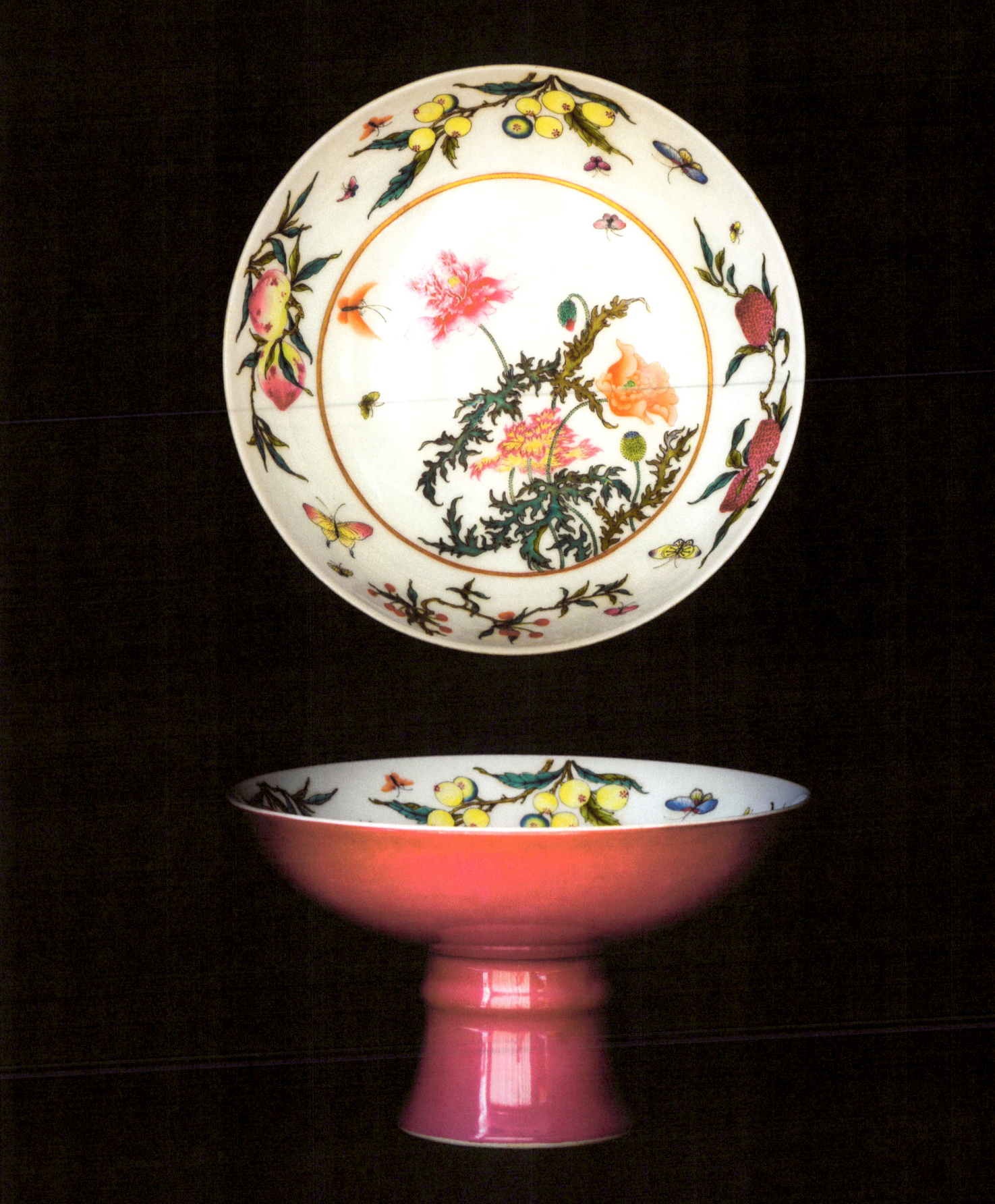

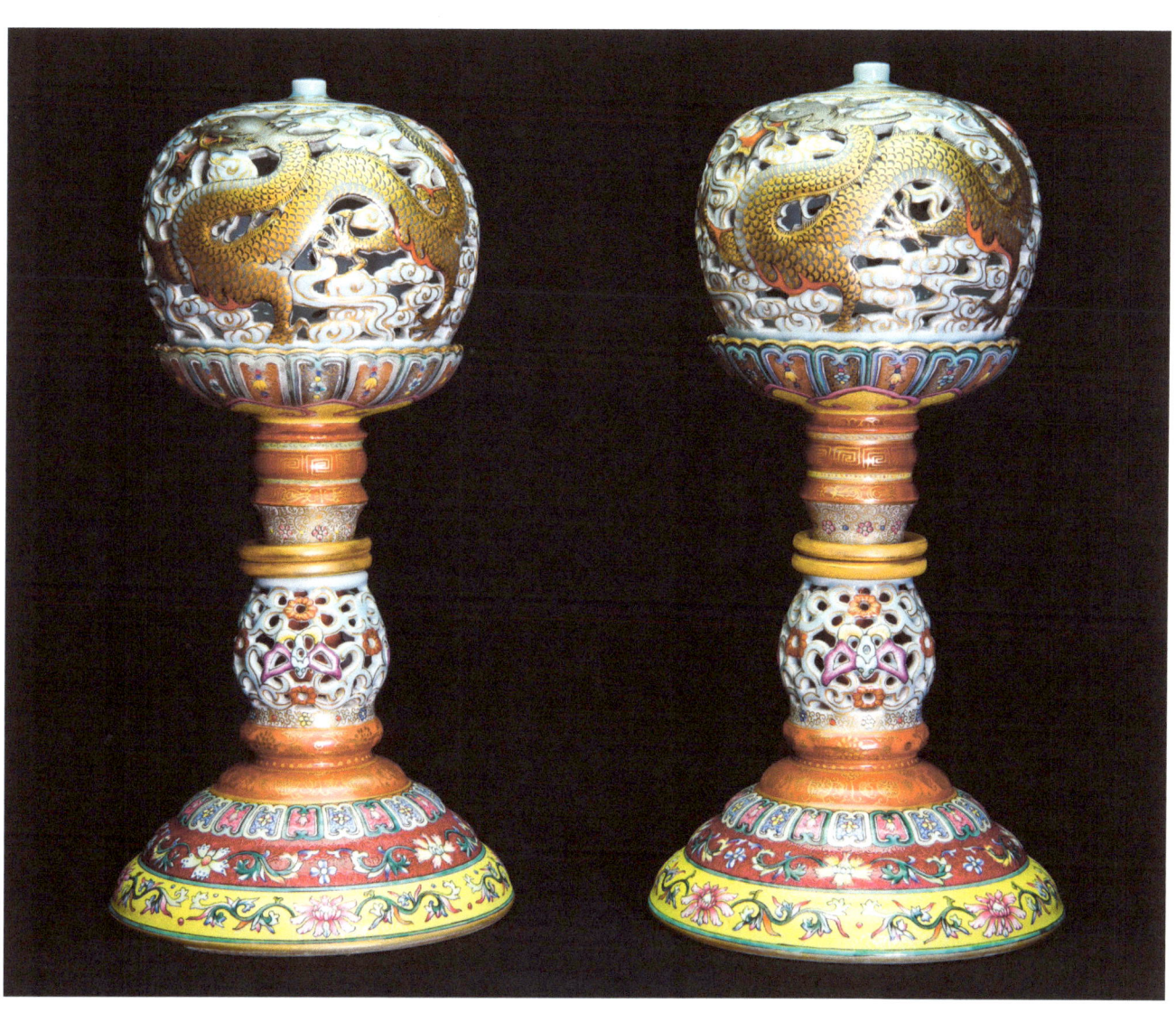

HONOURING THE UNKNOWN 97

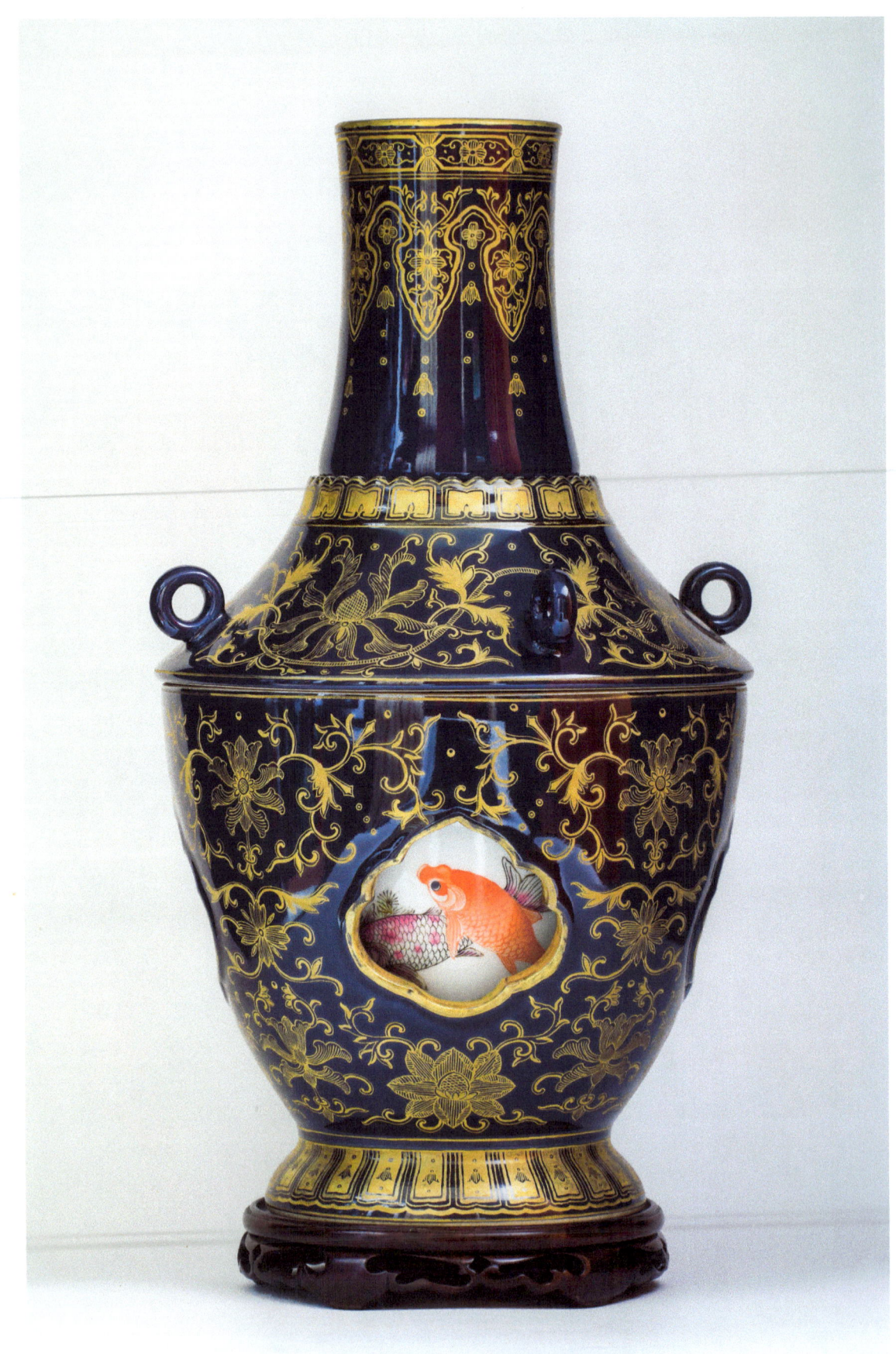

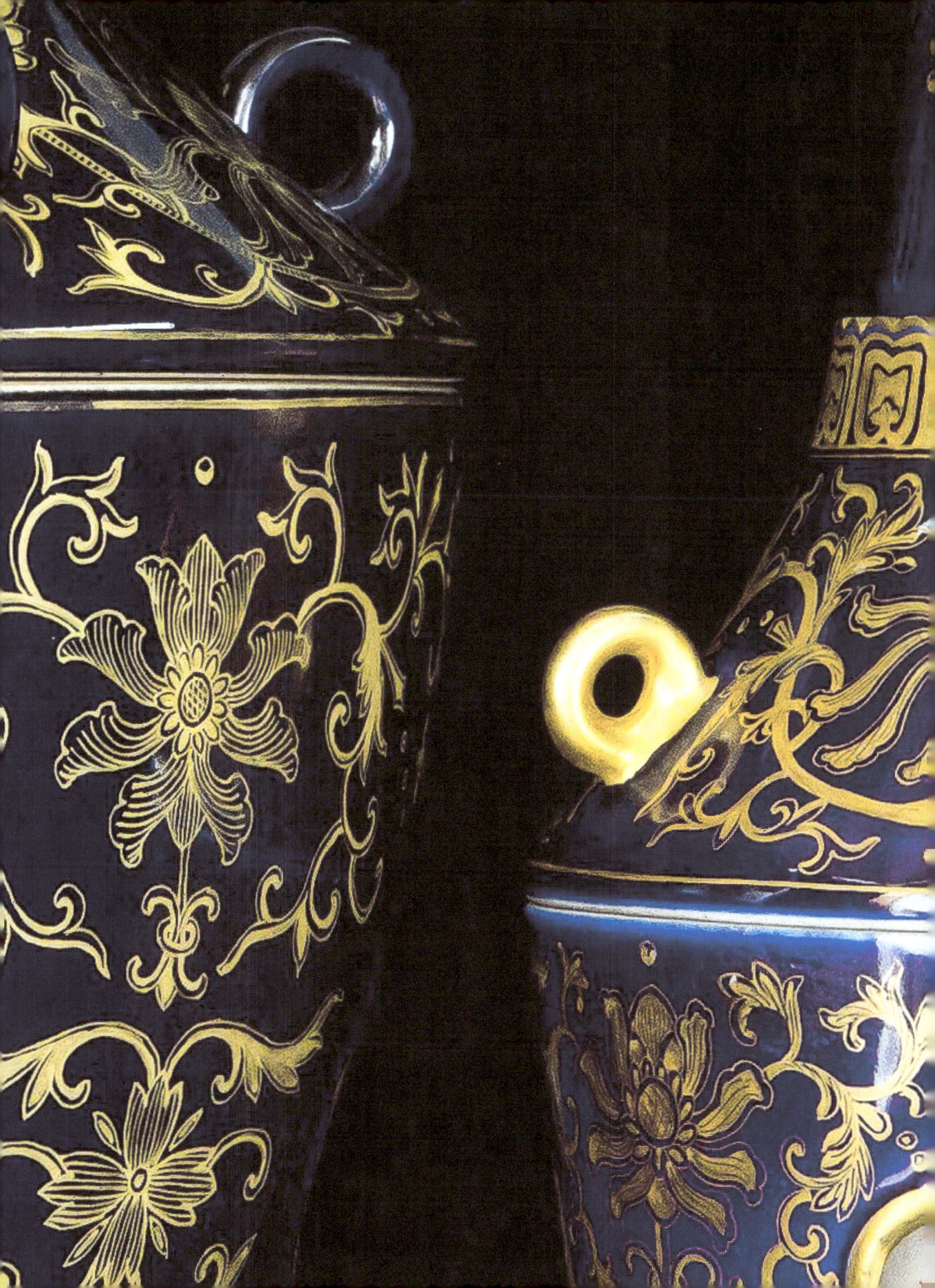

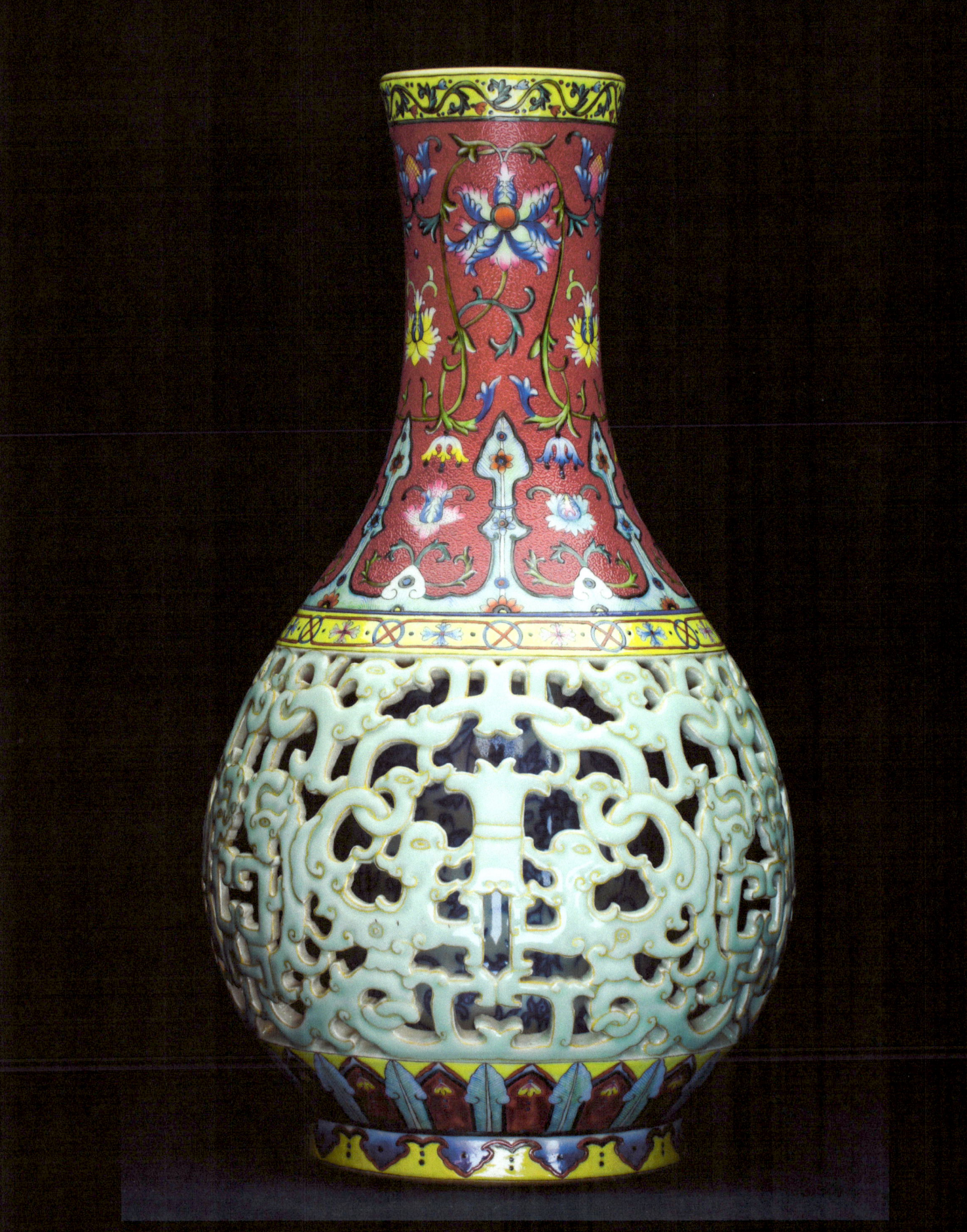

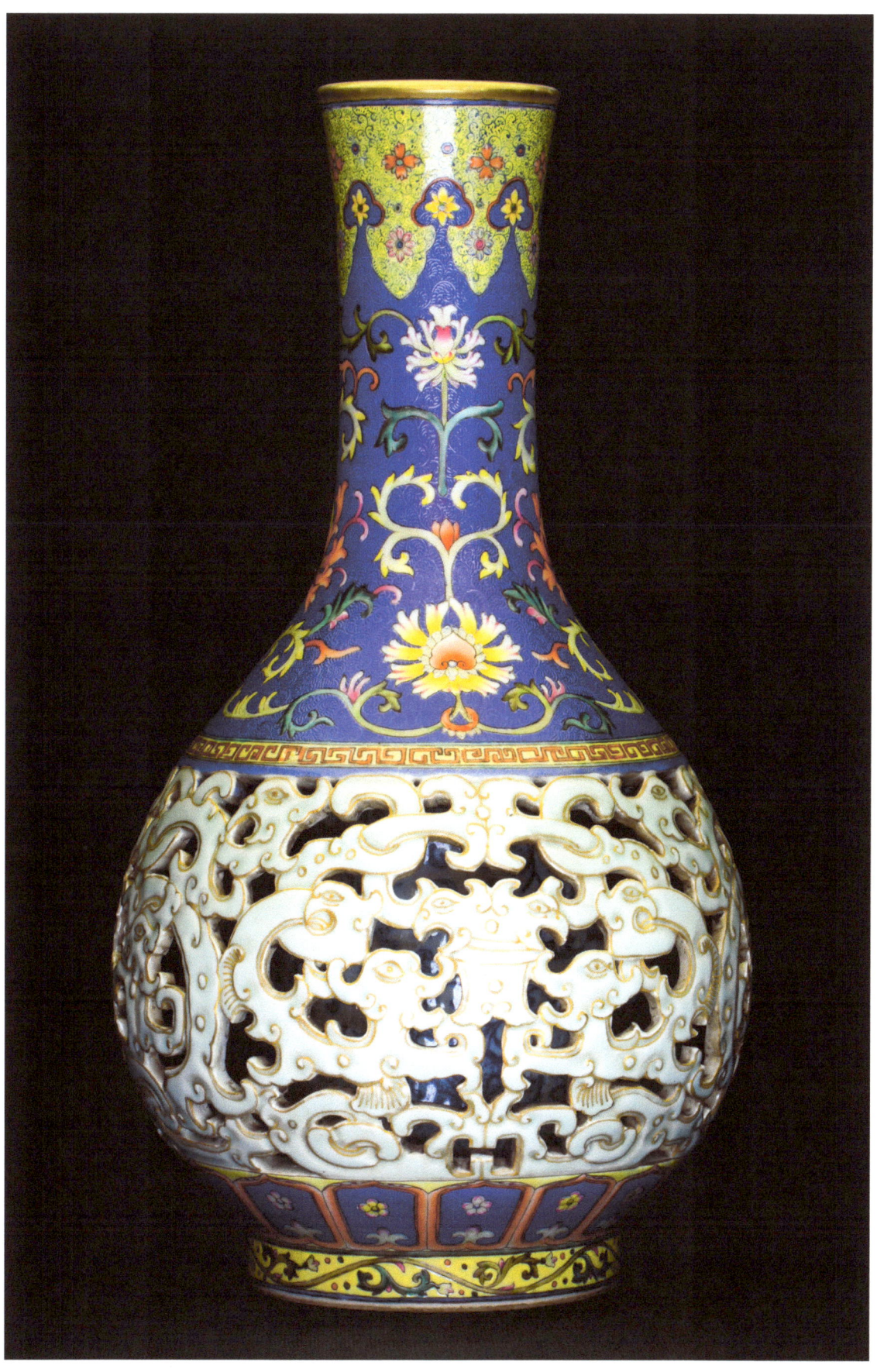

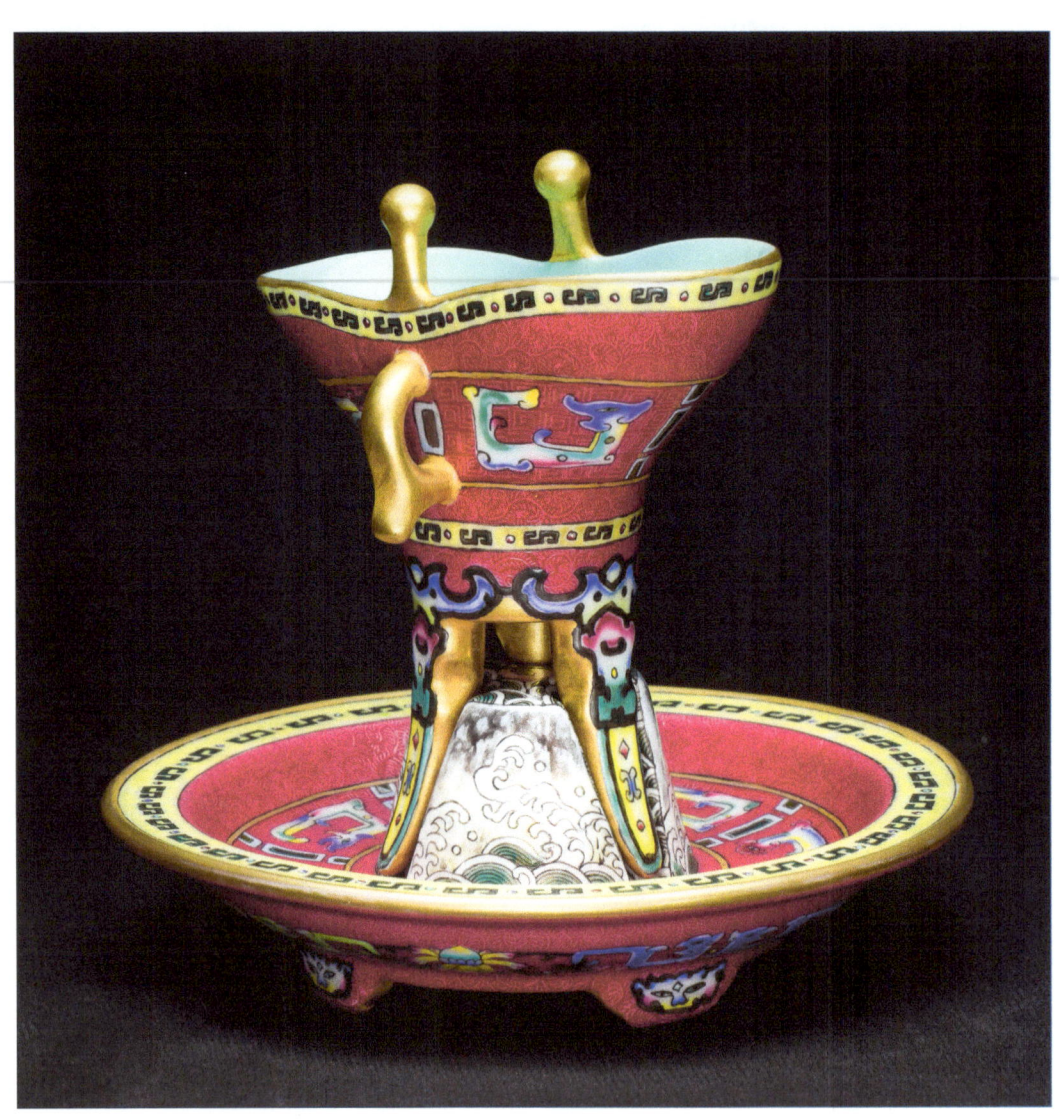

102 FORBIDDEN REPLICAS

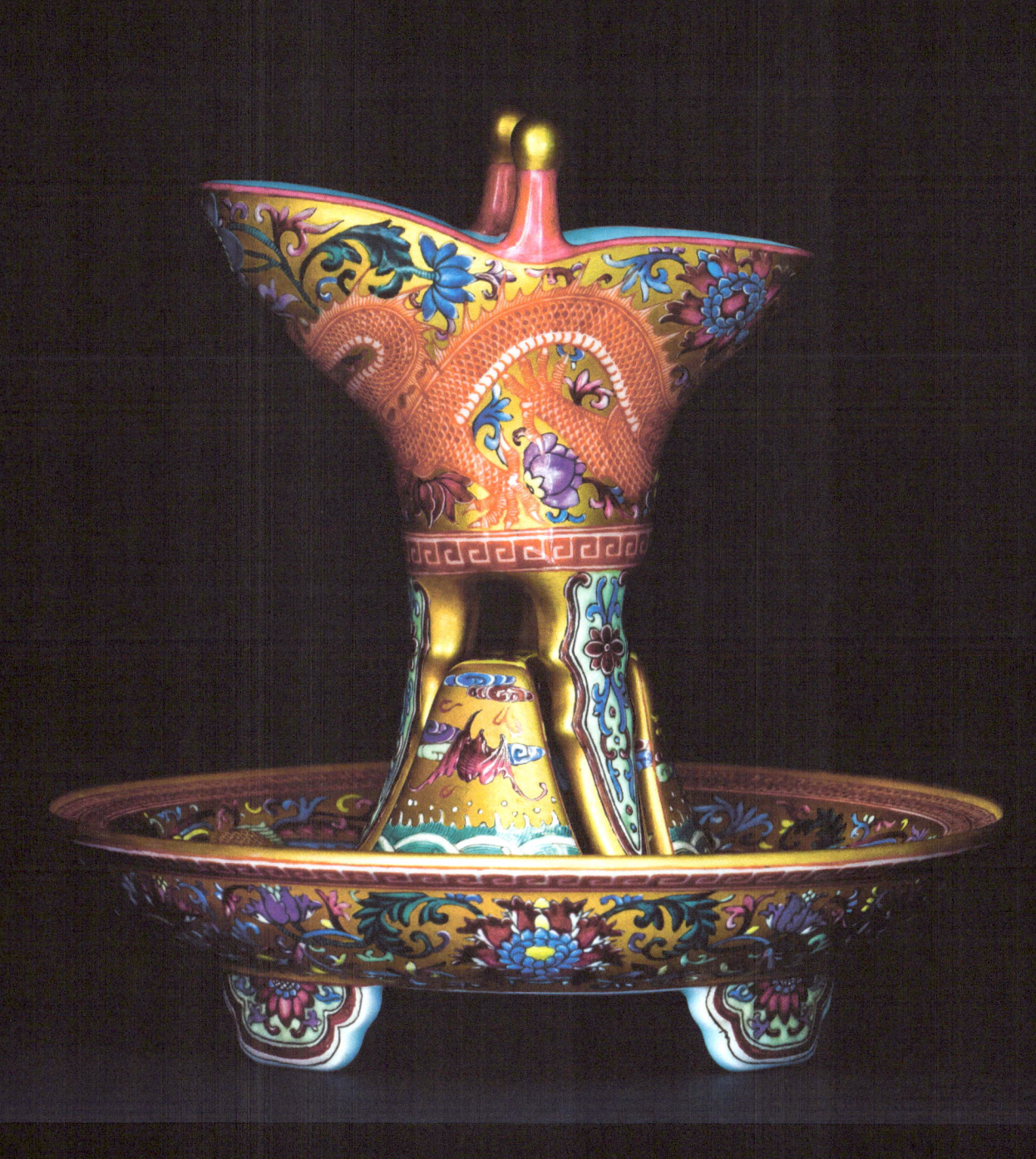

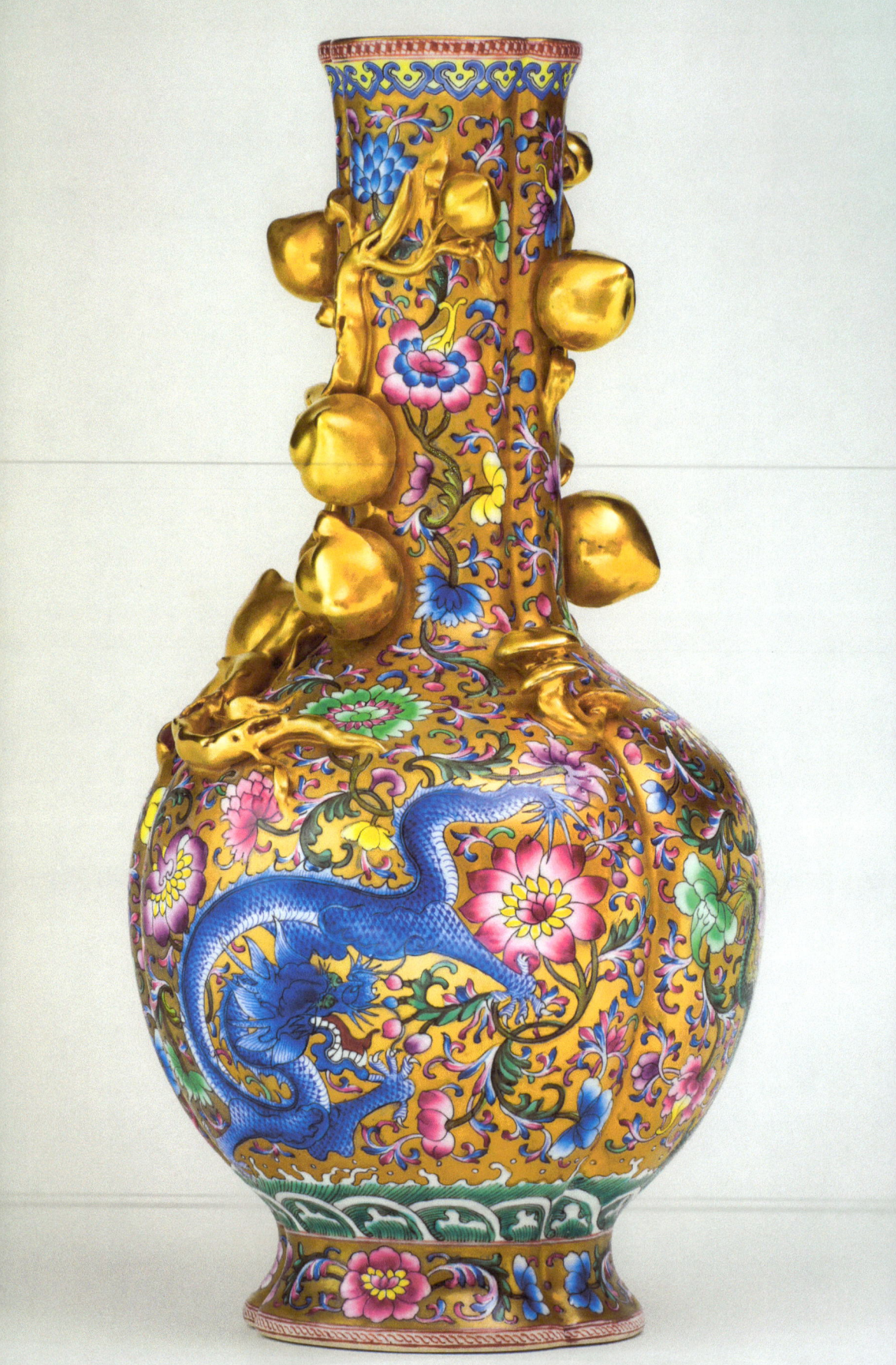

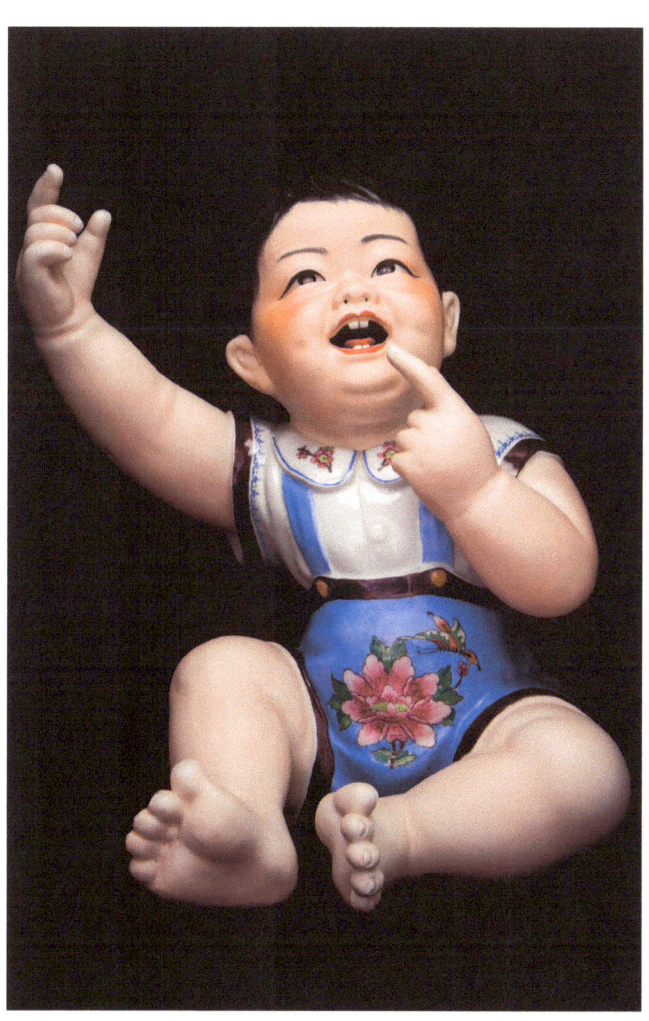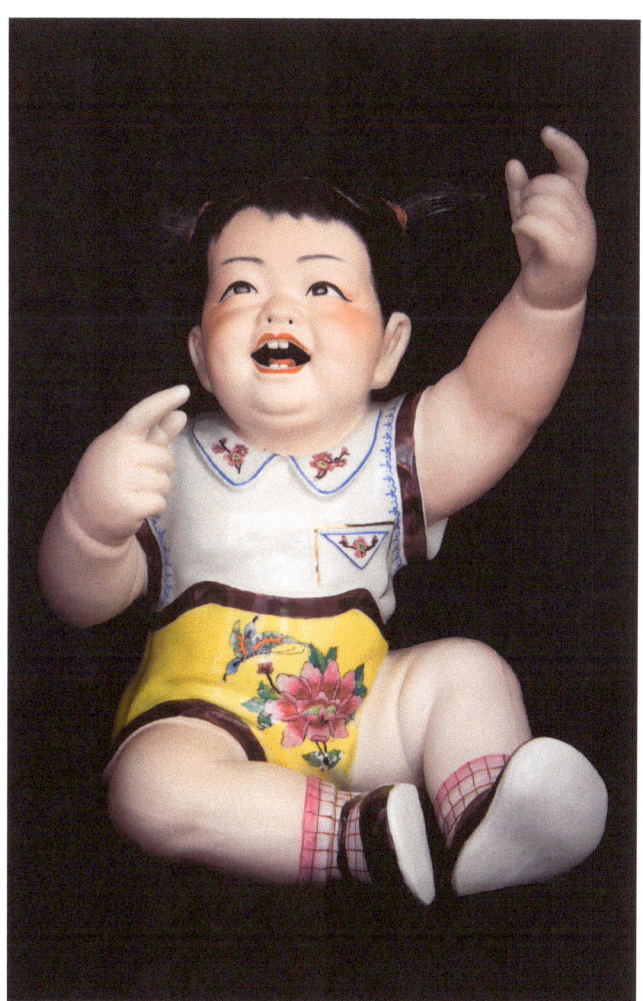

HONOURING THE UNKNOWN 105

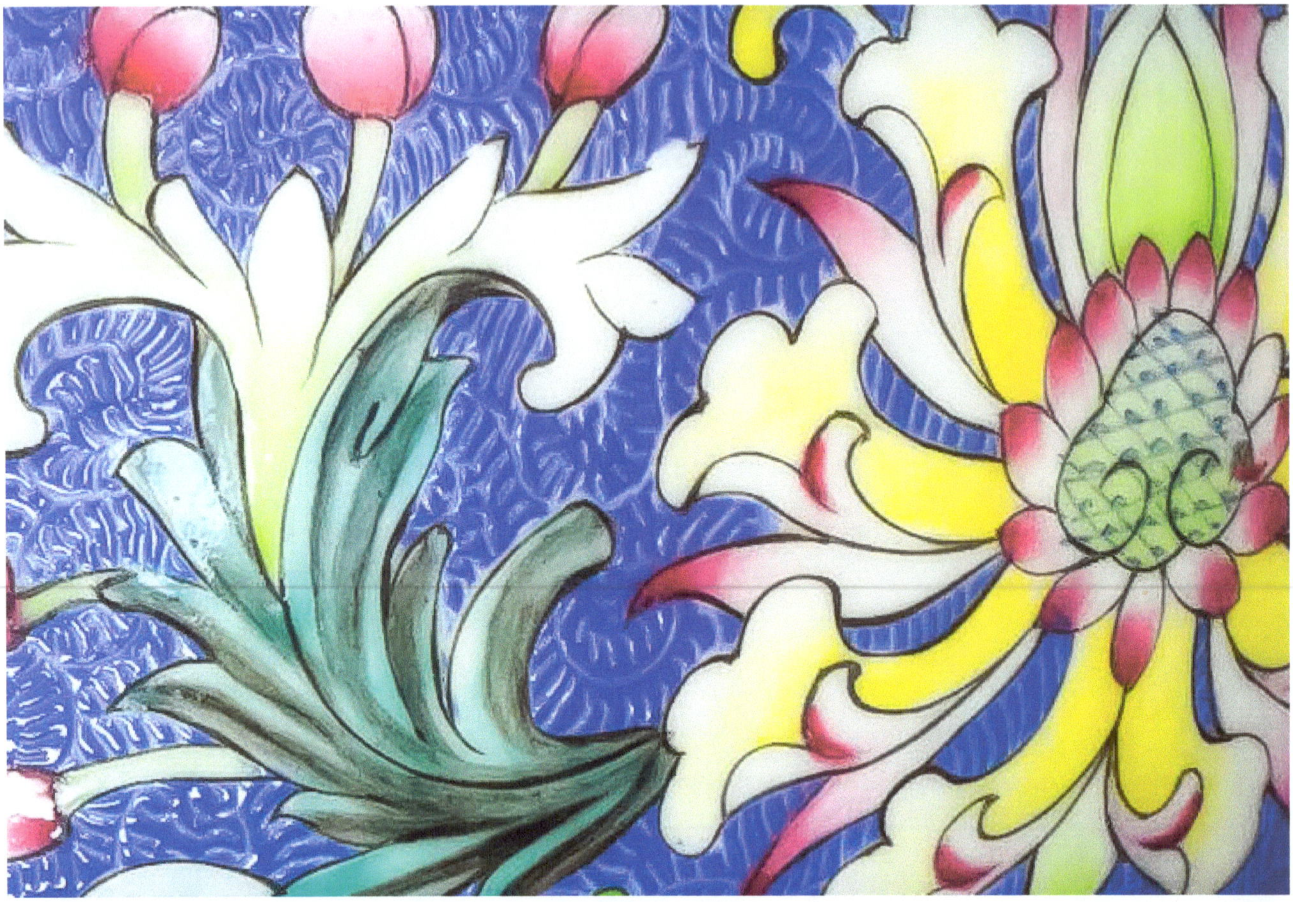

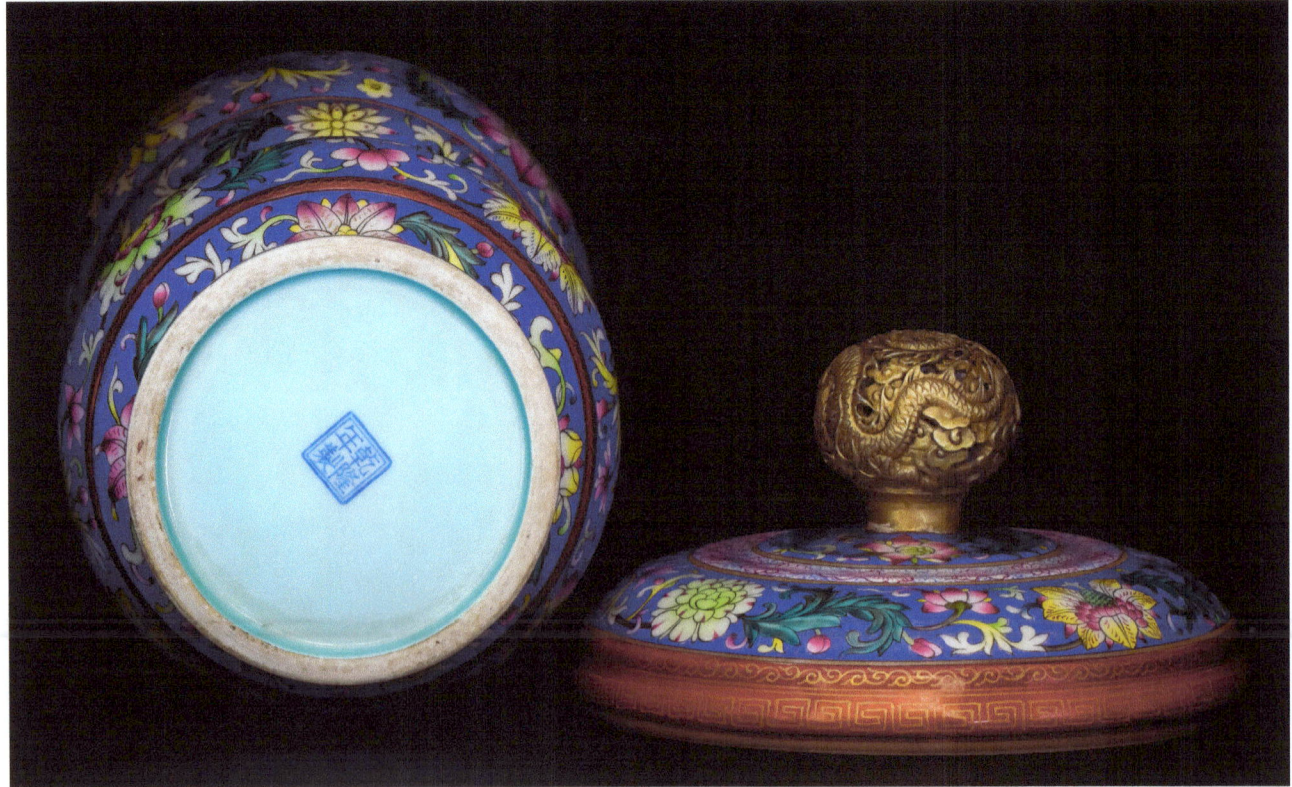

106 FORBIDDEN REPLICAS

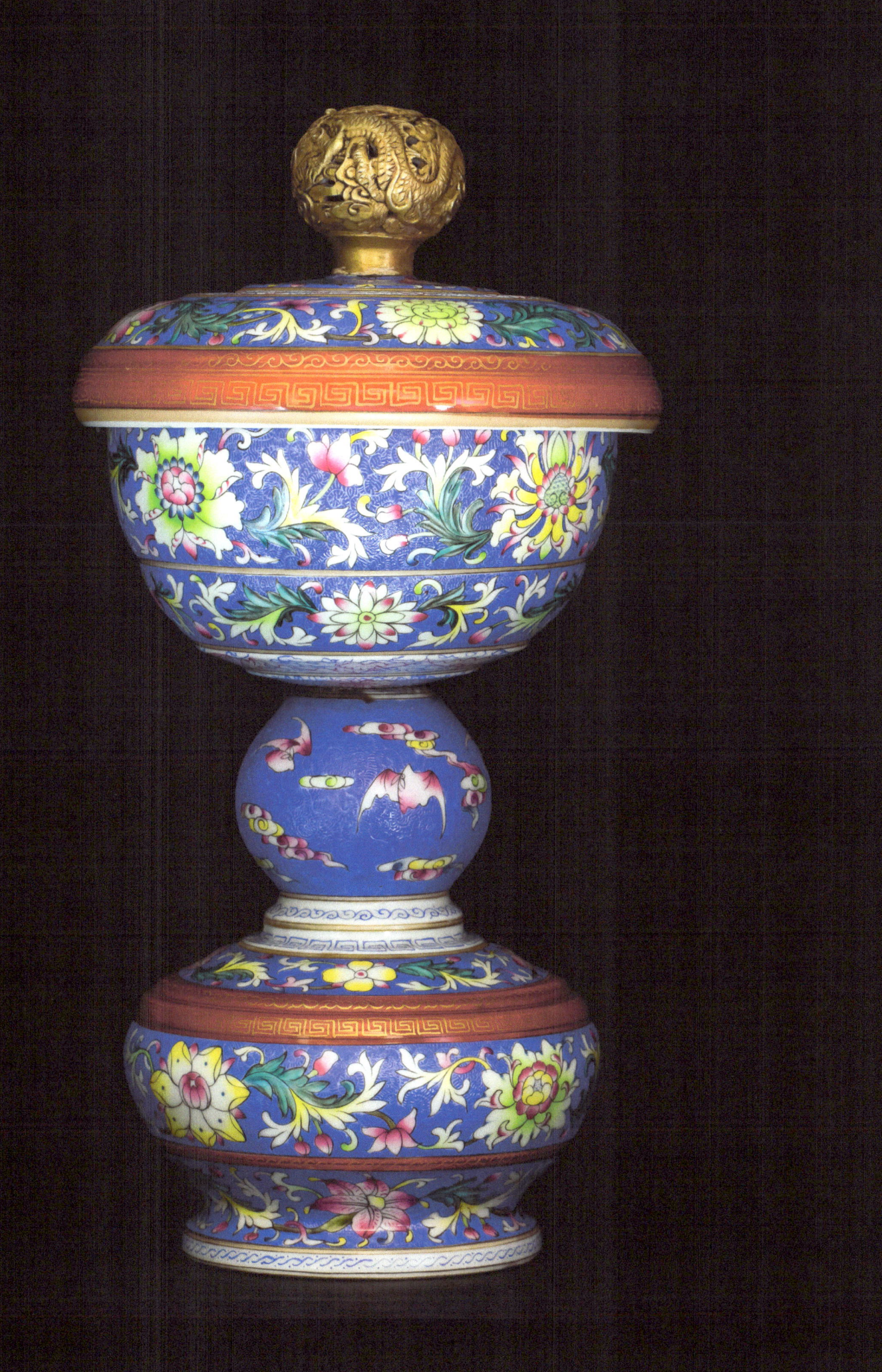

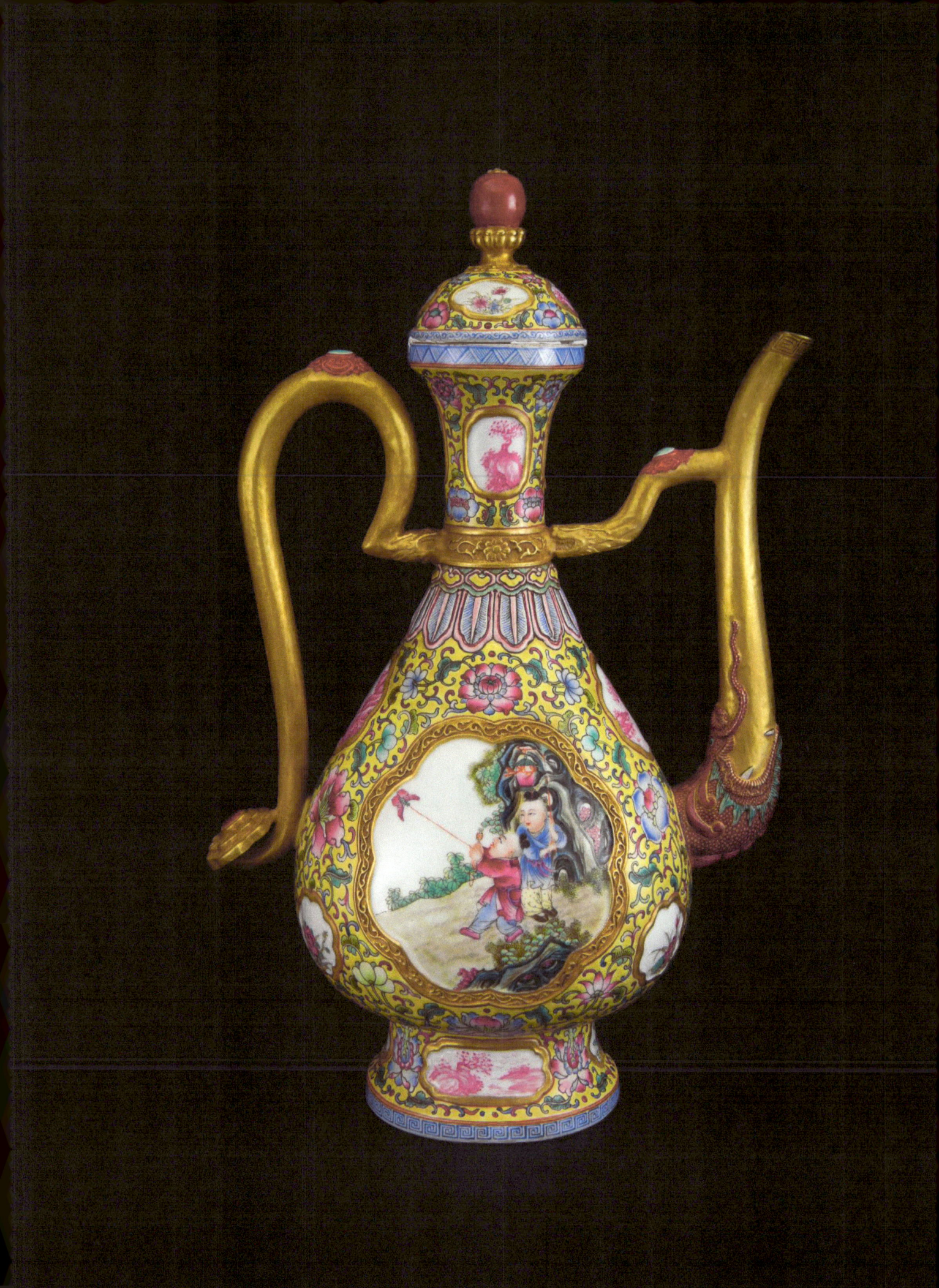

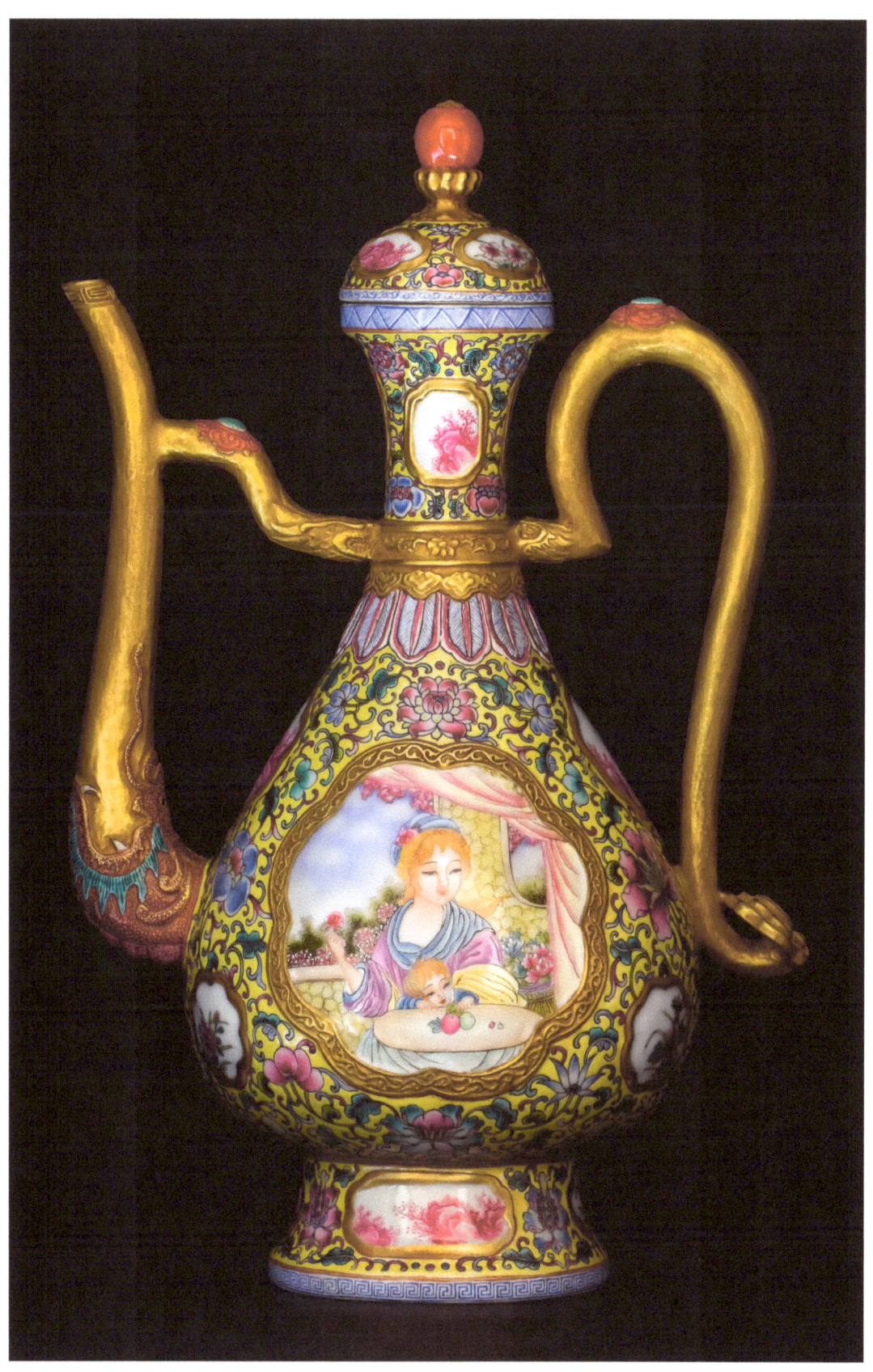

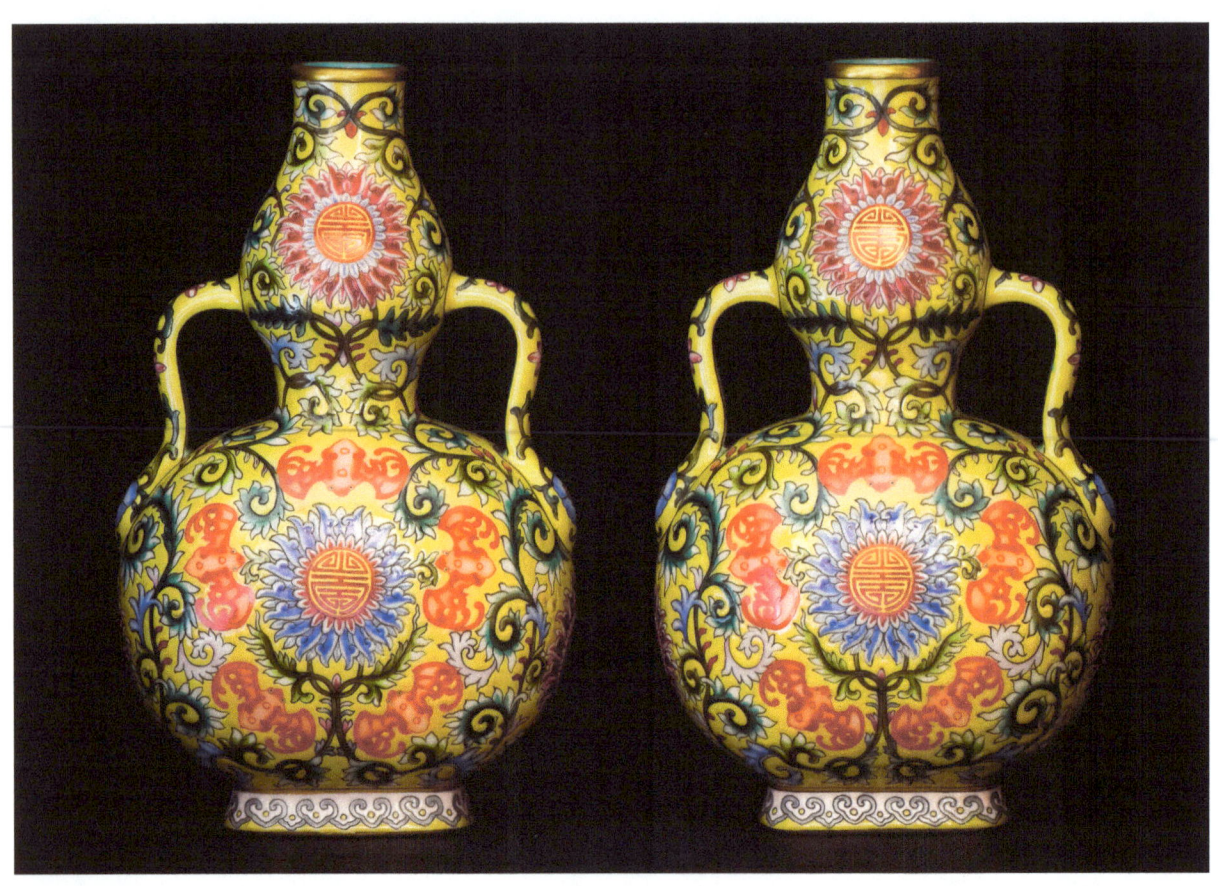
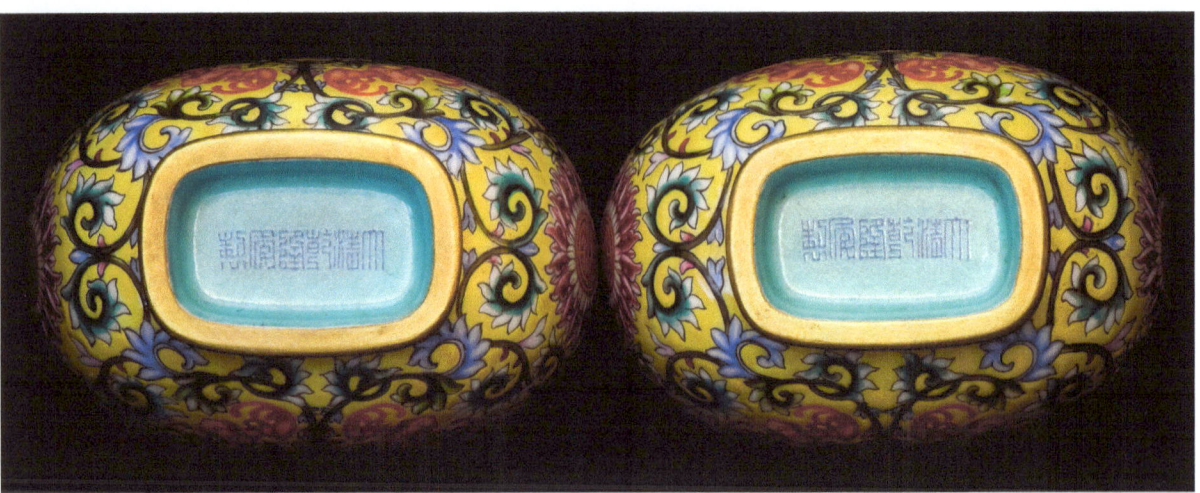

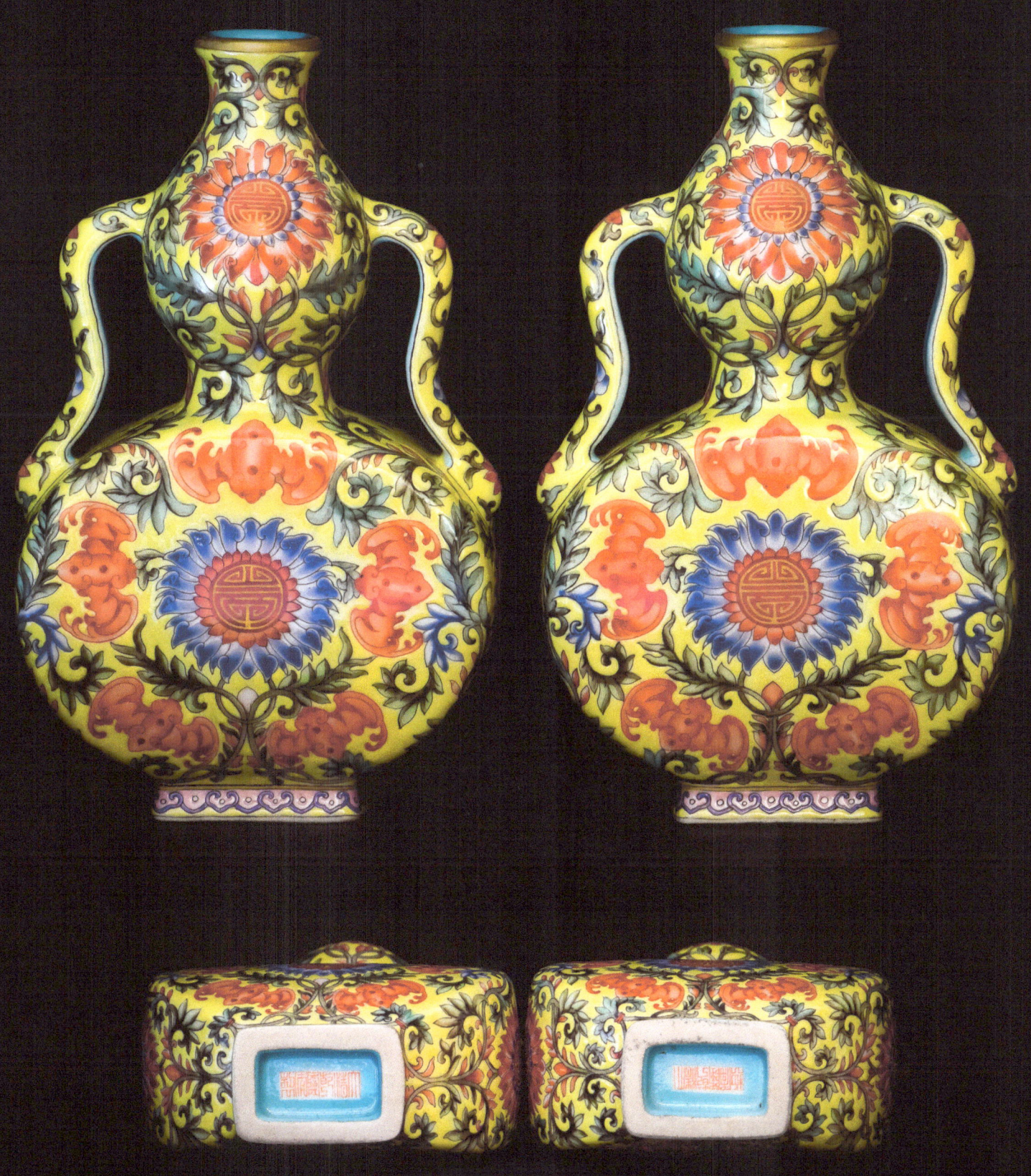

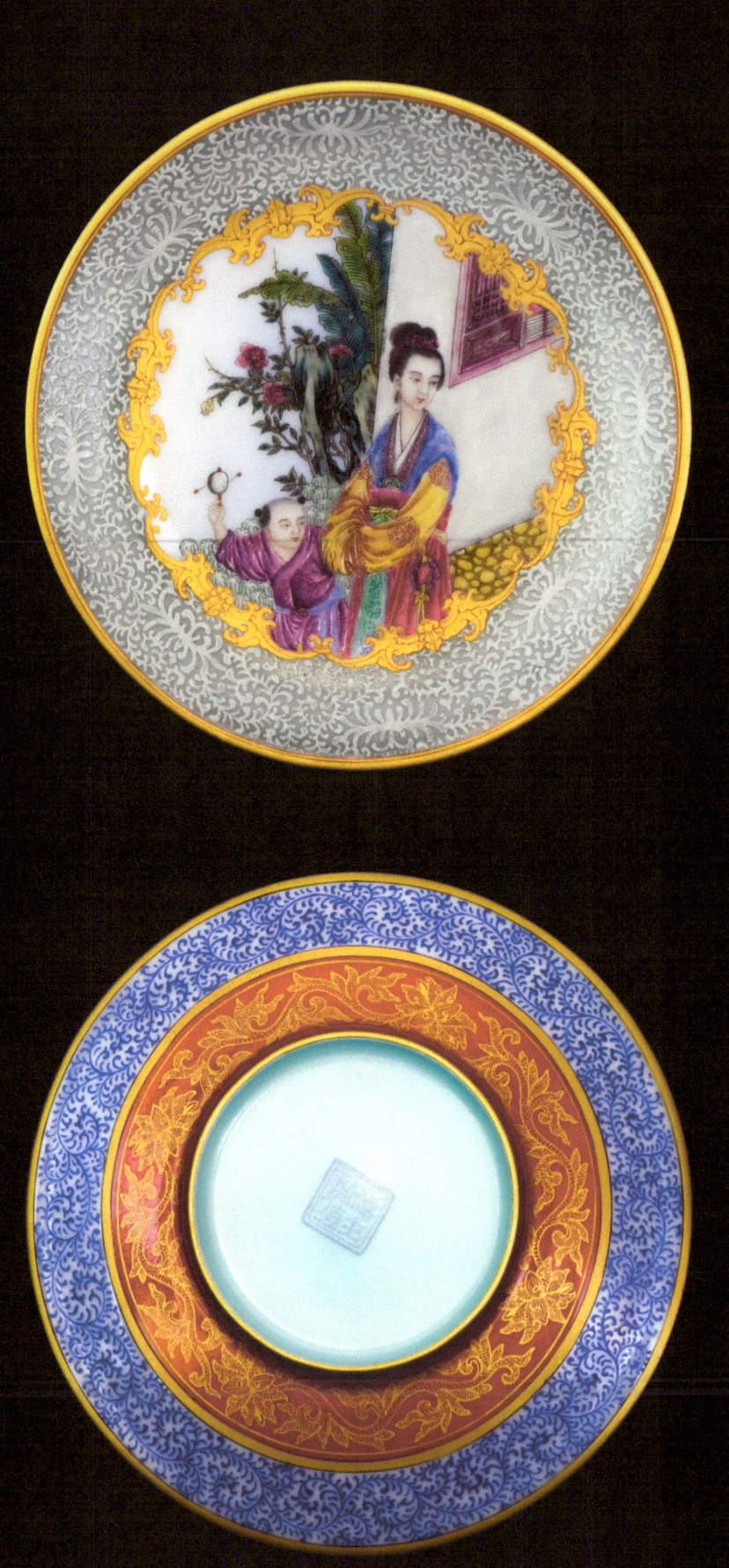

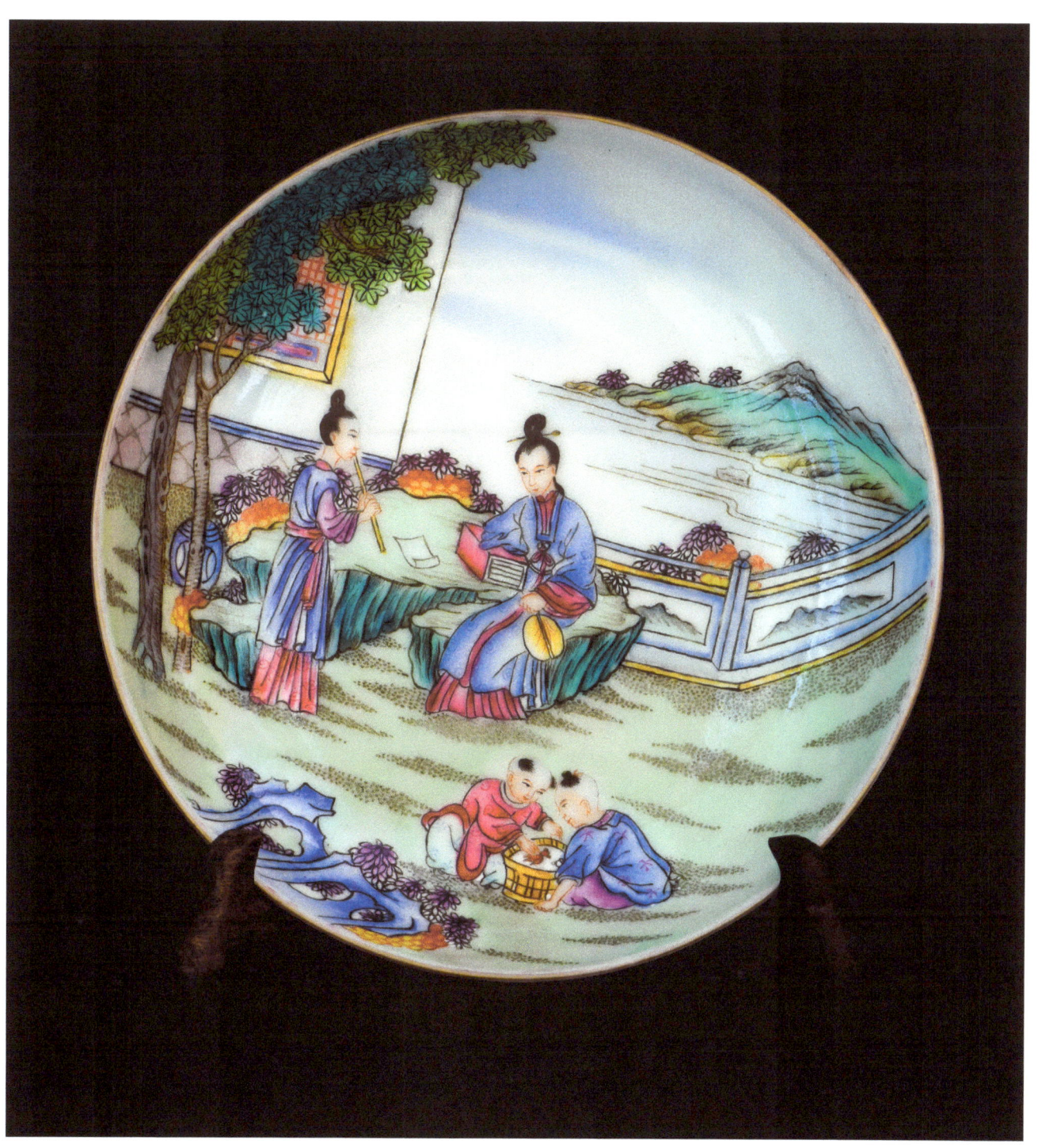

HONOURING THE UNKNOWN 113

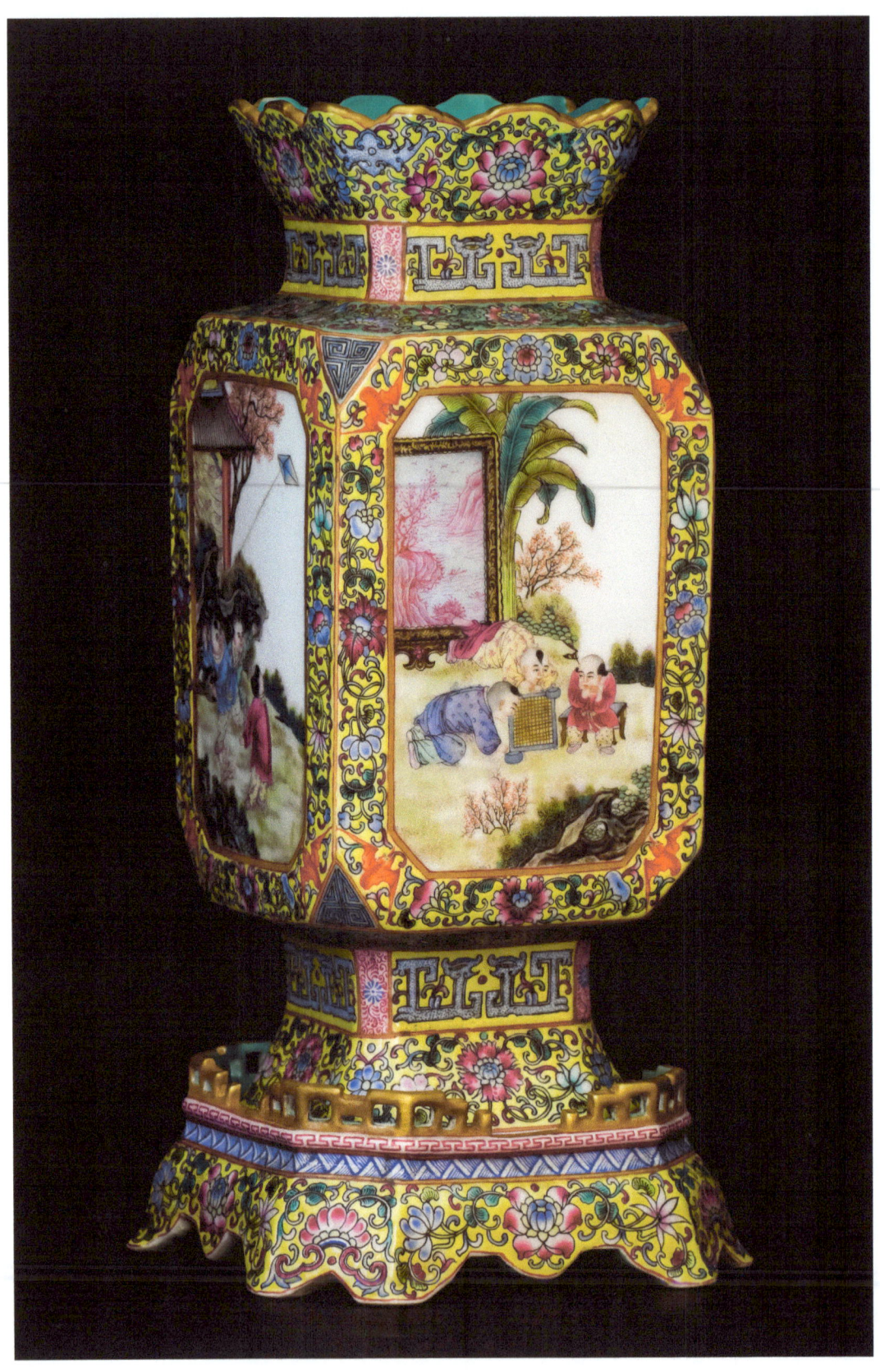

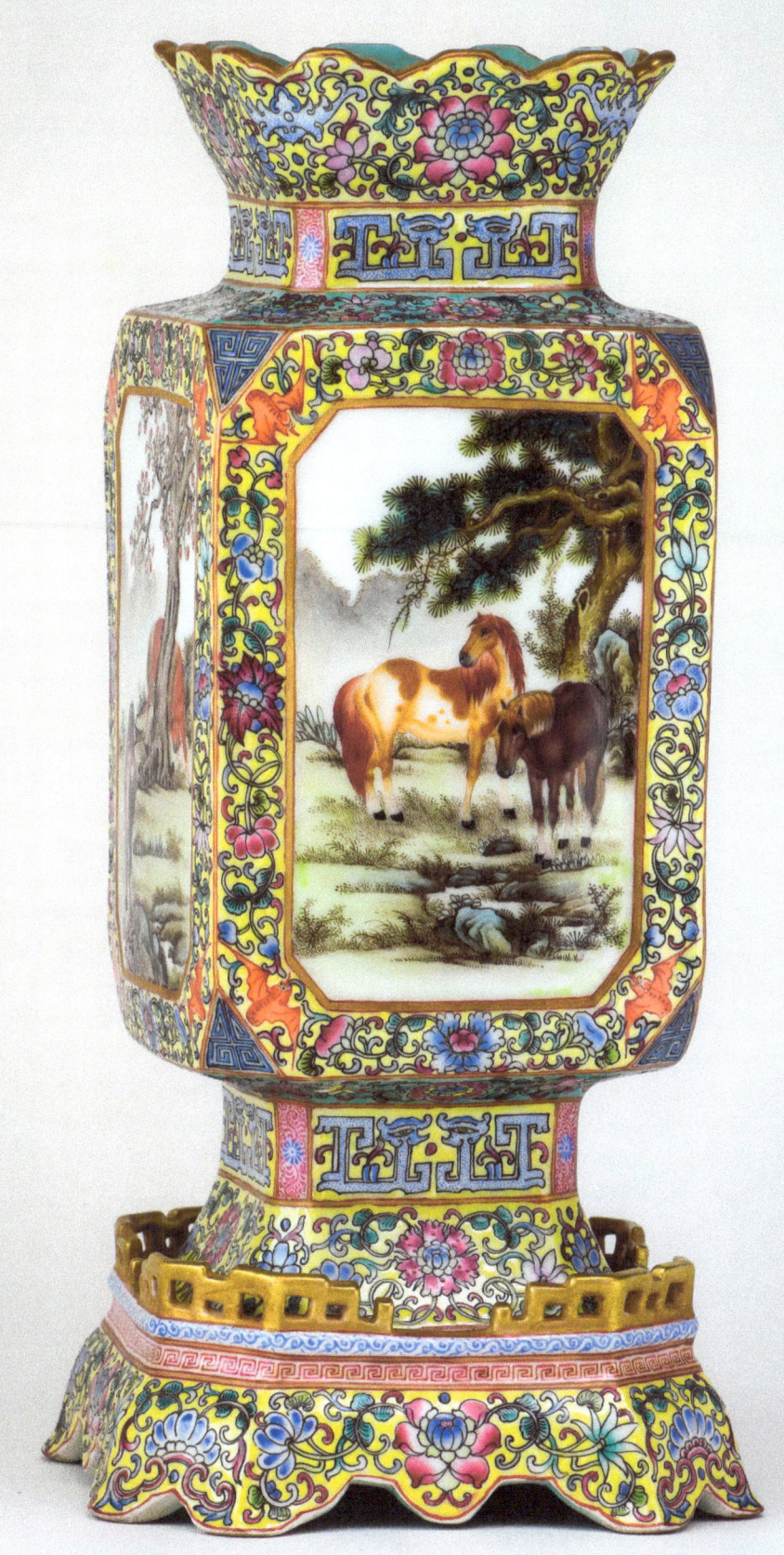

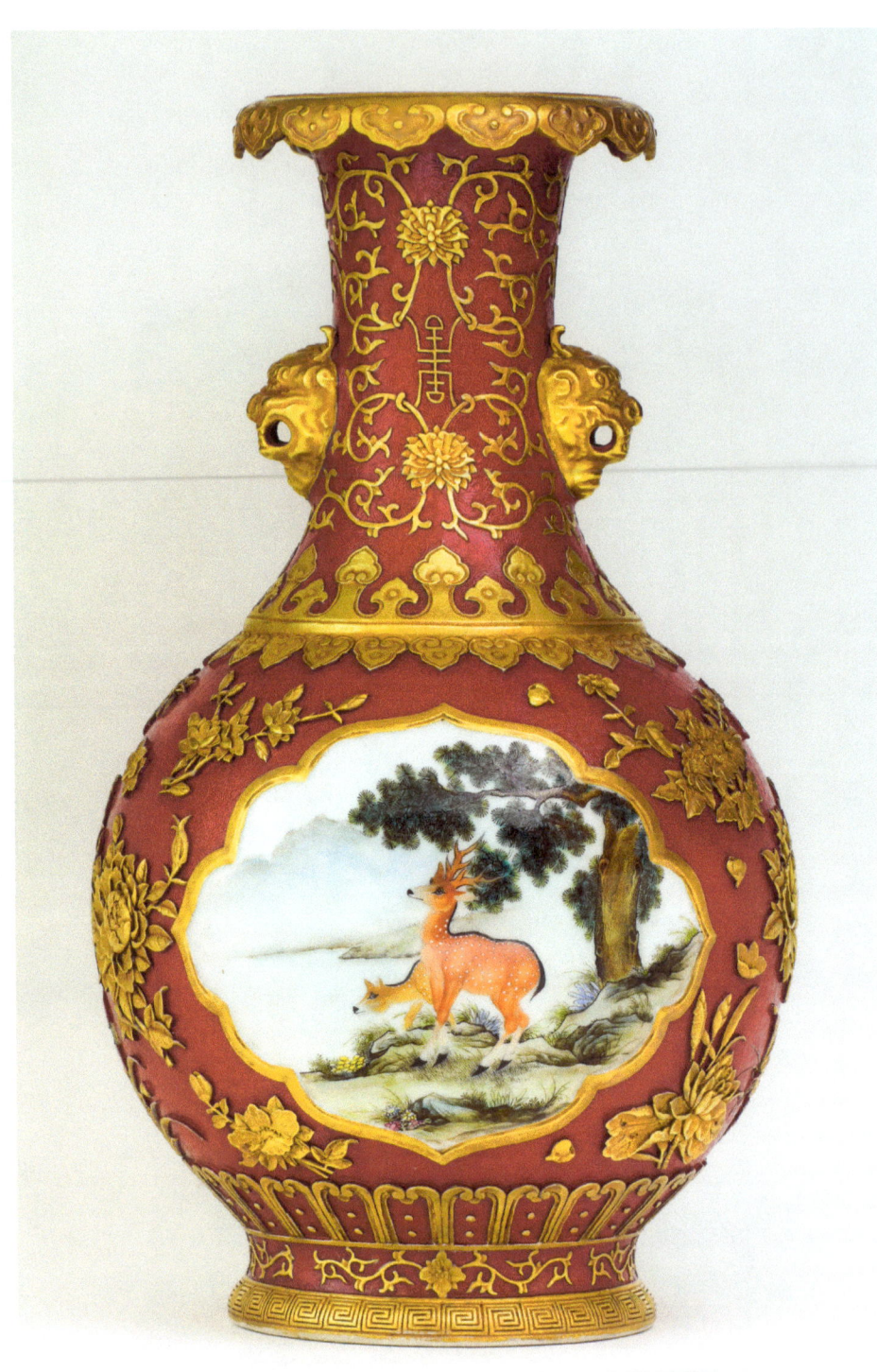

116 FORBIDDEN REPLICAS

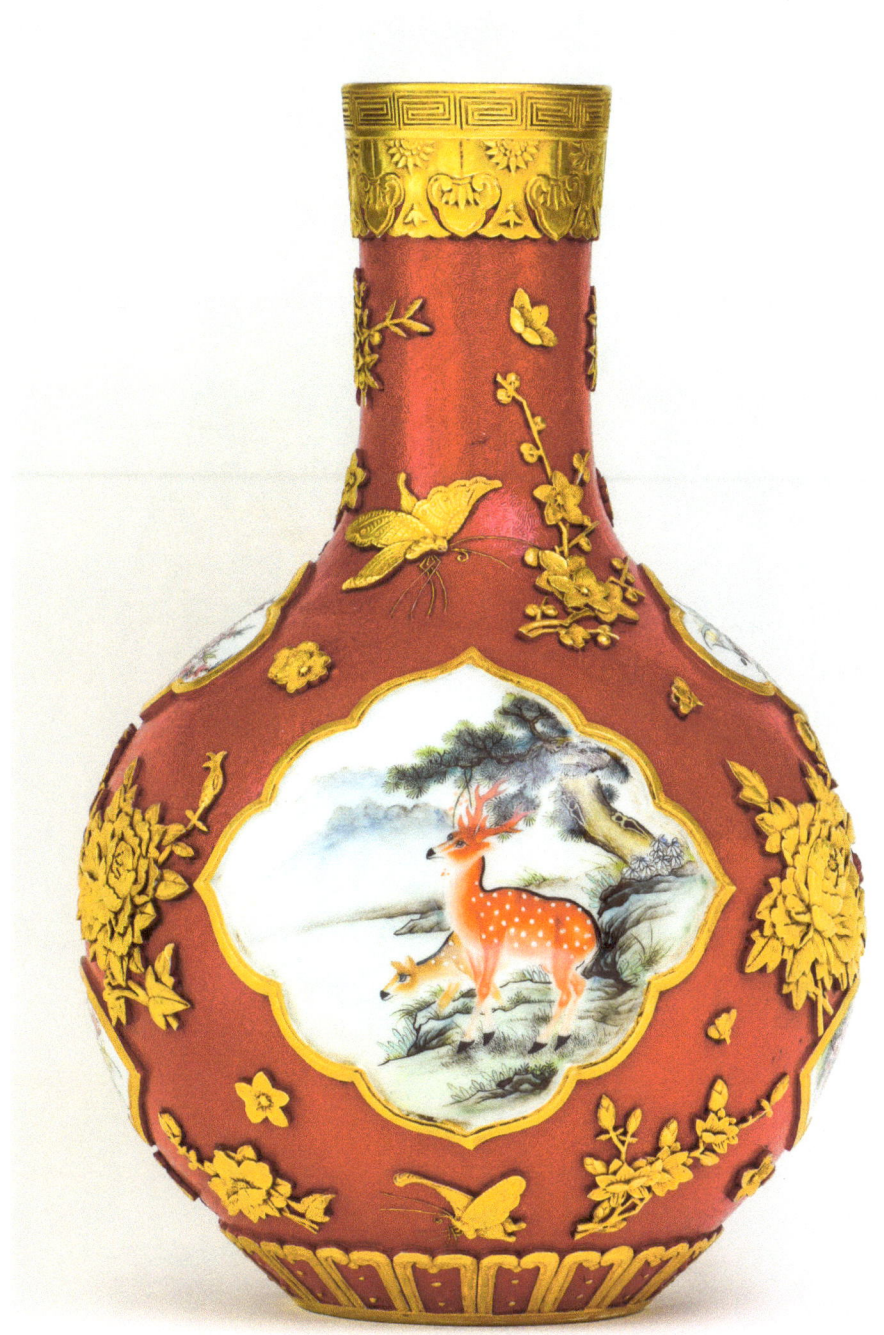

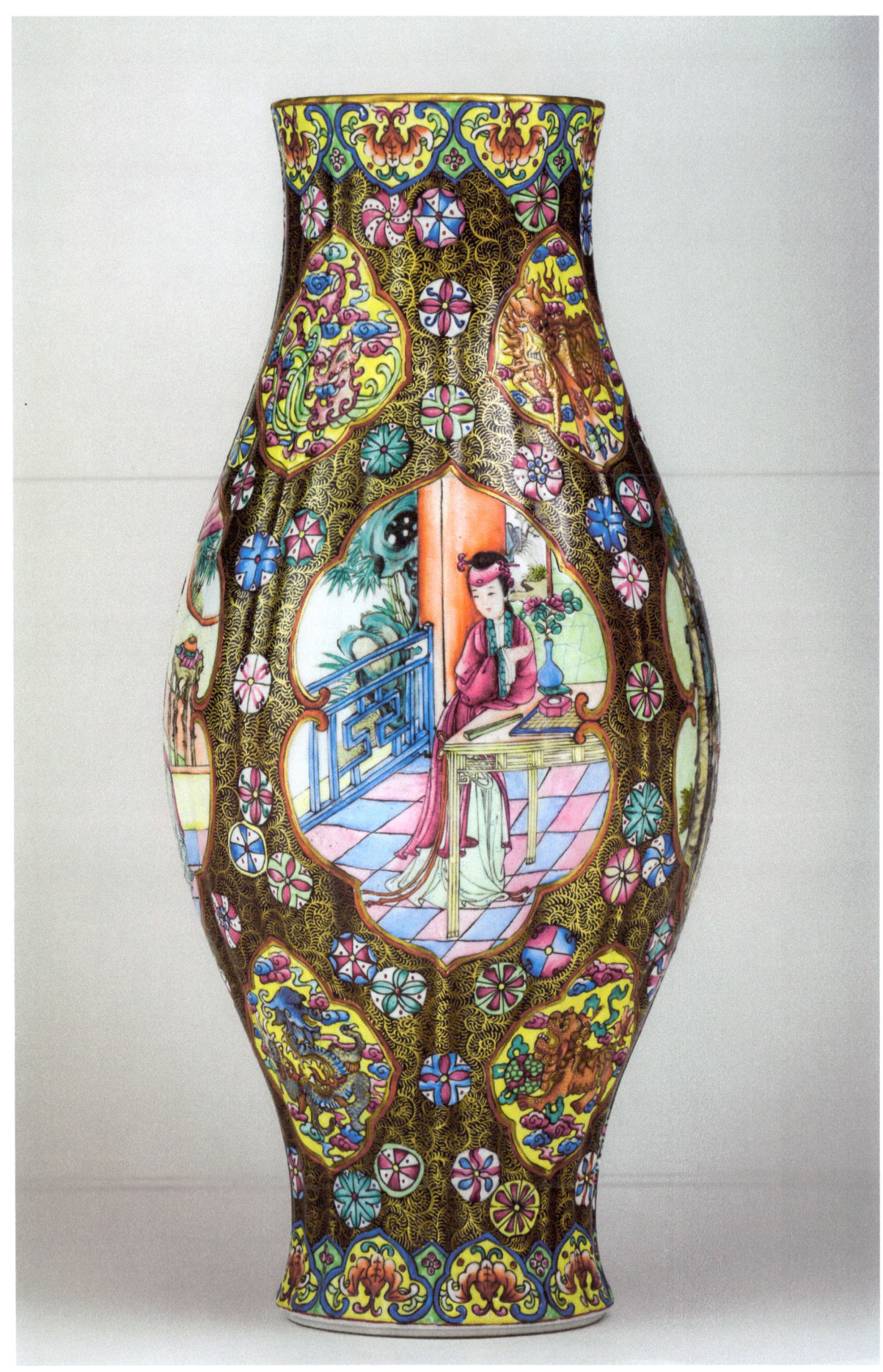

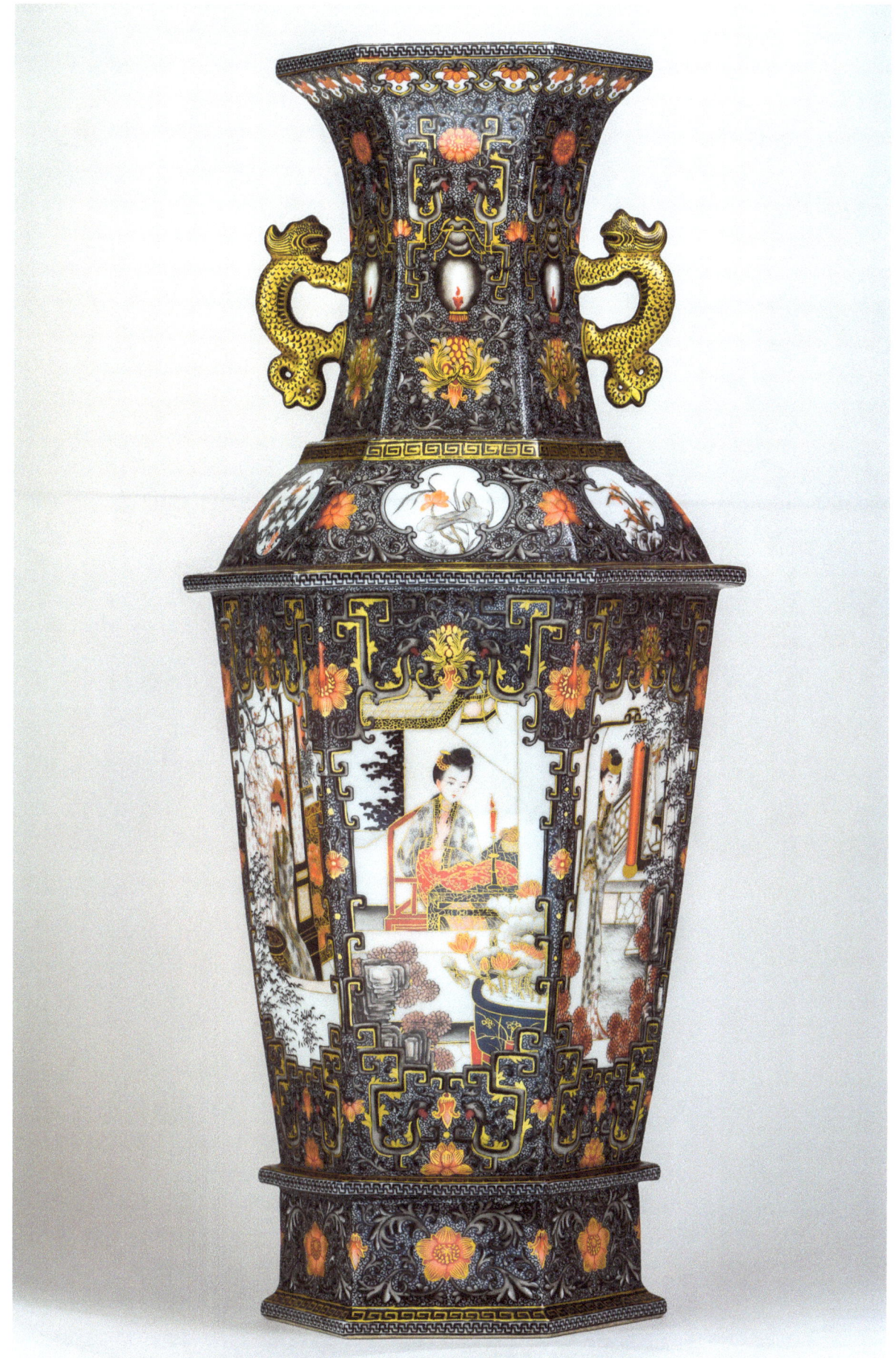

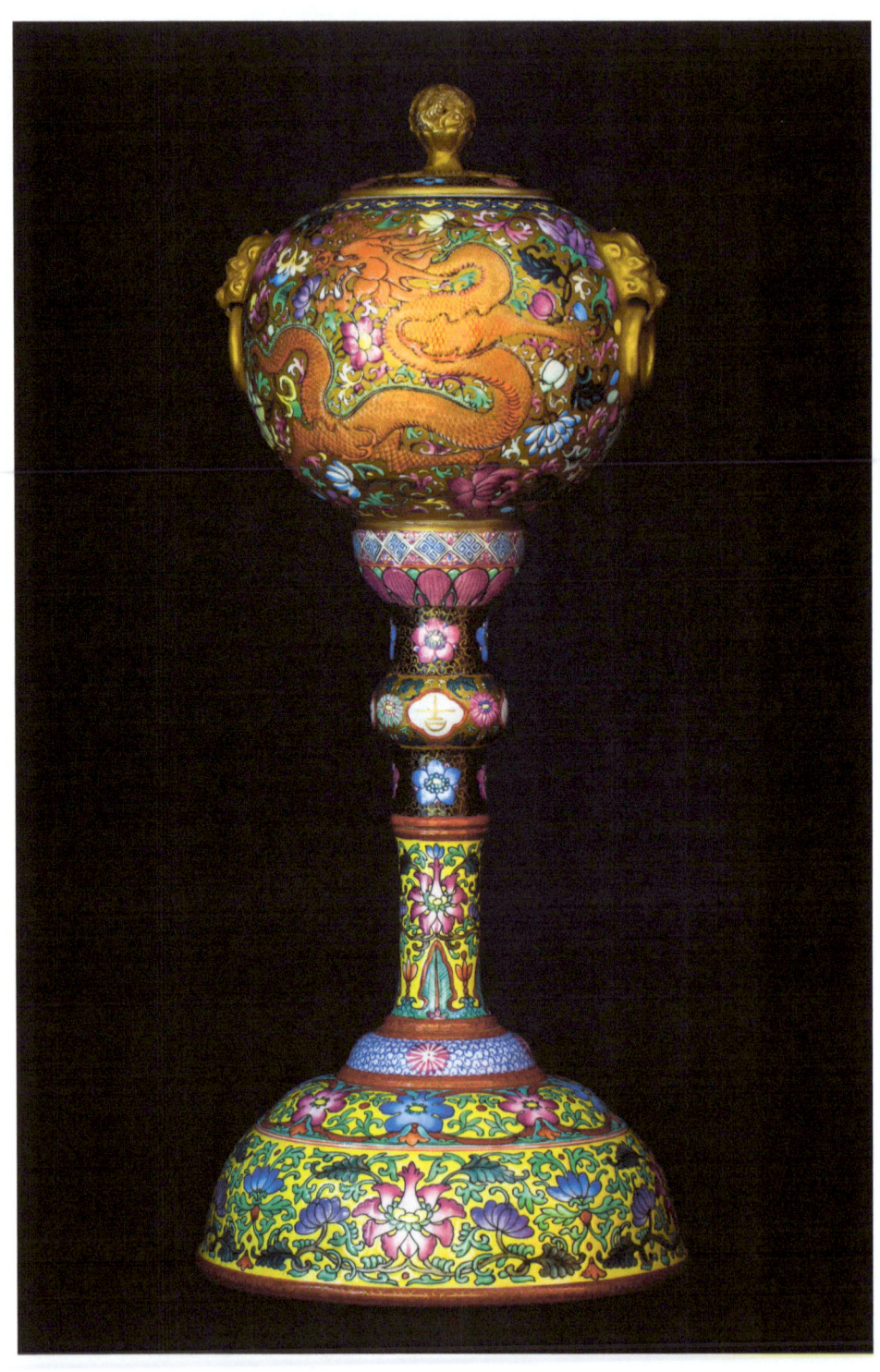

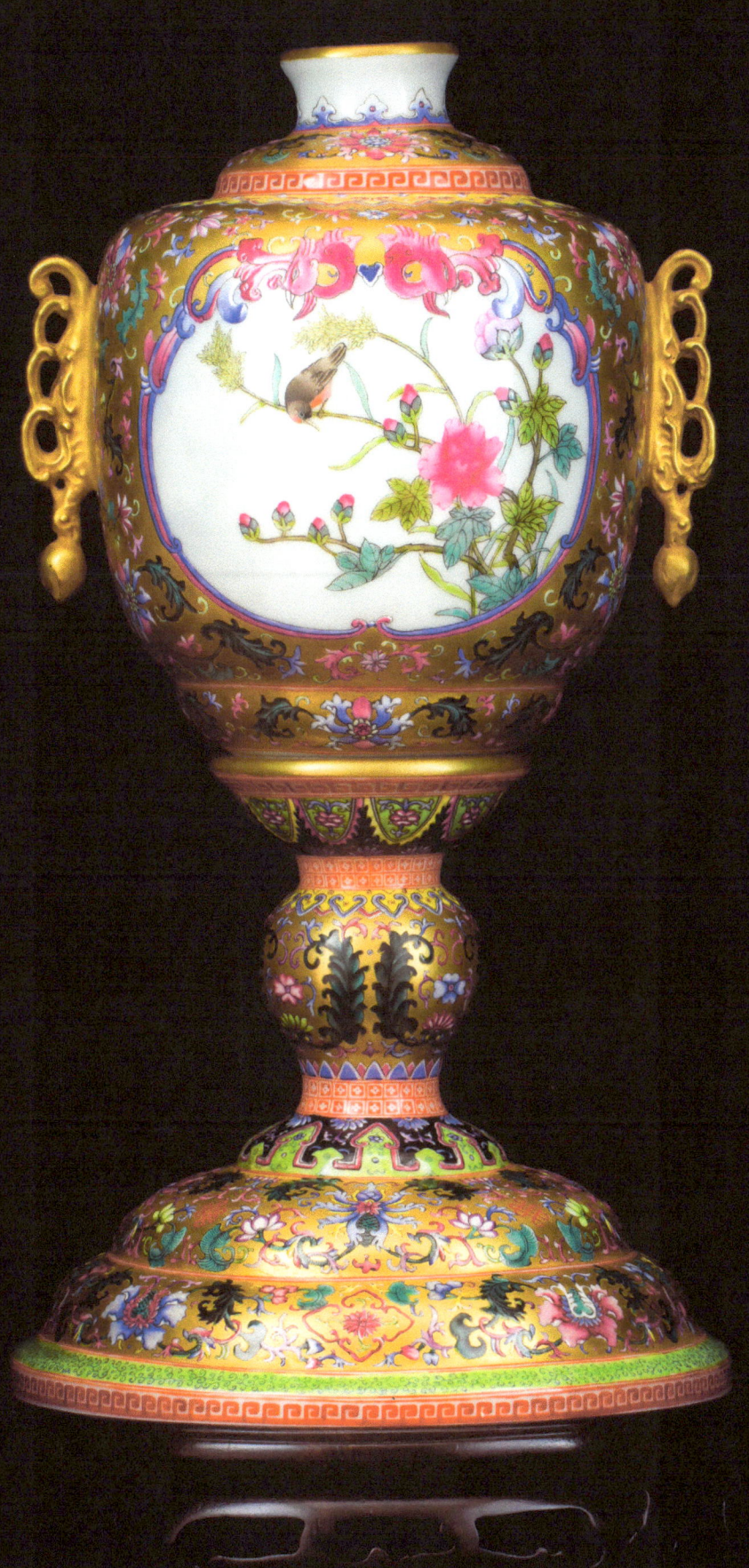

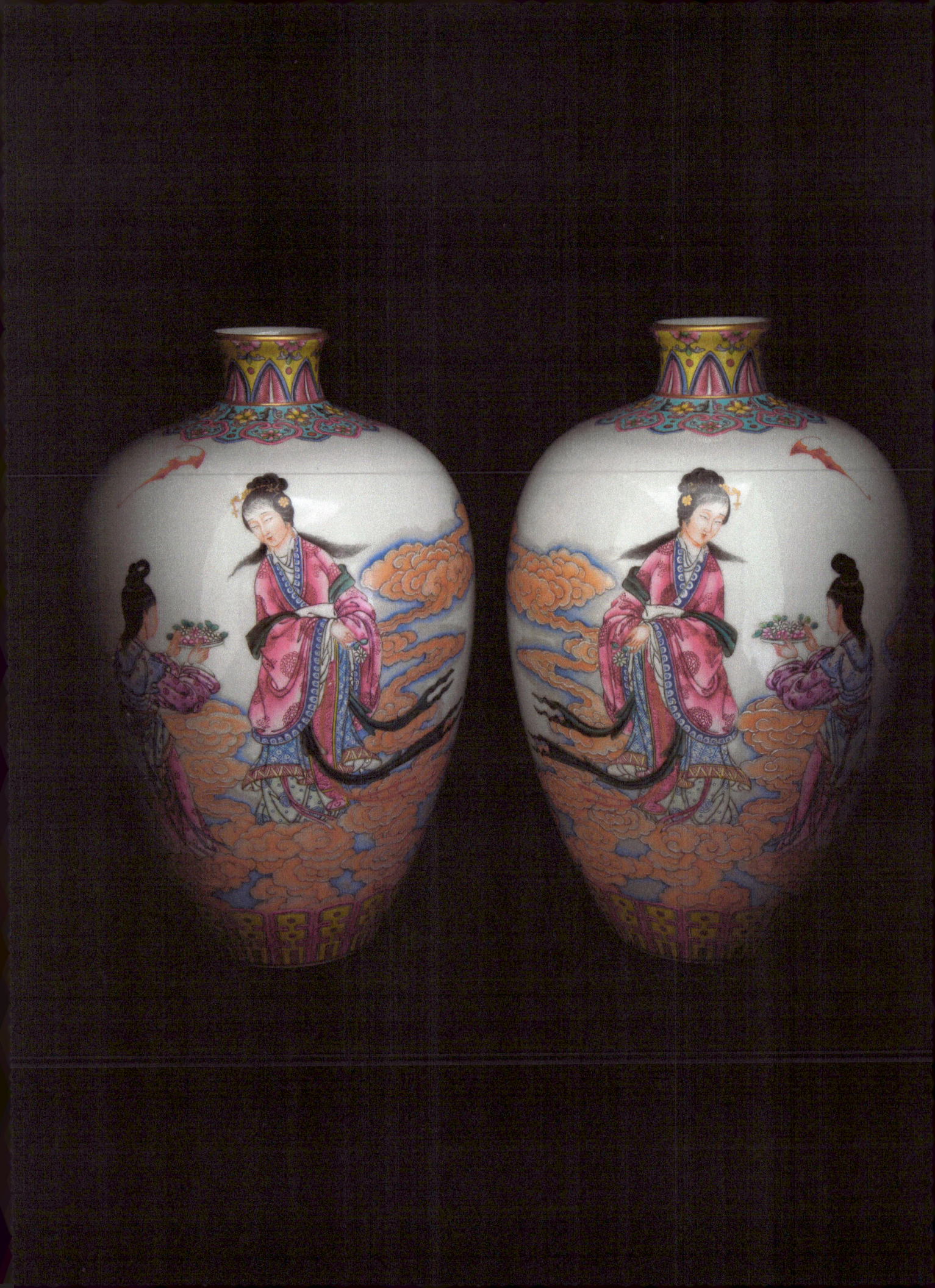

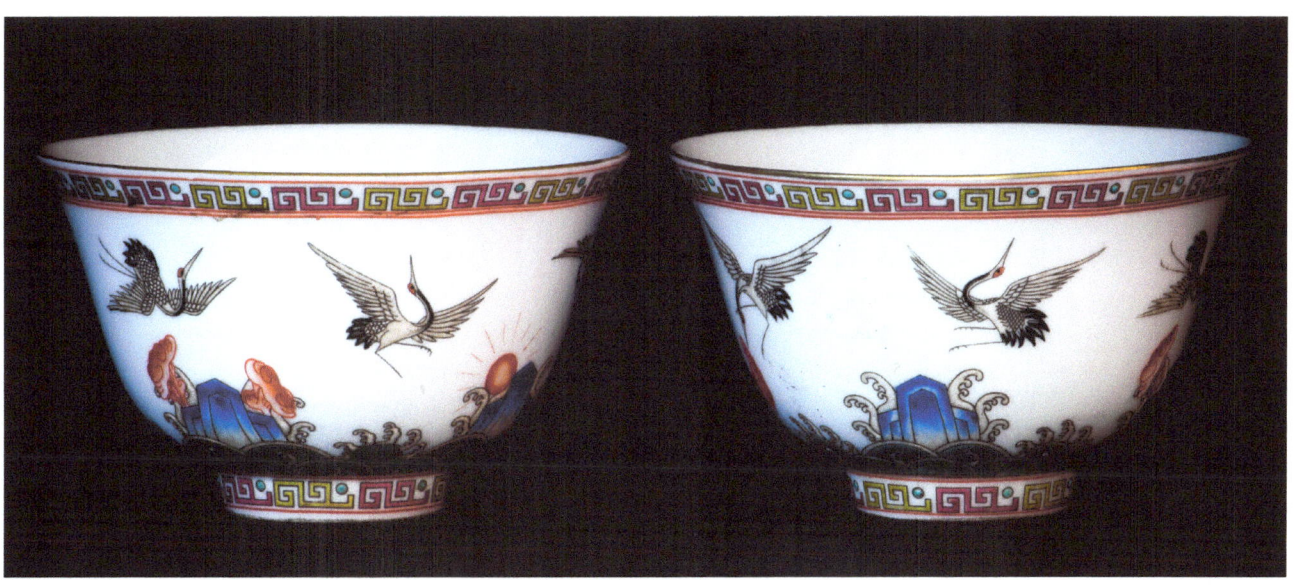

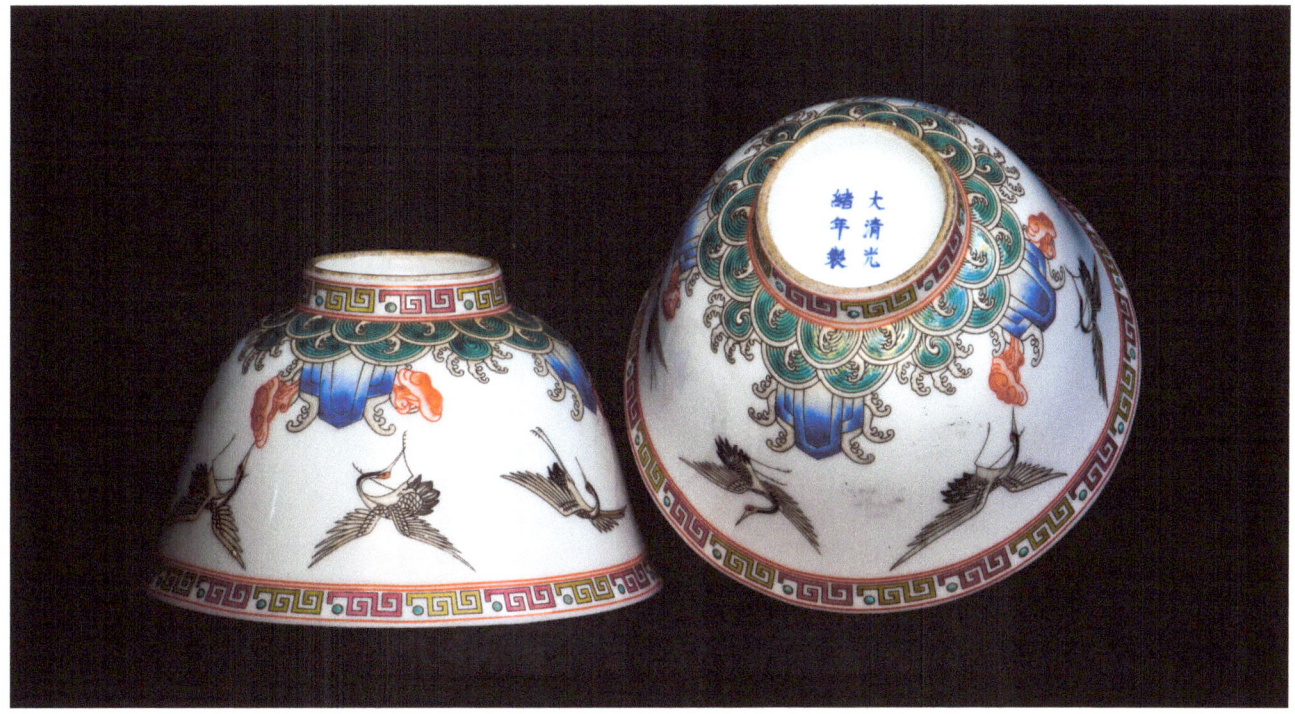

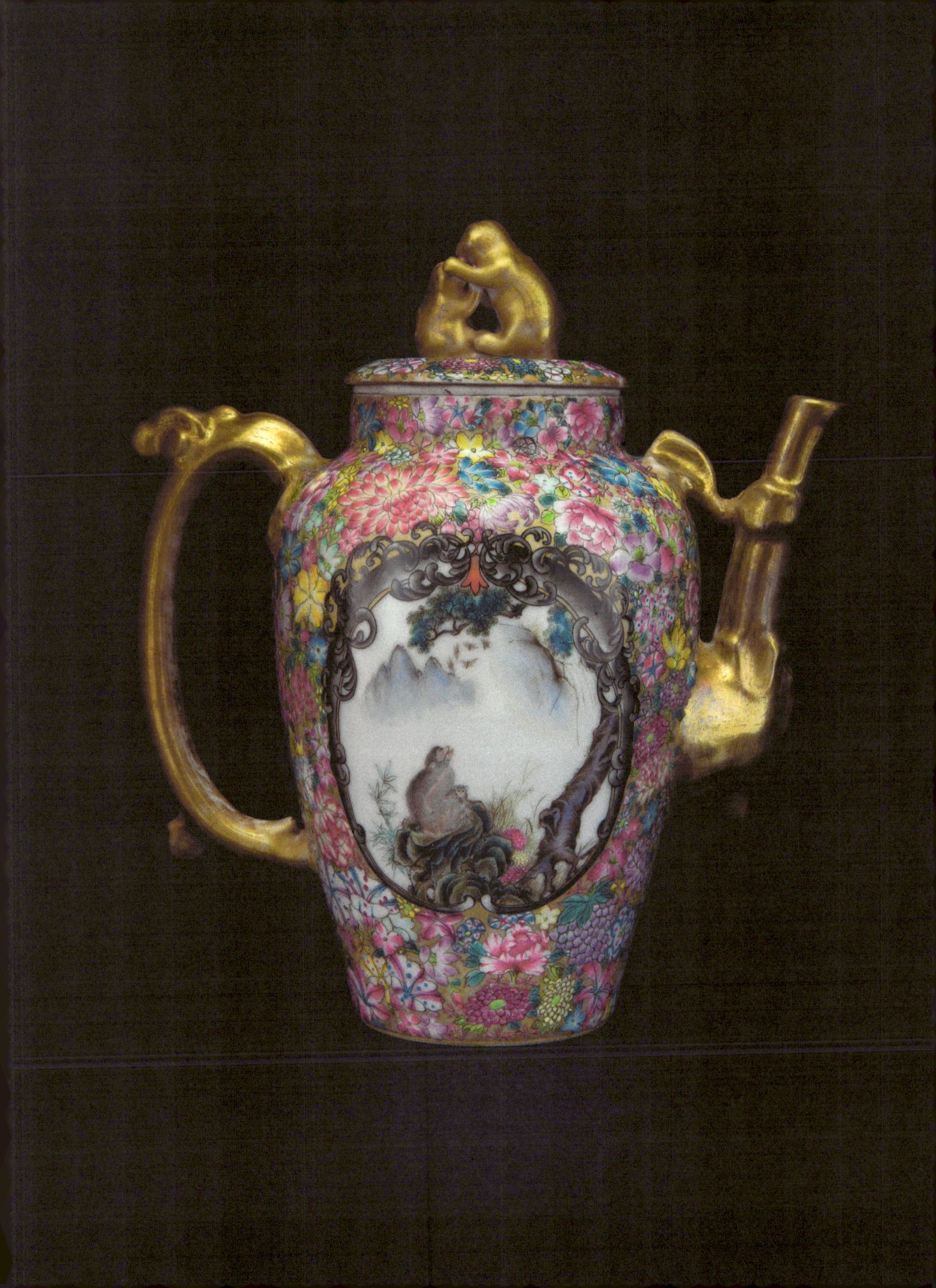

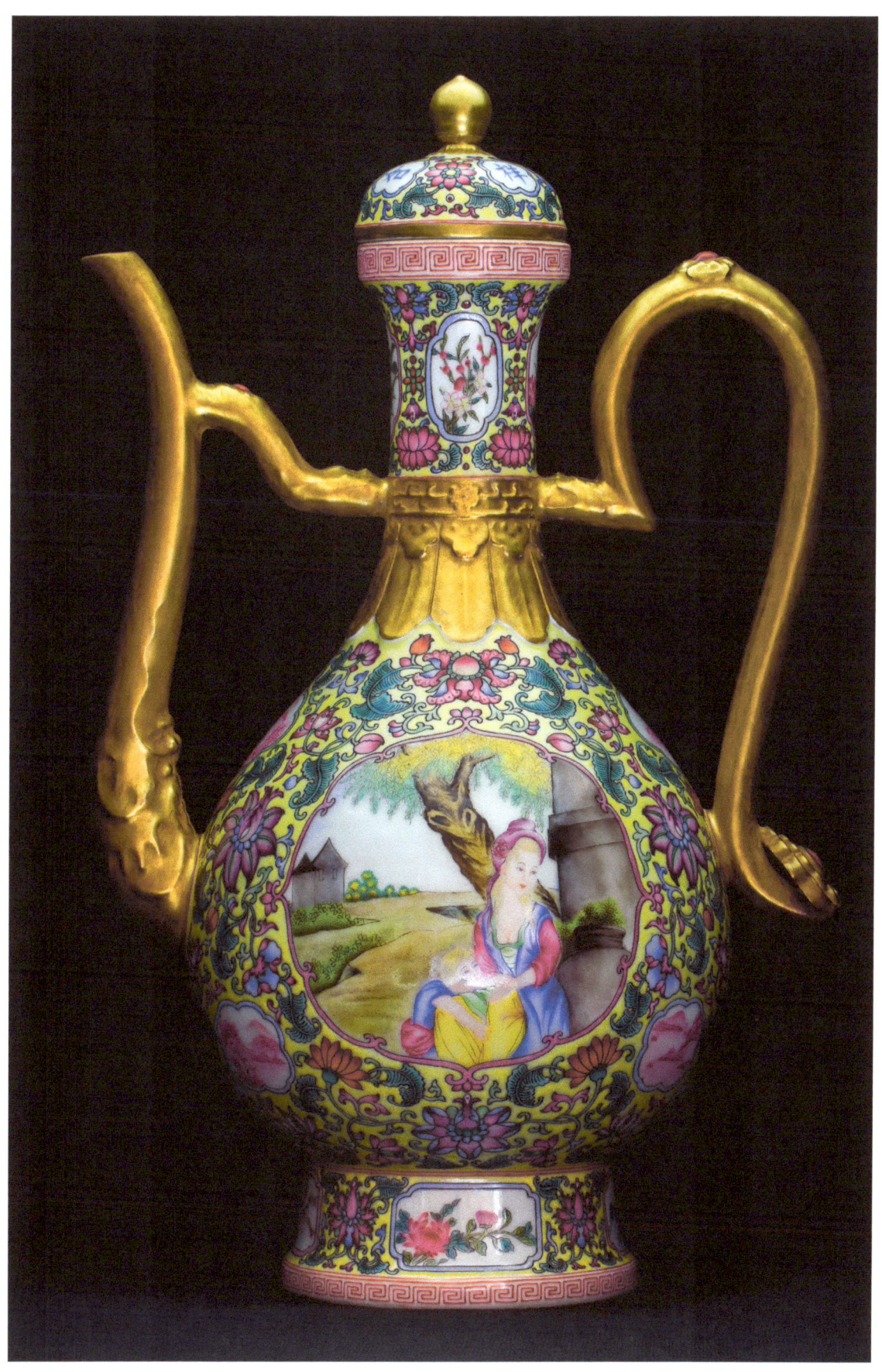

HONOURING THE UNKNOWN

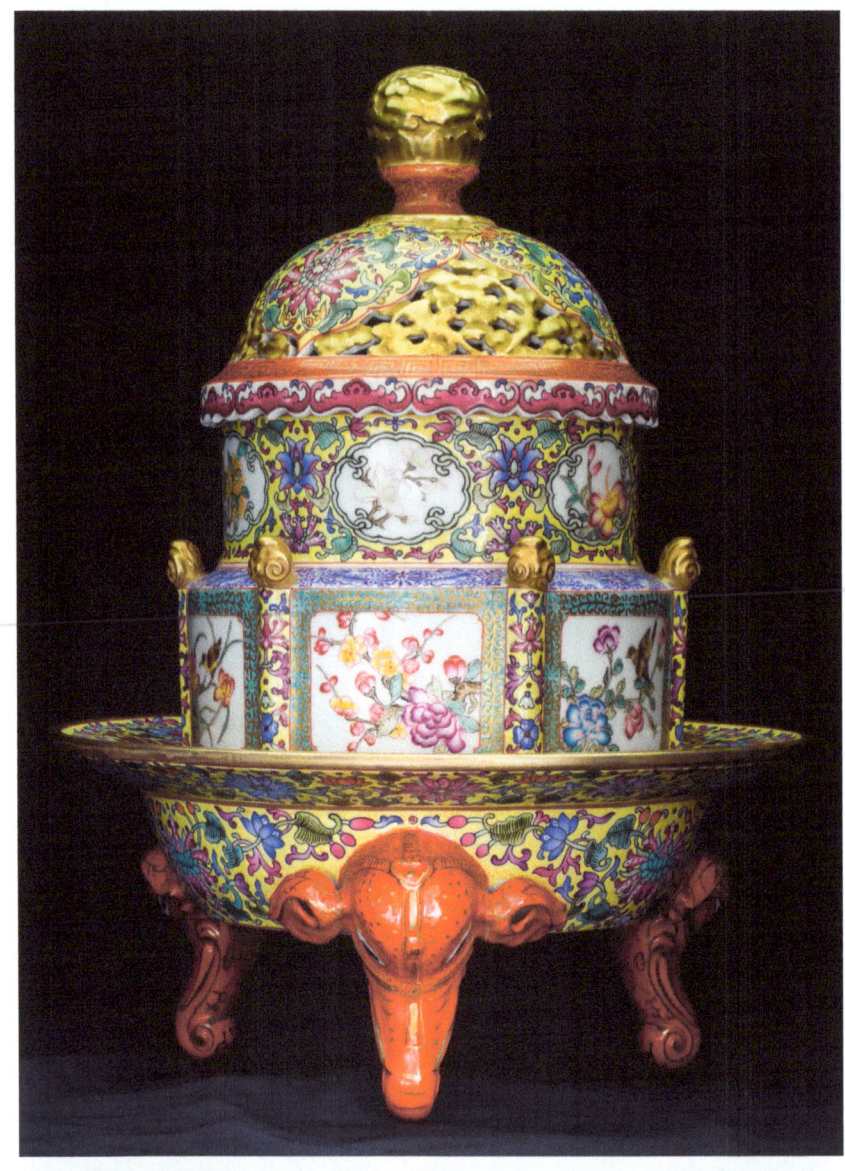
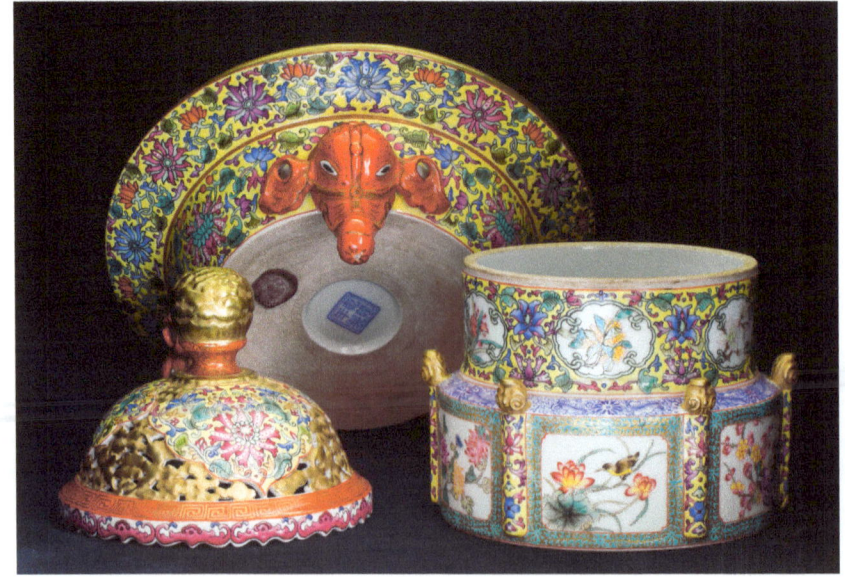

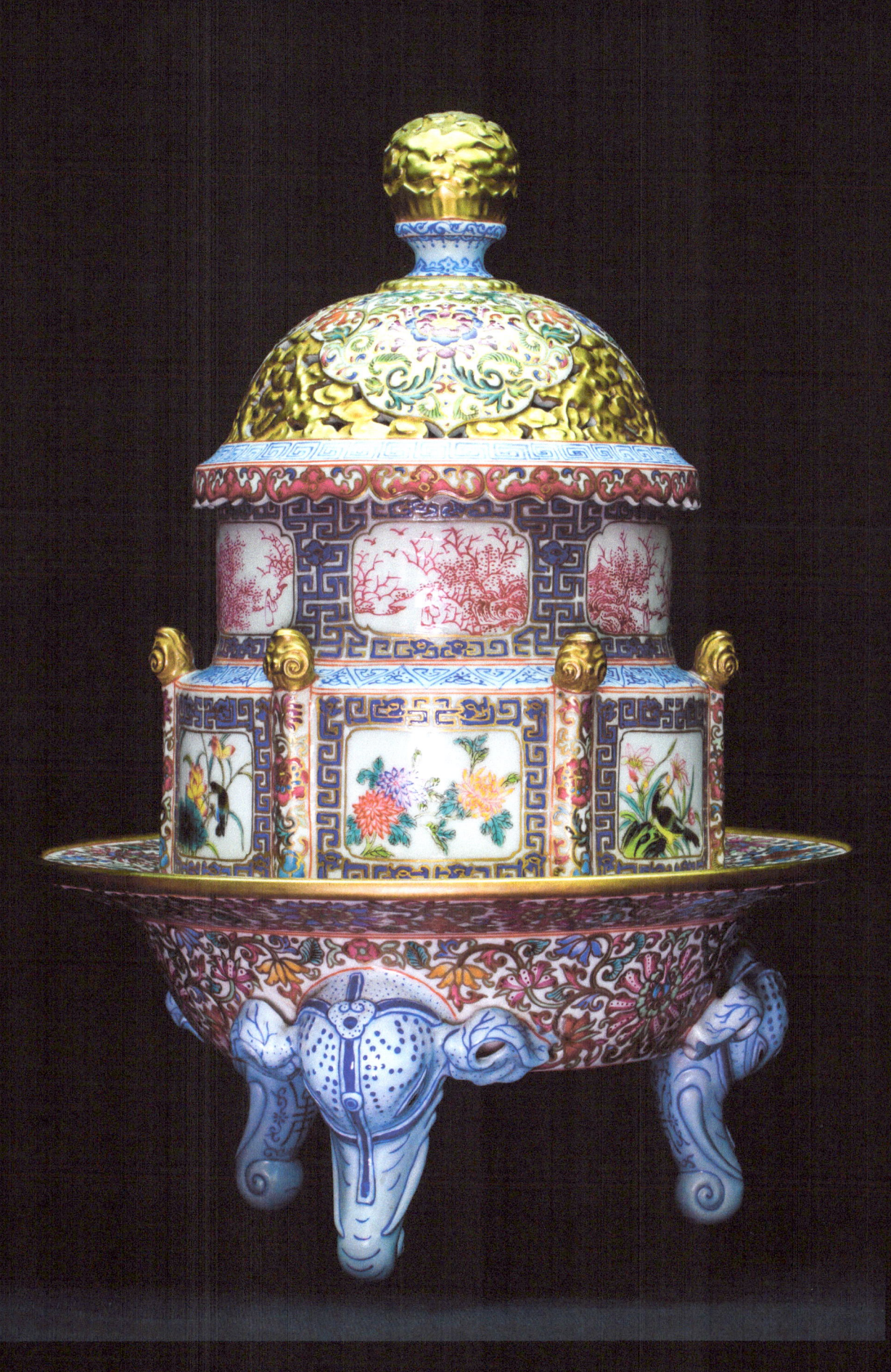

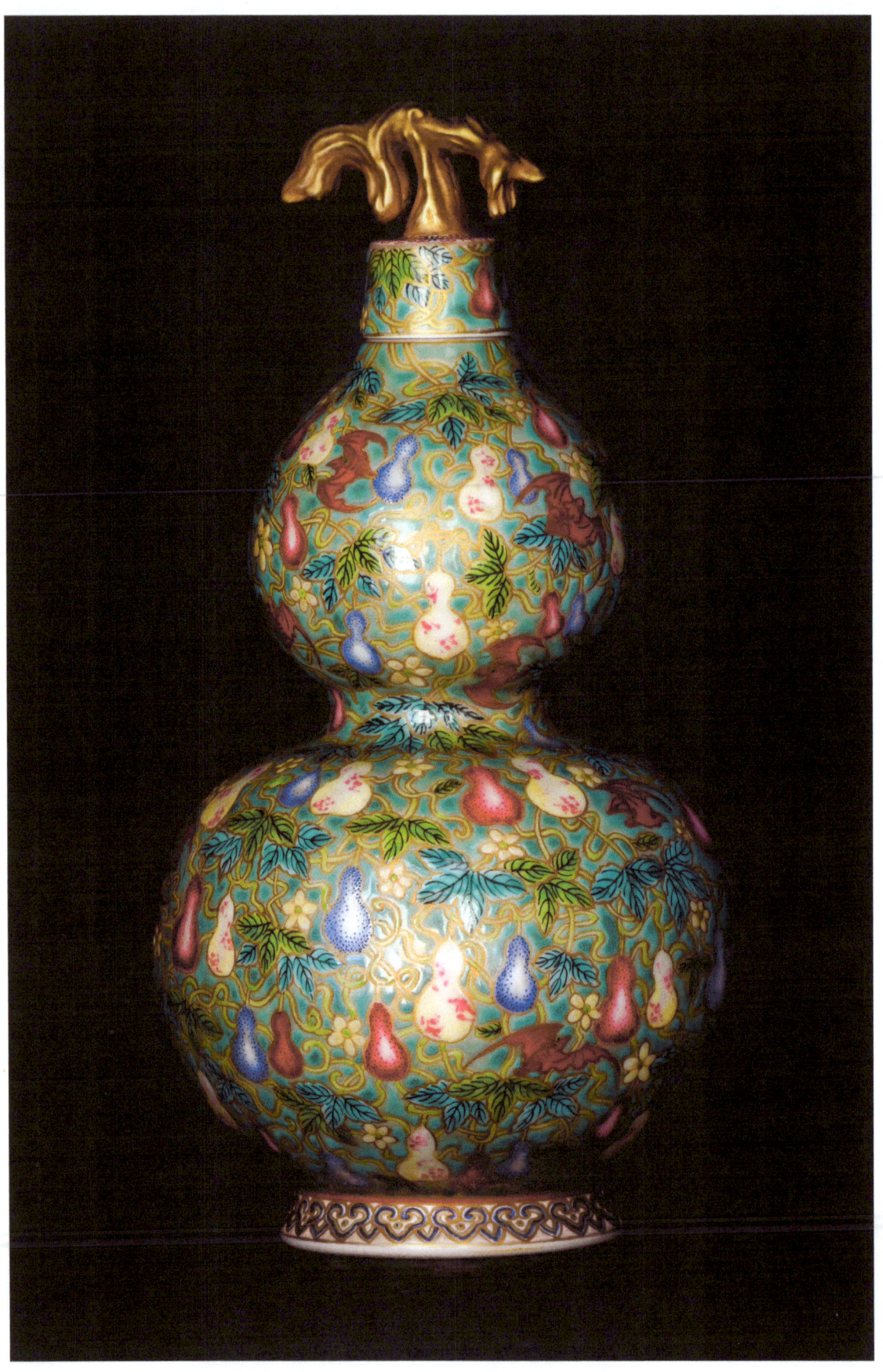

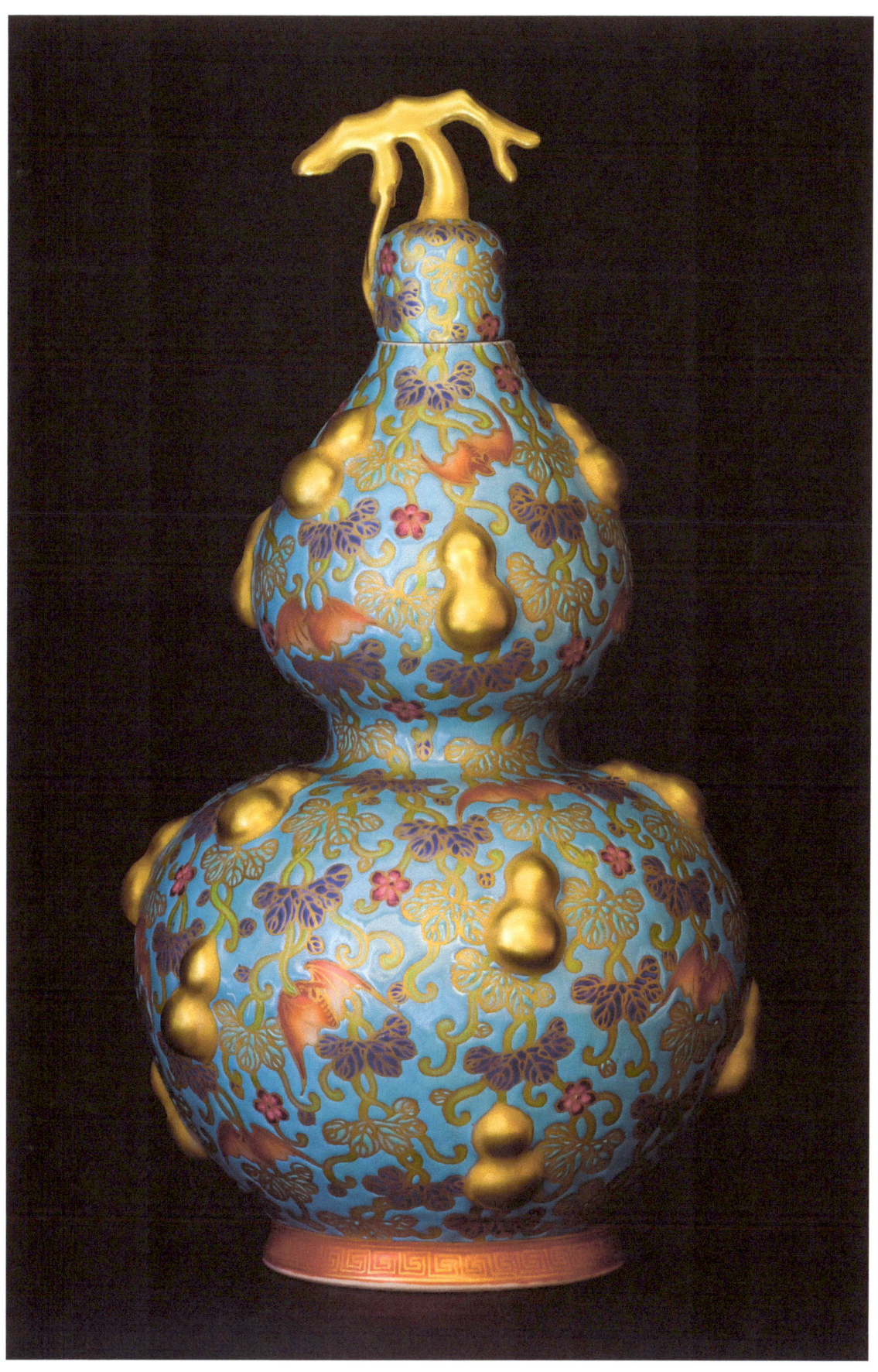

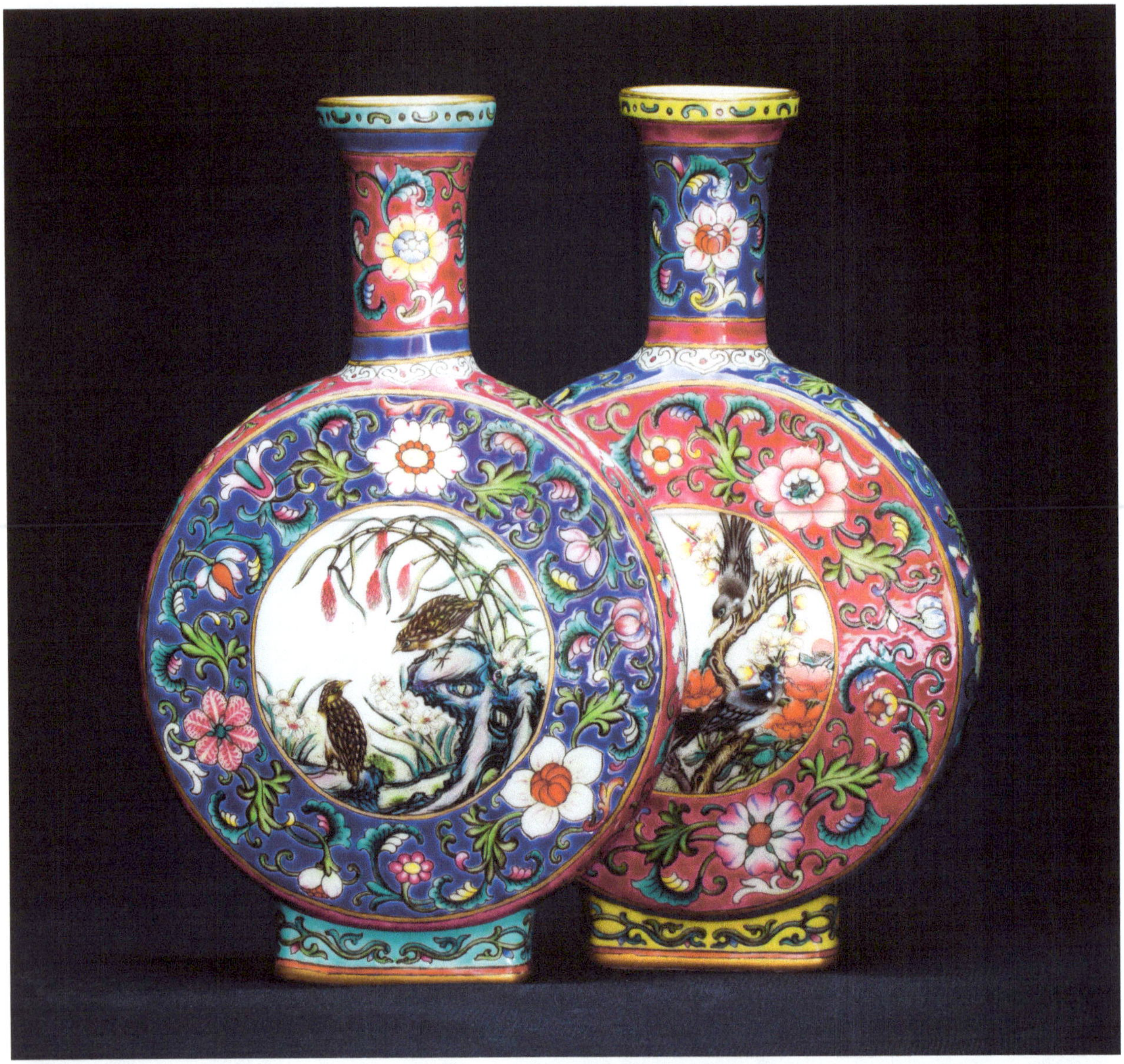

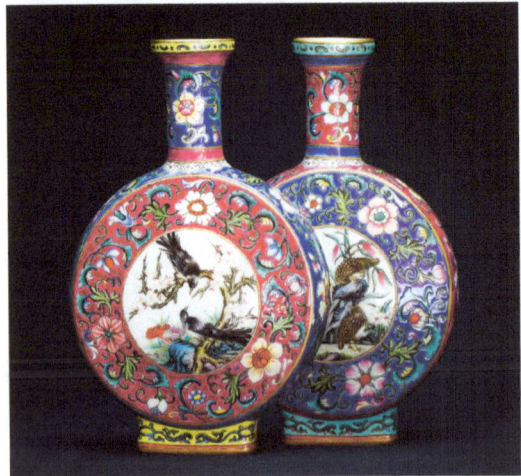
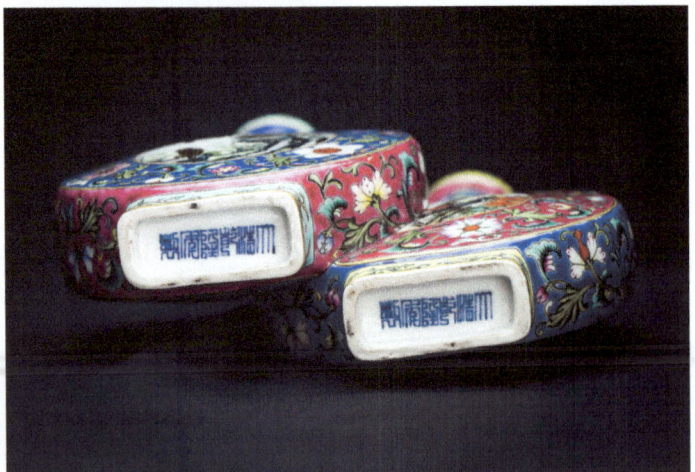

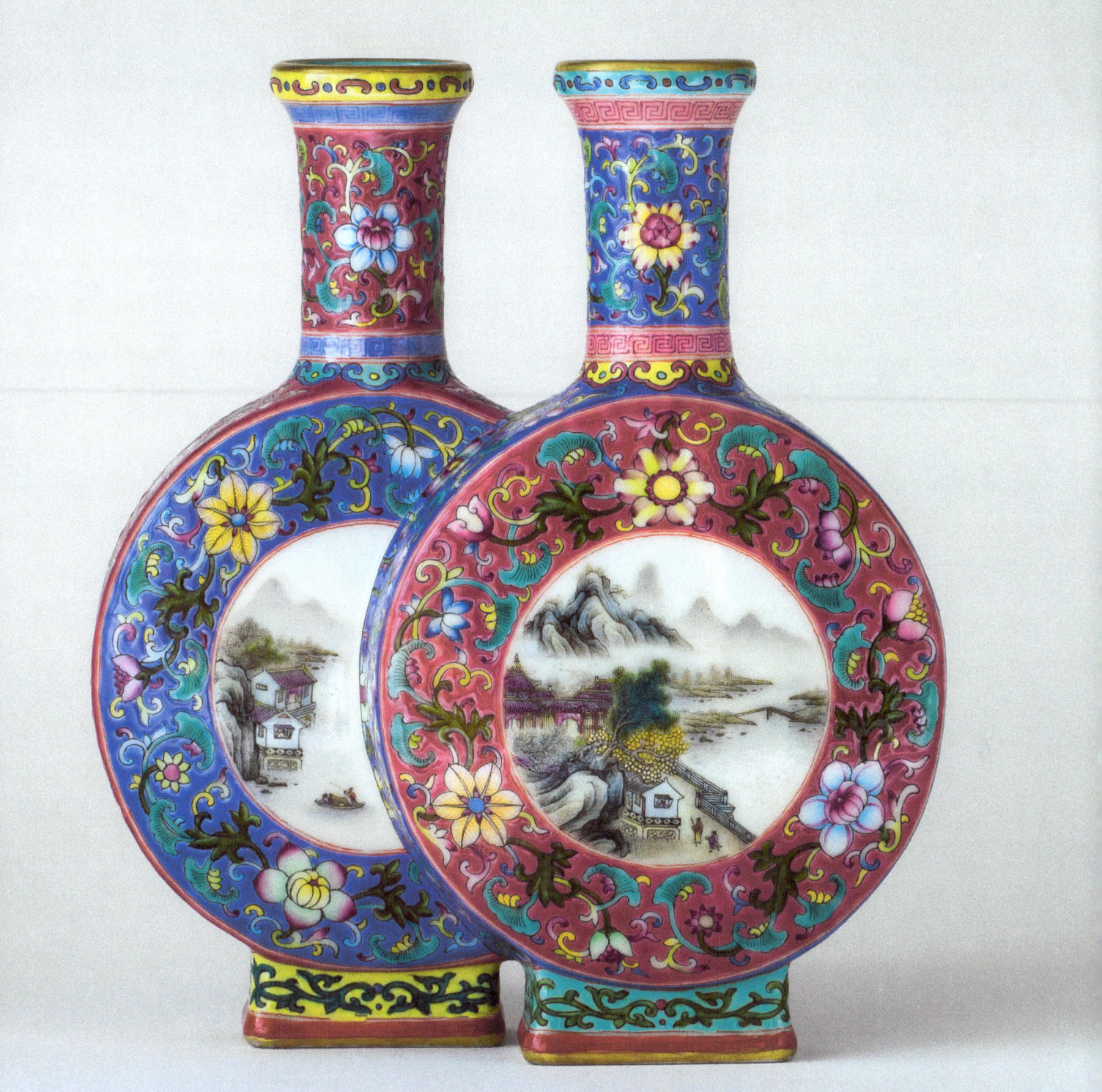

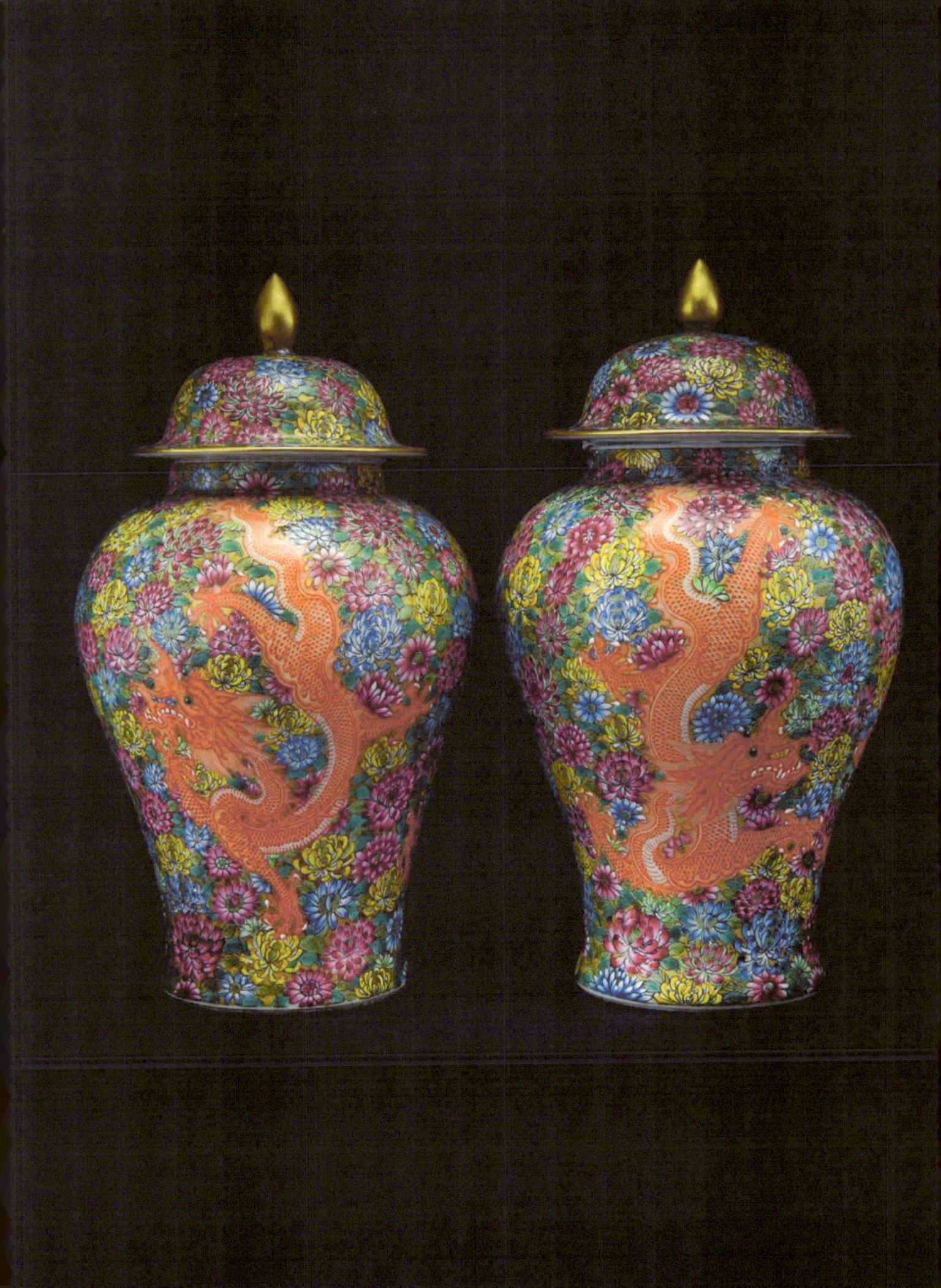

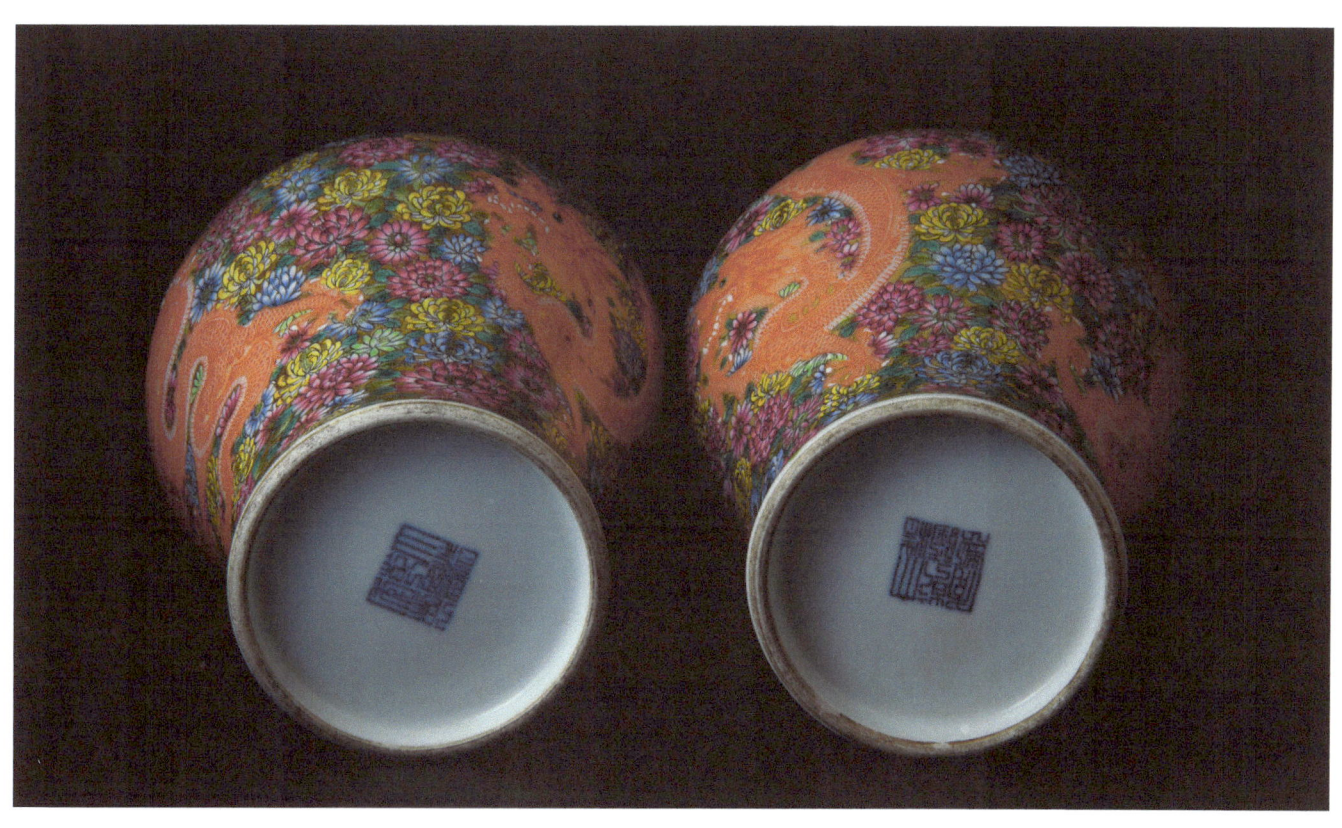

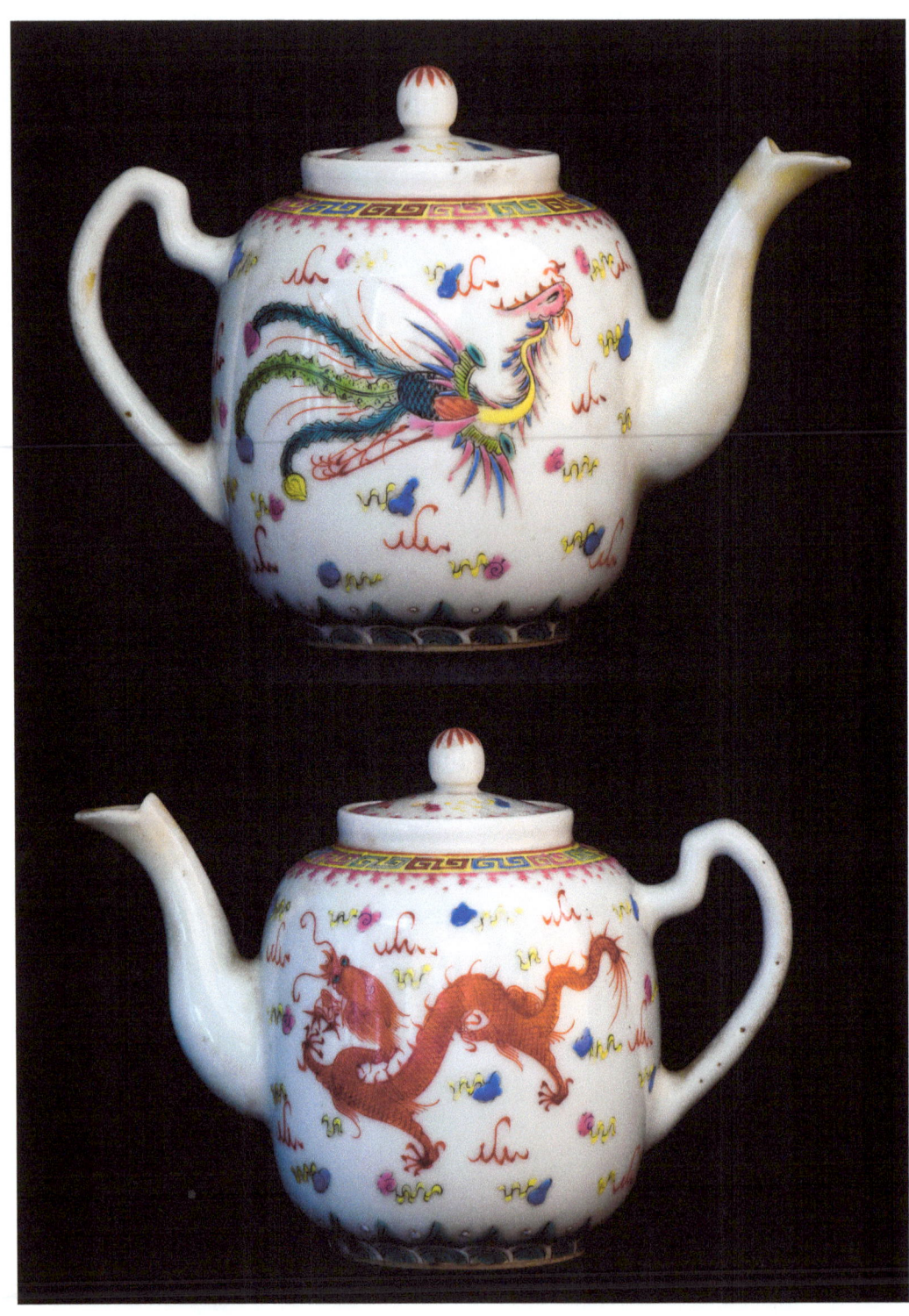

134 FORBIDDEN REPLICAS

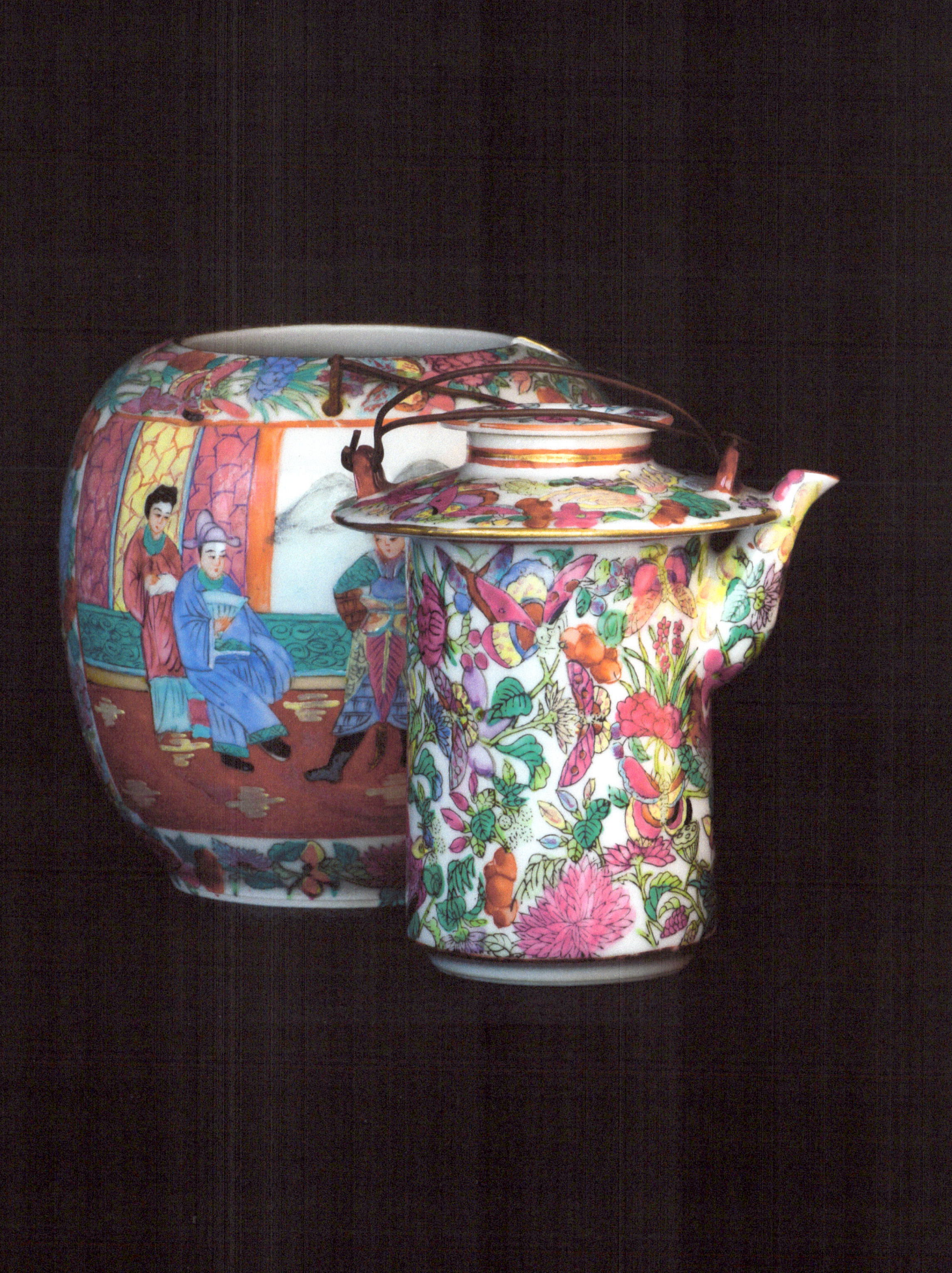

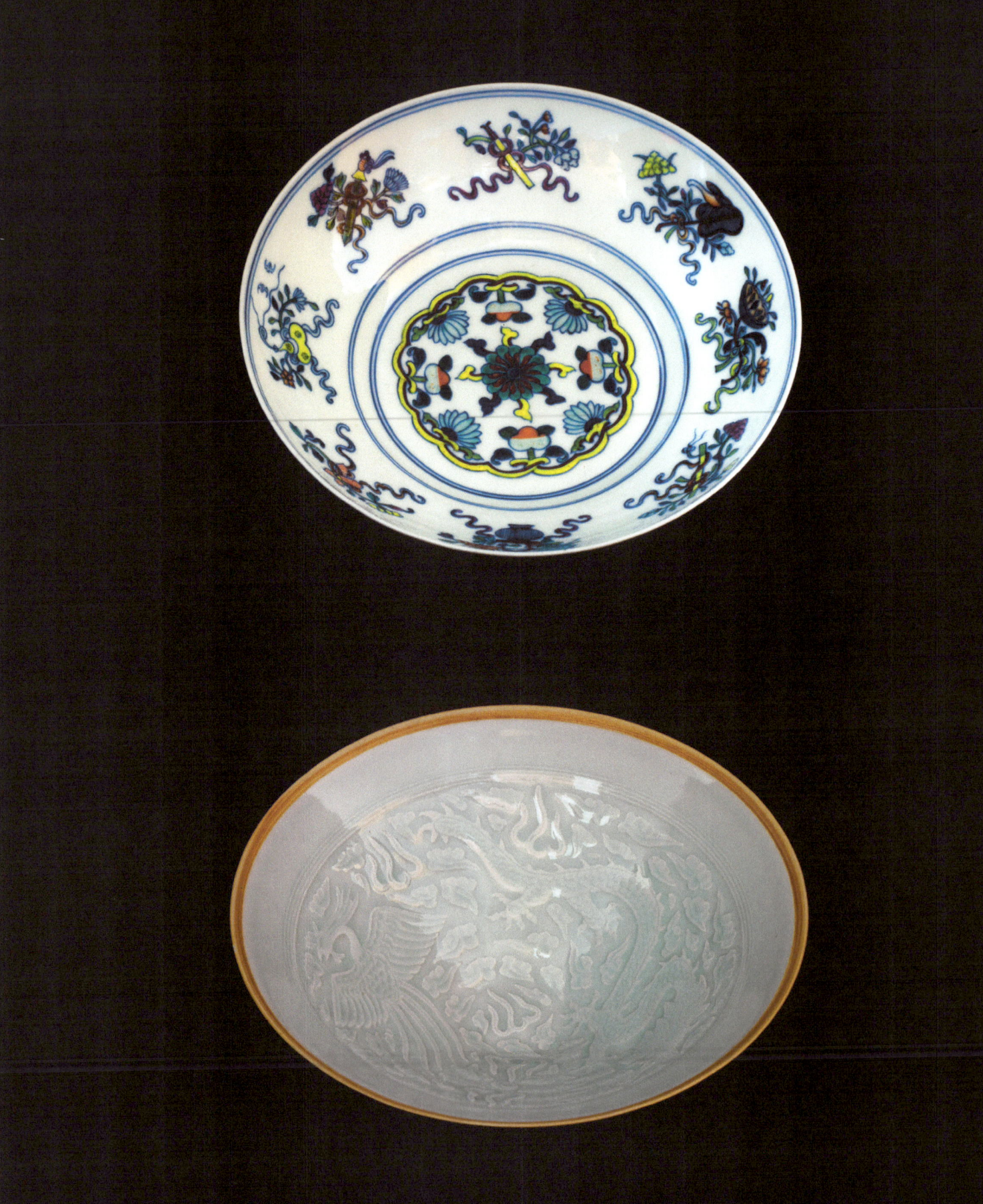

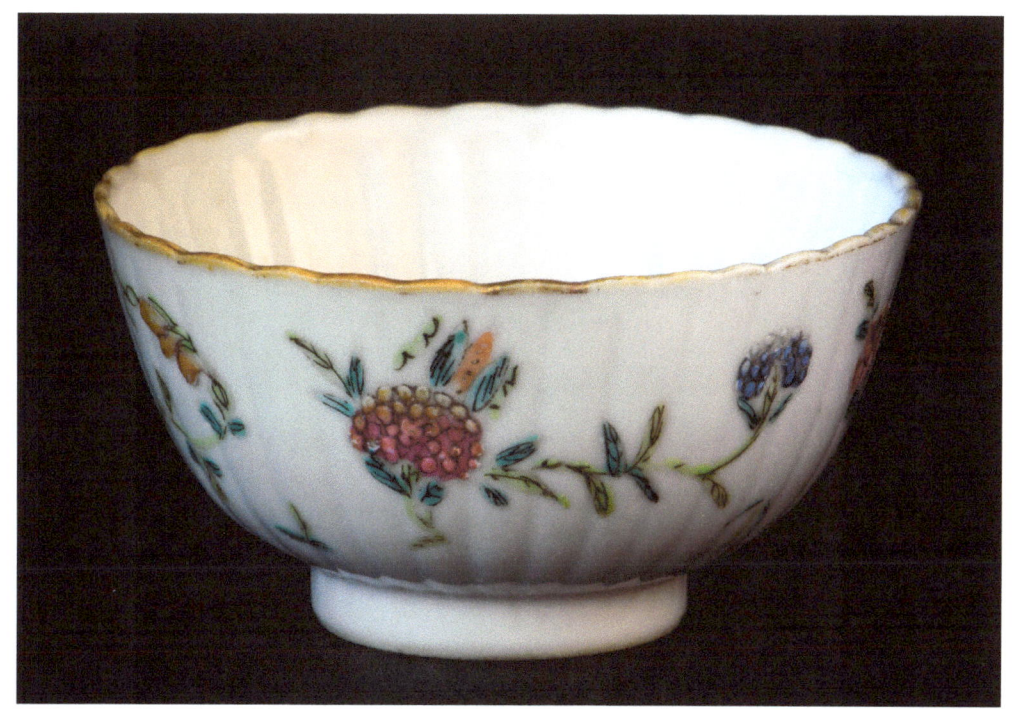

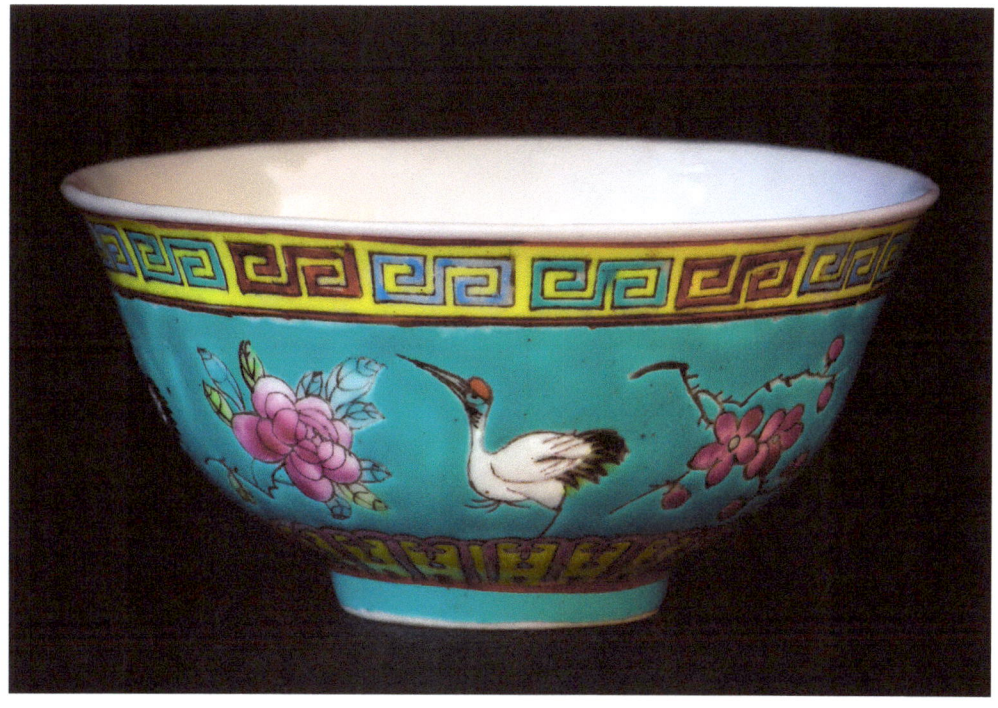

HONOURING THE UNKNOWN

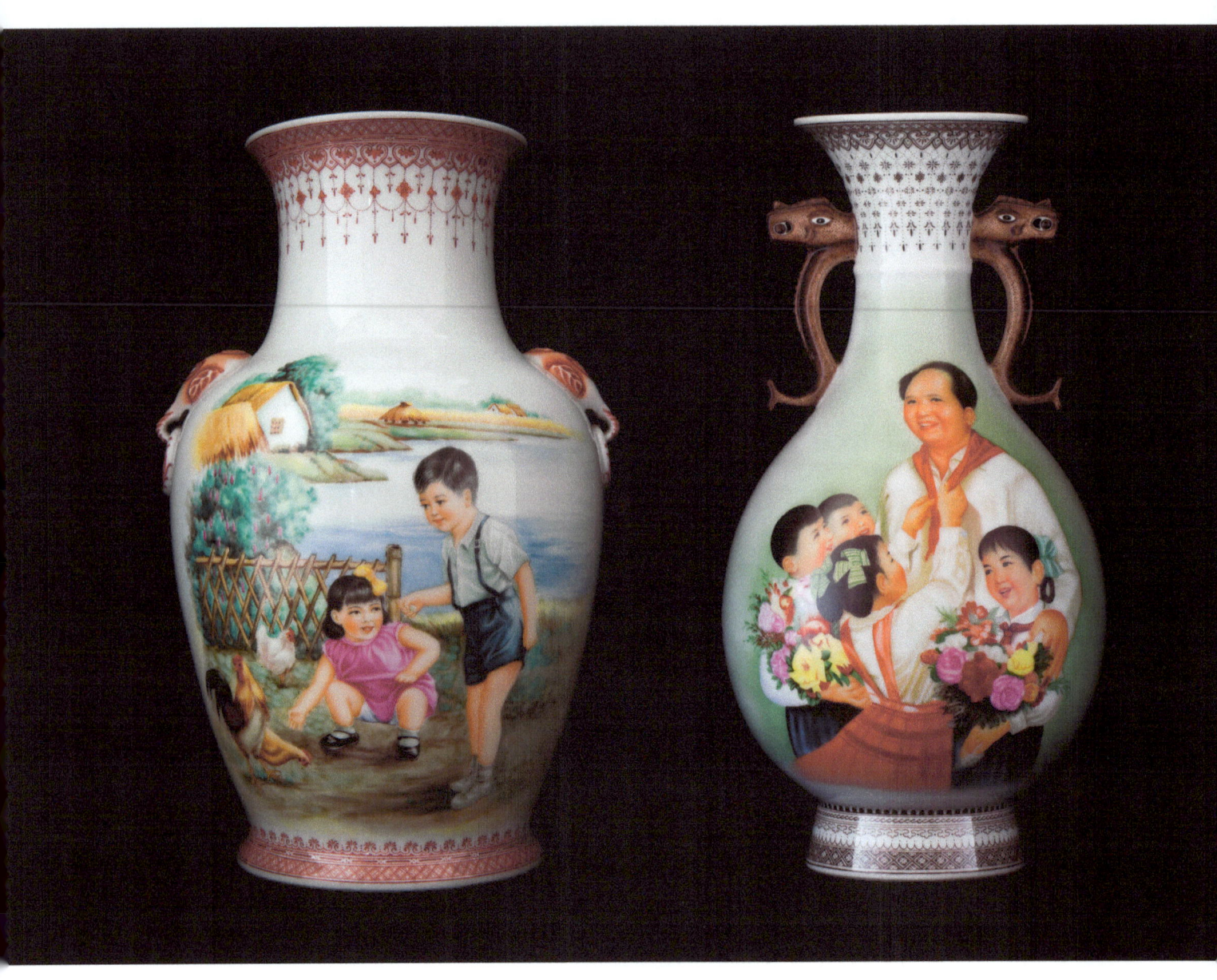

138 FORBIDDEN REPLICAS

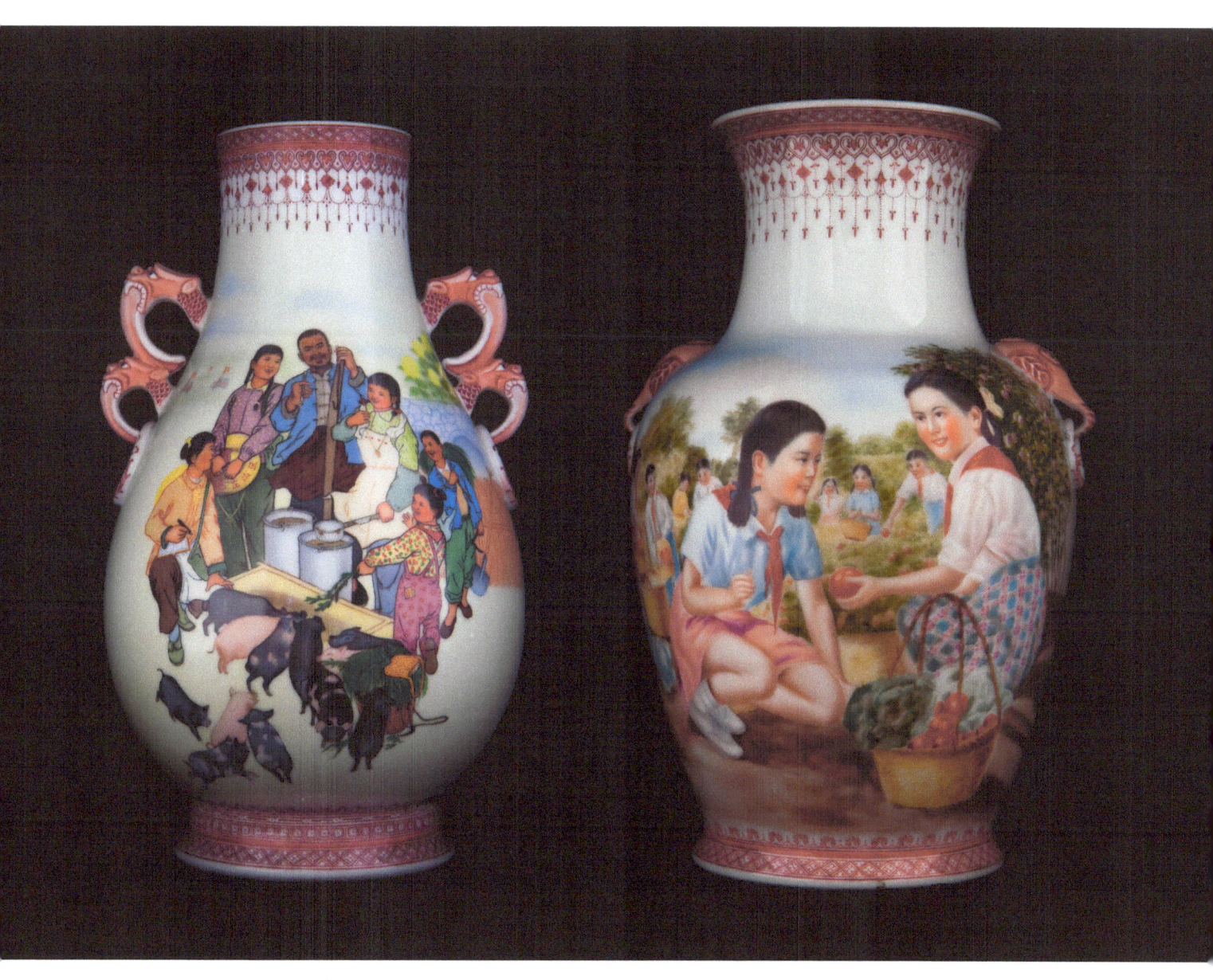

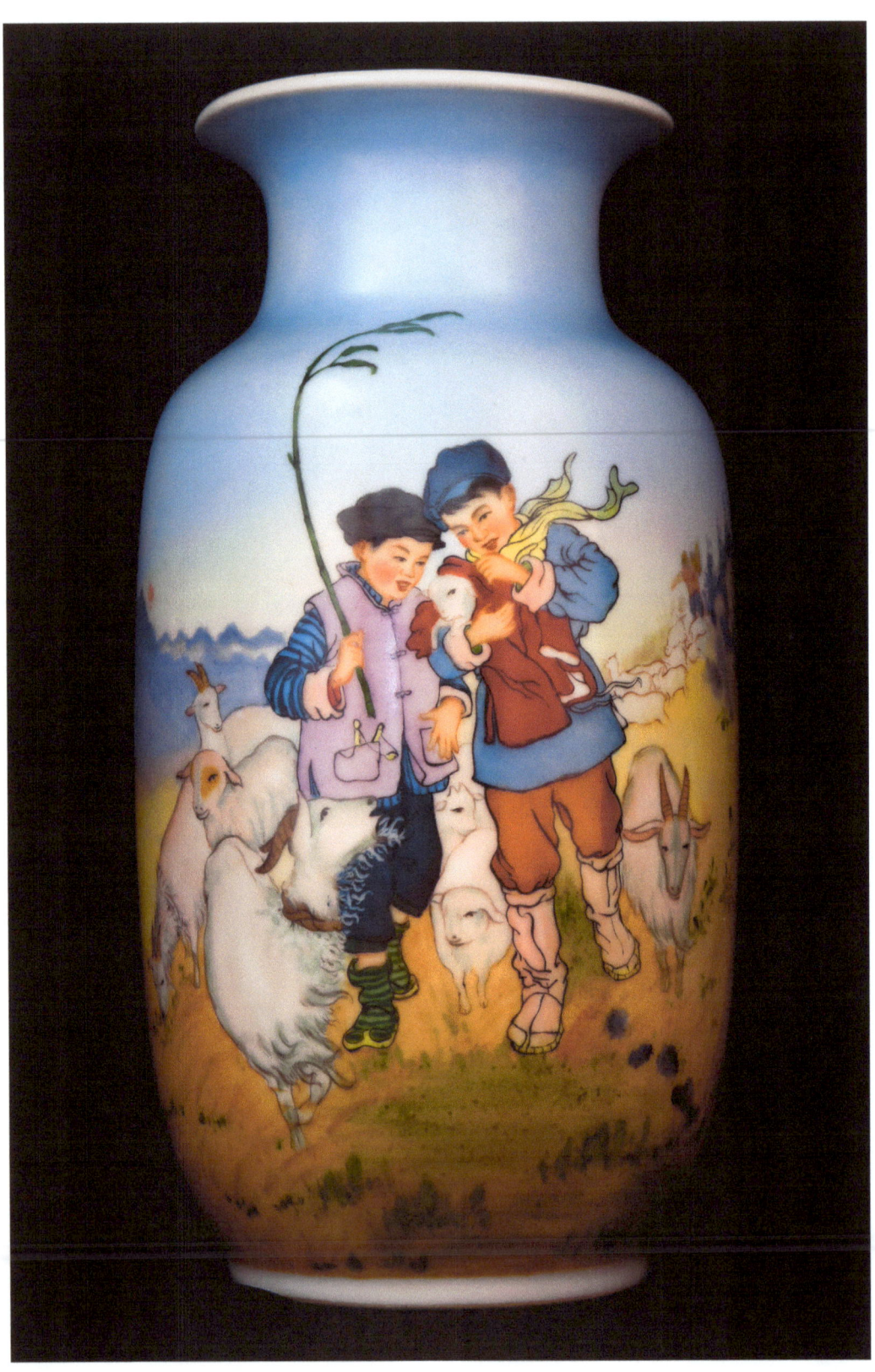

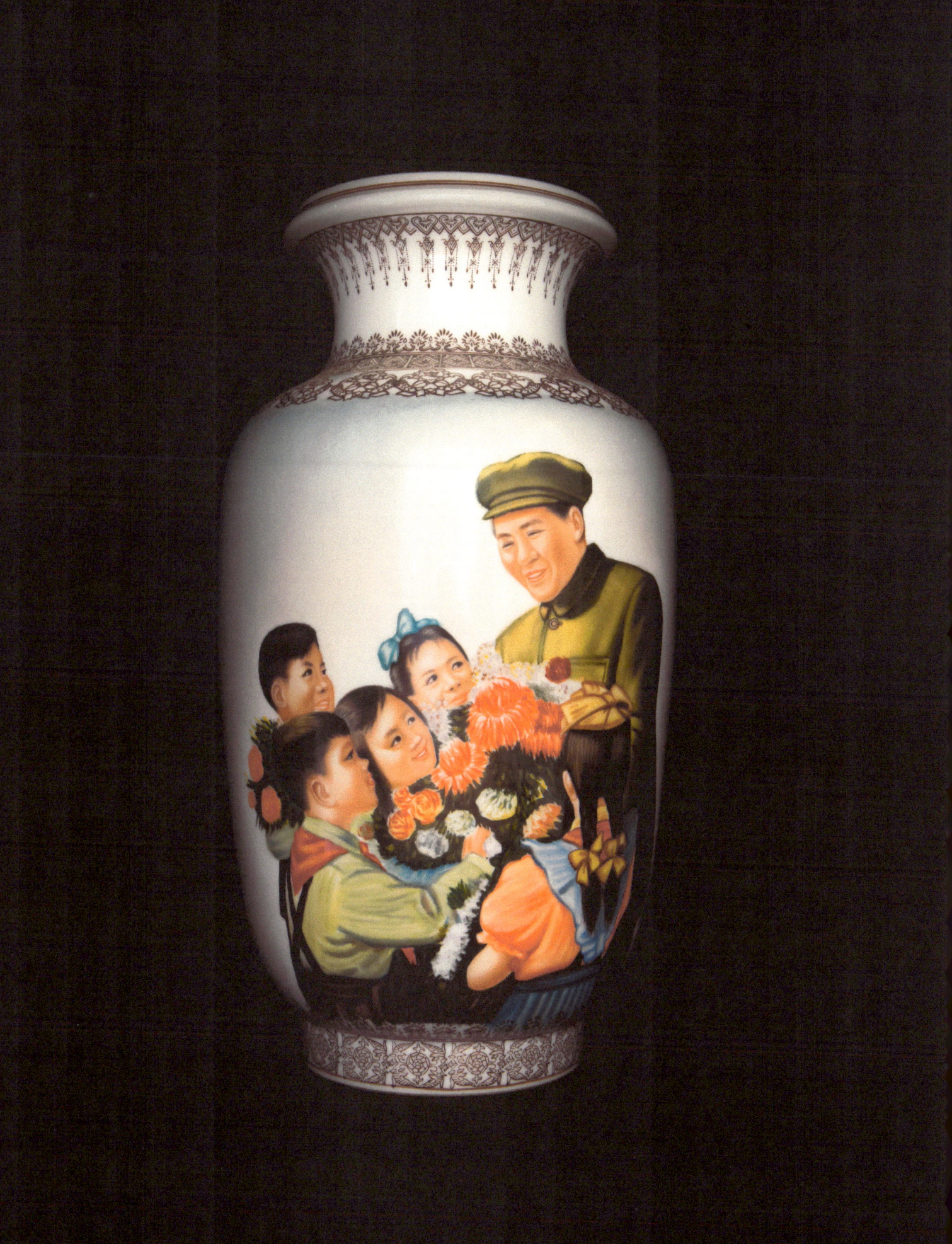

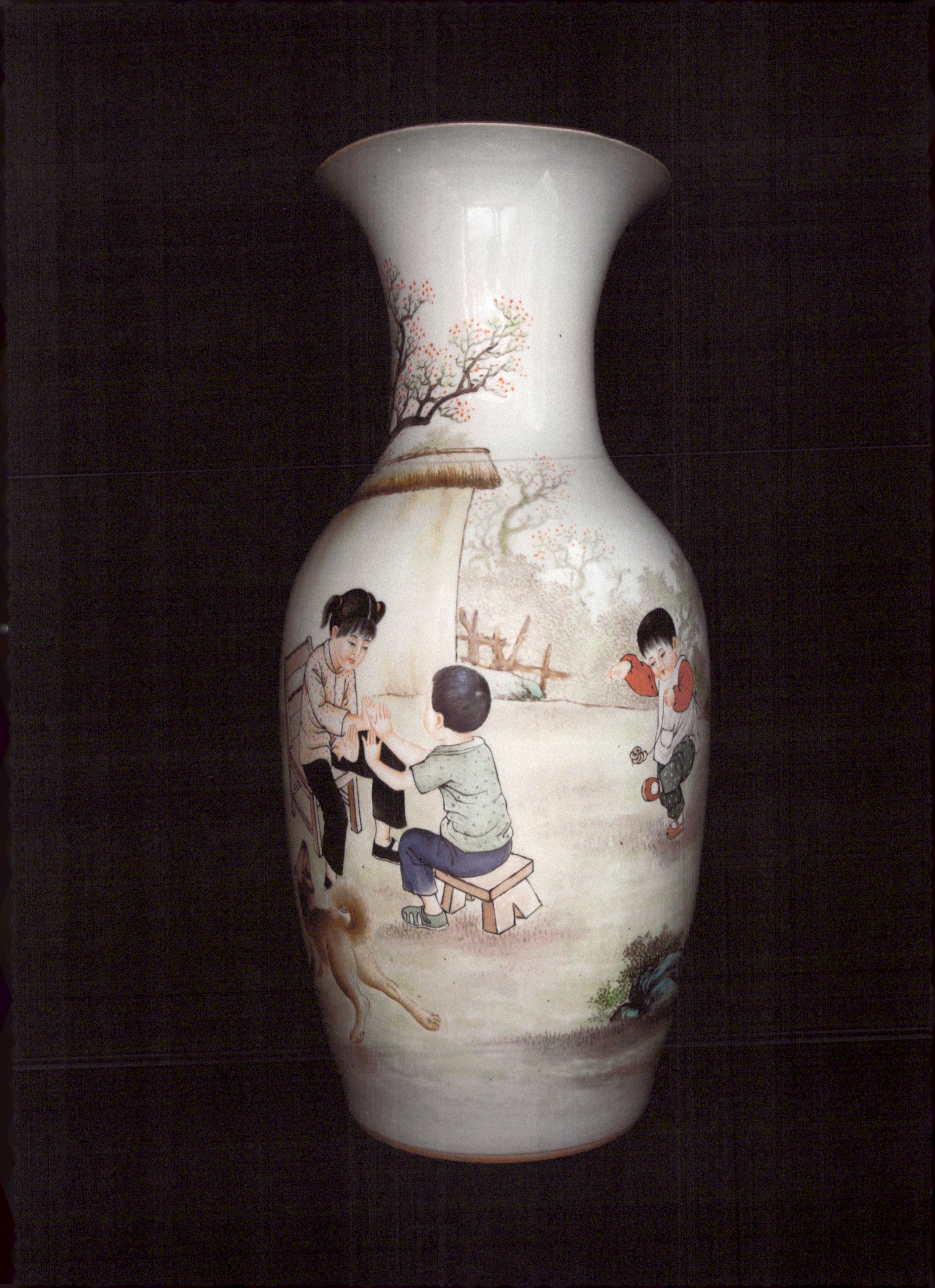

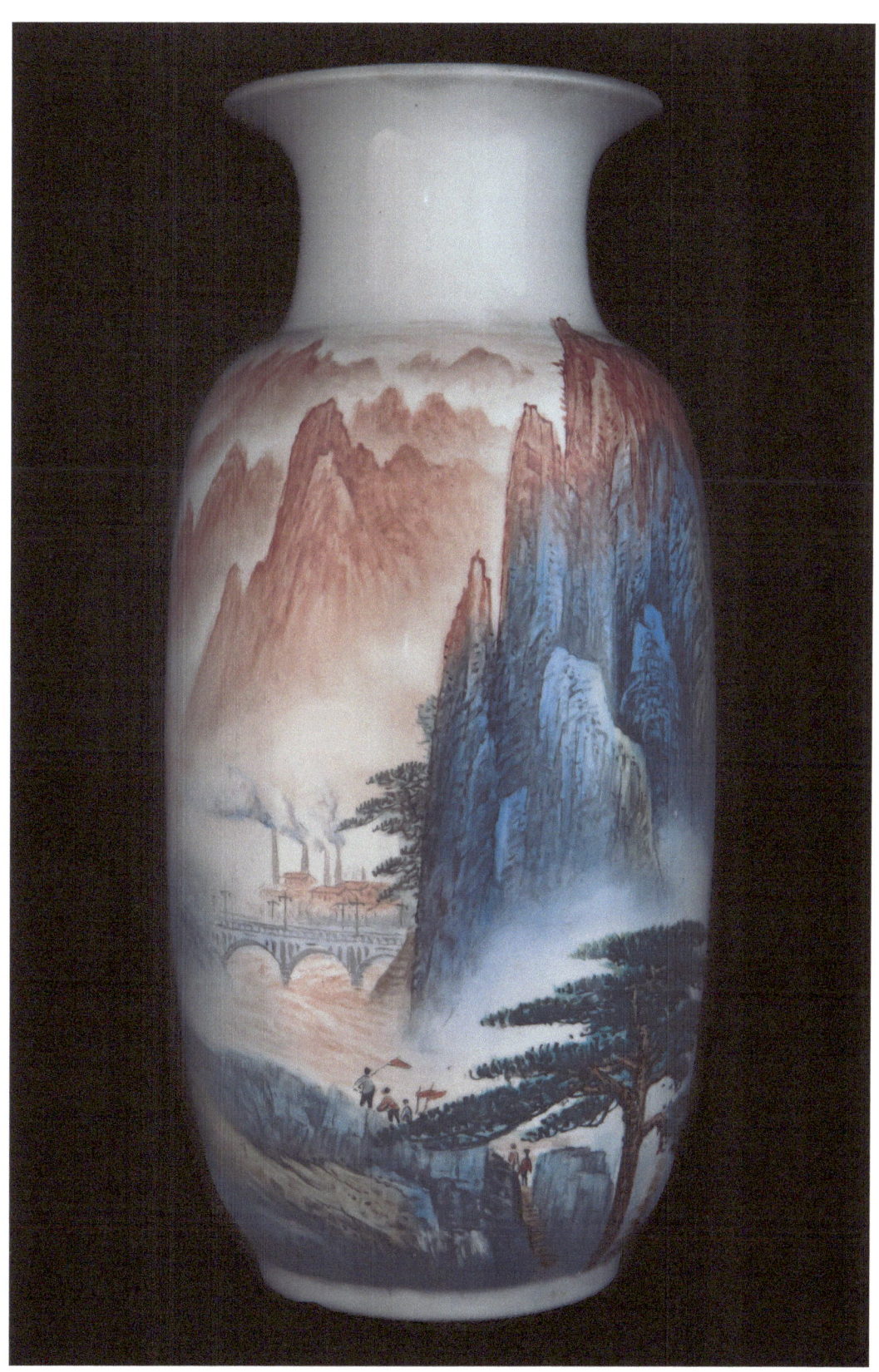

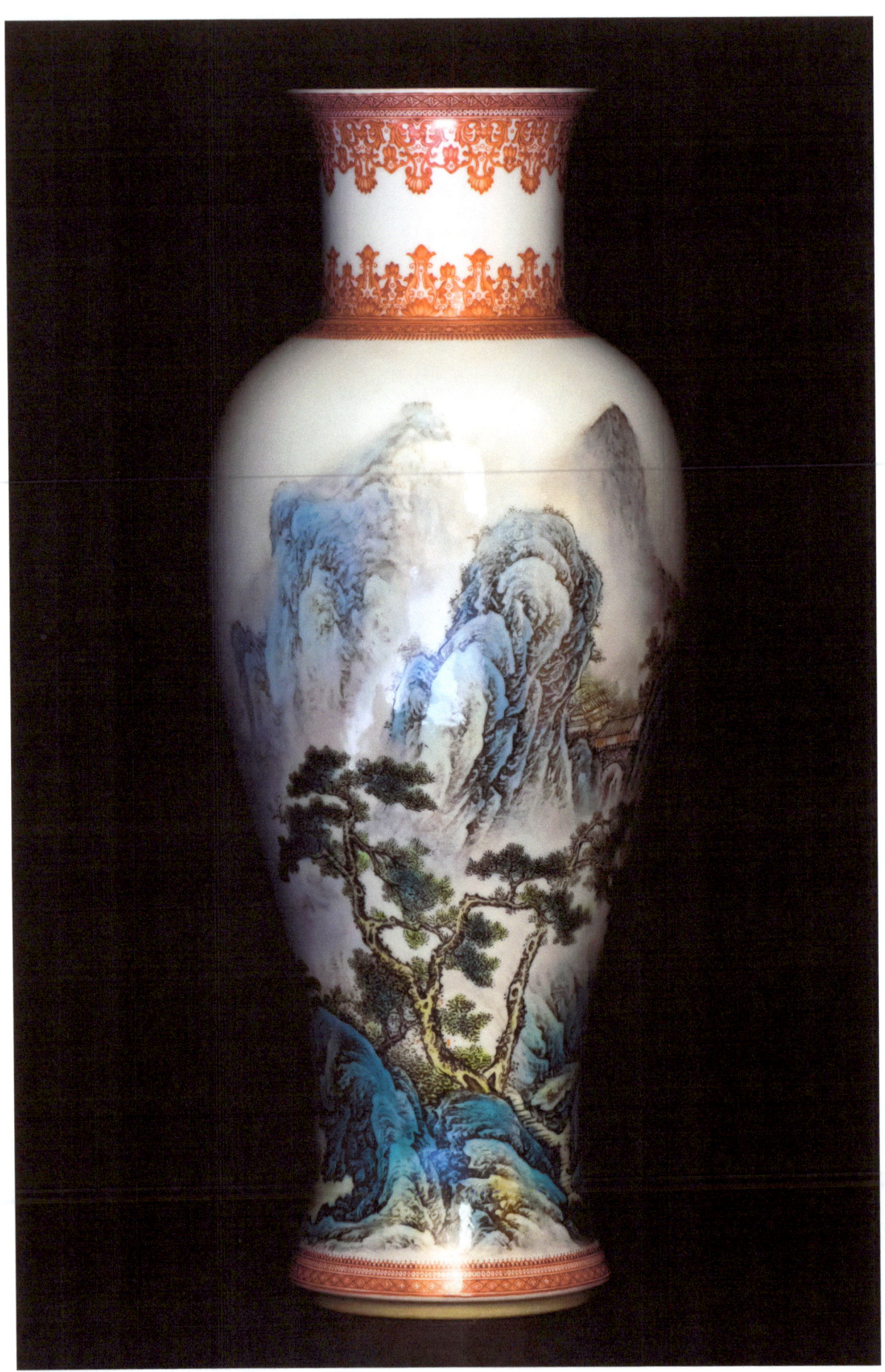

144 FORBIDDEN REPLICAS

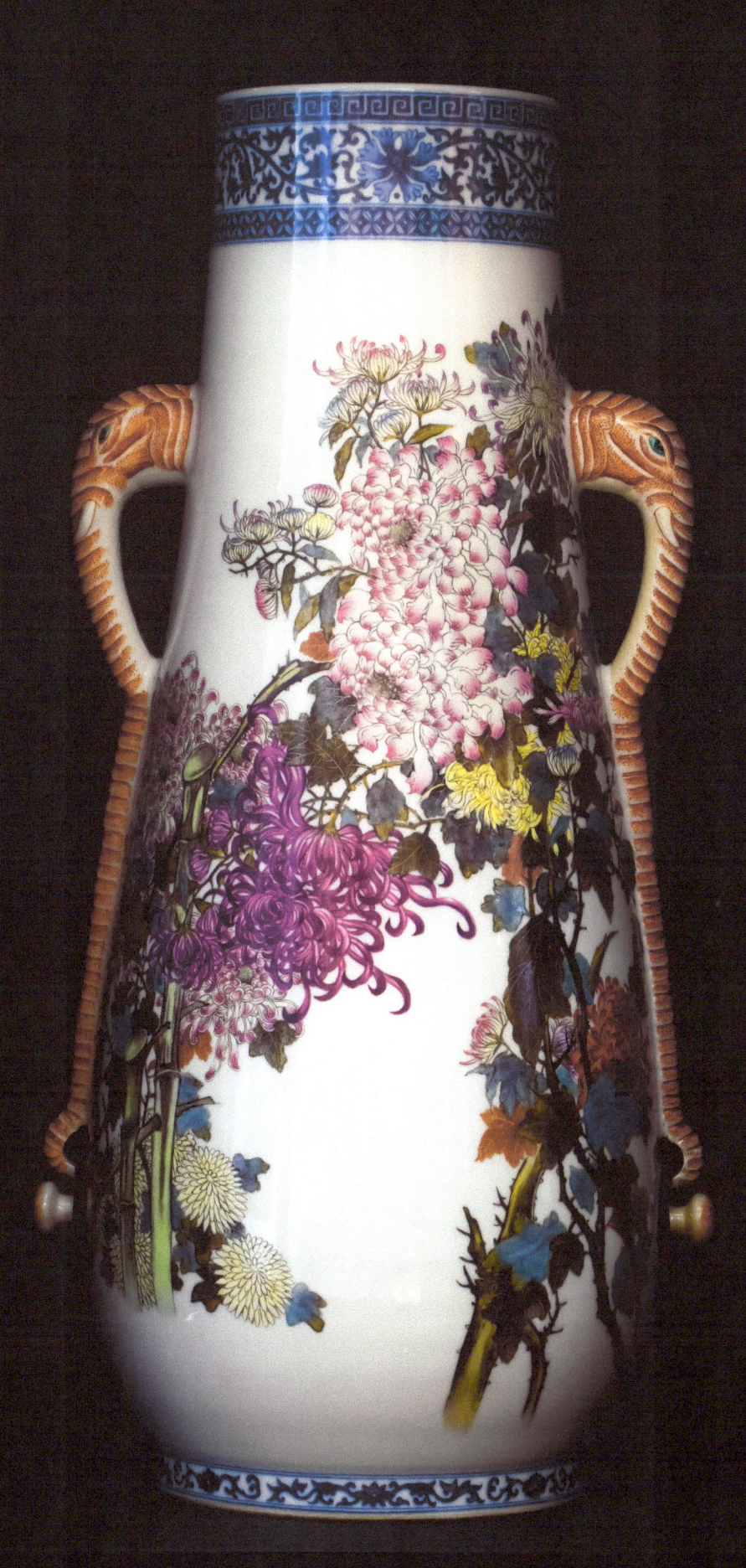

BIBLIOGRAPHY

1. Forbidden City The Great Within-May Holdsworth and Caroline Courtauld photography by Hu Chui-Frances Lincoln Limited Publishers.

2. Stunning Decorative Porcelains from the Ch'ien-lung Reign published by the NATIONAL PALACE MUSEUM, TAIWAN.

3. Traditional Jingdezhen Wares from Contemporary Kilns published by the University Museum and Art Gallery and University of Hong Kong.

4. China's Best Arts and Crafts, Volume 2 Number I 1981.Catalogue.

5. Wikipedia, internet sources, CCTV documentary titled "National Treasures Lost and Found. Part 1 and 2".

CHRONOLOGY OF QING EMPERORS

QING DYNASTY	1644 - 1911
Shunzhi	(1644 - 1661)
Kangxi	(1662 - 1722)
Yongzheng	(1723 - 1735)
Qianlong	(1736 - 1795)
Jiaqing	(1796 - 1820)
Daoguang	(1821 - 1850)
Xianfeng	(1851 - 1986)
Tongzhi	(1862 - 1874)
Guangxu	(1875 - 1908)
Xuantong (Puyi)	(1909 - 1911)

ABOUT THE WRITER AND COLLECTORS

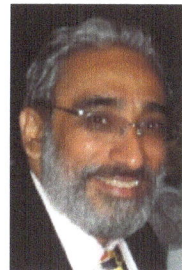

Ravinder Singh Manocha is a retired Senior Regional Counsel for a US multinational corporation. A cancer survivor, who paints, collects art and writes books and articles on art collection. His personal collections range from paintings, ceramics, jade and sculptures and snuff bottles. He has designed authored and published books on modern inside painted snuff bottles. He has organised several art exhibitions, promoted and marketed his selected artists and sculptors both locally and regionally. He has trained under eminent Singapore watercolour artist Loy Chye Chuan in Singapore for two years. He is currently an artist-in-training under internationally known celebrity artist Professor Liu Guo, Dean of Chang Bai Shan Art Institute.

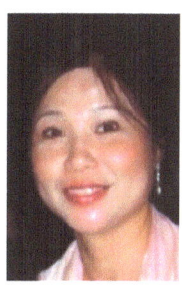

Grace Manocha/Tan Siew Poh is his Chinese wife and together they have pursued their passion for the arts. Grace comes from the famous lineage of the Tan Kah Kee family of Fujian that has inculcated in her a strong appreciation for the arts. They have four children, Tanisha, Rikhael, Sharmin and Ishshal.

They live in Singapore and can be contacted via
email   : clowns85@hotmail.com
or   : ravisinghmanocha@gmail.com
hand phone : 65 9617 2085

ACKNOWLEDGEMENTS

This book is similar to replica production and has passed through many young, capable and diligent hands. We would like to thank all of the following individuals who are no less than members of our extended family. Their patience and hard work contributed significantly to raise the quality and standard of this publication beyond our highest expectations.

Tanisha Manocha – Chief Editor
She executed her role as Chief Editor with flair, passion and objectivity despite the many discussions on the writing and style of the publication. Her research helped weed out the many errors of questionable sources and assumptions and clarified the analysis and facts in the publication. She did not let her personal relationship interfere with the task of ensuring a professional outcome and her parents are extremely proud and grateful for her contribution.

Derek Tse – Principal Photographer
Derek is the son of our dear friends Cody and Delia Tse. Derek was only a few months old when we held him in our arms for the first time. As a competent young man of twenty seven, he dedicated more than a year of evenings to do most of the photography in this book. As an amateur photographer, every skill from lighting to editing the pictures was something he learnt by trial and error since he was twenty-one. He experimented and modified lighting designs and created several lighting boxes to test and try out different original lighting conditions. The final outcome is no less than excellent quality from a young man who prides himself to do his best in everything.

Cheryl Tan Sok Lin – Cover Photographer
We have known Cheryl as a teenager and she is close friend of our daughter Tanisha. She is working in a media development Company and was our natural choice to help us with the design and photography of the front and back cover of the book. She has also individually photographed and edited the cover pieces in the book. Photography is her passion since she was young and she has the natural ability to translate complex ideas to simple and striking images. Her photography, design and editing skills have created a unique book cover that will capture the reader's attention and imagination.

EM Art Design Print – Book Layout and Formatting Specialist
EM Art Design Print, a Singapore company has provided the necessary services in formatting, editing and designing the layout of documents and pictures in this book. They have created a professional looking book and we are very grateful for their excellent support.

Ravinder Singh – Writer and Publisher

www.ingramcontent.com/pod-product-compliance
Lightning Source LLC
Chambersburg PA
CBHW051148220526
45473CB00003B/695